Additional Praise for *Retire Secure!*

"*Retire Secure!* is a very practical investment guide on how to defer taxes and efficiently plan for retirement and your estate."

—Roger G. Ibbotson
Professor, Yale School of Management
Chairman, Ibbotson Associates

"Keeping your investment expenses low and following Jim Lange's tax savings strategies are the surest routes to a comfortable retirement."

—Burton G. Malkiel
Professor of Economics, Princeton University
Author, *A Random Walk Down Wall Street*

"Jim Lange's book is a must in the retirement library of anyone with a large IRA. Not only does it provide thorough coverage of a difficult topic, but it does so with crisp writing, surrounded with charts and tables to help you understand your options. I wholeheartedly recommend *Retire Secure!*"

—Robert S. Keebler, CPA
Author, Educator

"Everyone planning for retirement should read this book."

—Dr. Allan Meltzer
Political Economy Professor, Carnegie Mellon University

"Written for the sophisticated and successful layperson (and a great guide for professionals working in this field), *Retire Secure!* is like a master class in the subject with the instructor taking the student by the hand through each step of the process. Jim Lange, a practicing CPA and attorney, provides key real-world questions and answers—as well as numerous examples, illustrations, and practical sidebar comments."

—Stephan R. Leimberg
CEO, Leimberg Information Services, Inc. (LISI)

"*Retire Secure!* shows how to maximize retirement income while explaining IRA and retirement plan rules in language you can understand (and that is no easy task). Every retiree should read James Lange's chapter on optimal spending strategies for retirees."

—Gregory Kolojeski
President, Brentmark Software
Editor, www.rothira.com

"There are few areas of financial planning more complex than making decisions about retirement plans. *Retire Secure!* not only explains many of these issues in plain English, but provides the reader with common sense guidance in making choices. As advocates of the important role that philanthropy plays in raising financially responsible children, we especially appreciate the inclusion of a chapter on charitable estate planning with IRA and retirement assets."

> —Eileen Gallo, PhD and Jon Gallo, JD
> Authors, *Silver Spoon Kids* and *The Financially*
> *Intelligent Parent*

"Jim Lange has updated and improved his material in the second edition of this fine book. I have always said that the planning comes before the doing. He tells you how to plan your retirement, maximize your wealth, and minimize your taxes."

> —Garry D. Kinder, CLU, RFC
> Author, Lecturer, and Financial Industry Consultant
> The KBI Group

"IRA and other retirement plan assets comprise a huge and growing component of so many people's wealth, yet the growth of these important assets requires sound, practical, and, most important, understandable advice. All had been lacking until the publication of this excellent book, *Retire Secure!*, by James Lange. James brings to the fore practical information usable by both attorney and accountant on how to deal with these critical assets. Topics that he delves into, including using trusts to protect beneficiaries are topics that few lay people are aware of and most professionals don't address. Protect yourself and your family with the insightful comments of *Retire Secure!*"

> —Martin M. Shenkman, Attorney
> Author, *Inherit More*

"This new version of *Retire Secure!* is even better than the first. It shows you more great ideas to help you achieve the most important financial goal of your life. Make your money last and go further than you ever thought possible."

> —Brian Tracy, Speaker, Sales Trainer
> Author, *Getting Rich Your Own Way*

"*Retire Secure!* is highly recommended reading for all practitioners in the estate and retirement planning field, as well as for those brave souls who take this task on as a do-it-yourself project."

> —Jack Gargan, Founder
> International Association of Registered Financial Consultants
> Author, *The Complete Estate Planning Guide*

"The flexible Lange's Cascading Beneficiary Plan offers a practical solution to the bewildering array of qualified retirement options, many of which are improperly used. Jim's book makes a valuable contribution to the field of personal finance—for both the consumers and the professional advisors who serve them!"

> —Edwin P. Morrow, CLU, ChFC, CFP, CEP, RFC
> Chairman and CEO International Association of Registered
> Financial Consultants (IARFC)

"Jim created the most flexible and effective estate guide for IRA and retirement plan owners."

> —Charles "Tremendous" Jones, RFC
> Author, *Life Is Tremendous*

"*Retire Secure!* should be in everyone's home who has money to invest. It is well written in language that anyone can understand. I plan to make this book available to my children and grandchildren to read."

> —Frank Thomas
> Former Pittsburgh Pirate (286 home runs)

"If taxes were the only consideration in financial planning, I'd give James Lange, JD, CPA, a 100 percent grade! Every financial advisor ought to have a copy of *Retire Secure!* at his or her fingertips, plus copies to give more serious clients. After clients have been taught how to save and where to place their investments, James Lange's book is the definitive answer to the very important tax considerations."

> —Vernon D. Gwynne, CFP, RFC
> Chairman Emeritus, and Former Director of International
> Association for Financial Planning (now Financial Planning
> Association)

"James Lange is a genius at making the most difficult subject of estate/retirement planning easy to understand. His book is an absolute must for anyone who wants the peace of mind that comes from knowing they will retire secure."

> —Eleanor Schano
> Former TV News Anchor, Host *LifeQuest* (WQED Multimedia)

"Like the original, the updated second edition of *Retire Secure!* does a fine job of explaining why, when, and how folks should move money into, out of, and between the myriad tax-advantaged employer-sponsored retirement savings plans and IRAs. The key points are summarized clearly, and a more thorough, equally clear explanation is also offered for those who want it. The book is well-organized, with plenty of practical examples. It will be a valuable resource for people in both the accumulation and distribution of their retirement assets—and to their advisors, as well."

> —Michael T. Palermo, Attorney, CFP
> Author, *AARP Crash Course in Estate Planning*

"Read this book before you meet with any tax or financial advisor about how to get the most out of your IRA, 401(k), or other retirement plans. *Retire Secure!* will help you ask the right questions and find out if your advisors really know what they're talking about."

  —Paul Merriman
  Founder, Merriman Berkman Next
  Author, *Live It Up Without Outliving Your Money*

"You've worked hard to build up your retirement funds—now finish the job and read the the new edition of Lange's *Retire Secure!* You should carefully examine each of his main points, and take full advantage of his suggestions to stretch your money as far as possible before paying taxes. In these troubled times, Lange's ideas are particularly relevant."

  —John A. Tracy, PhD, CPA
  Author, *How to Read a Financial Report*
  and *Accounting for Dummies*

"Nice girls eventually become old women who want to retire. Let this book help you to ensure you have all the money you need to live your life the way you want in retirement."

  —Lois P. Frankel, PhD
  Author, *Nice Girls Don't Get the Corner Office*

"A clear, concise, and well-written book that explains where and how to save for retirement so that you don't outlive your assets, pay too much in taxes, or have too little to pass on to your heirs. In non-technical terms, James Lange compares and contrasts various strategies for the accumulation, preservation, and the distribution of wealth. No one should invest in a retirement plan, or take a distribution from one, until he or she has first read *Retire Secure!*"

  —Gary S. Lesser, JD
  Author, *Roth IRA Answer Book*

"Jim Lange is a clear and concise communicator. He takes the complicated and makes it simple. *Retire Secure!* is a must read for anyone wanting a secure financial future."

  —Diane L. McCurdy, CFP
  Author, *How Much is Enough?*

RETIRE SECURE!

SECOND EDITION

RETIRE SECURE!

PAY TAXES LATER

THE KEY TO MAKING YOUR MONEY LAST

JAMES LANGE
CPA/ATTORNEY

WILEY

John Wiley & Sons, Inc.

Published by John Wiley & Sons, Inc., Hoboken, New Jersey.
Published simultaneously in Canada.

For general information on our other products and services or for technical support, please contact our Customer Care Department within the United States at (800) 762-2974, outside the United States at (317) 572-3993 or fax (317) 572-4002.

Wiley also publishes its books in a variety of electronic formats. Some content that appears in print may not be available in electronic books. For more information about Wiley products, visit our web site at www.wiley.com.

Cartoons by Michael McParlane.

Library of Congress Cataloging-in-Publication Data:

Lange, James, 1956–
     Retire secure! : pay taxes later : the key to making your money last /
James Lange. —2nd ed.
        p.   cm.
     Includes index.
     ISBN 978-0-470-40531-4 (cloth)
        1. Tax planning—United States.   2. Individual retirement accounts—Law and legislation—United States.   3. Pension trusts—Law and legislation—United States.
     I. Title.
KF6297.L36   2009
343.7305'238—dc22

2008041526

Printed in the United States of America
10 9 8 7 6 5 4 3 2 1

Contents

Part One

3. Traditional 401(k)s and 403(b)s versus Roth 401(k)s and Roth 403(b)s   49

Part Two

The Distribution Years: Spend the Right Funds First and Other Critical Decisions You Face in Retirement   71

9. Withdrawing Retirement Plans Funded with Company Stocks and Net Unrealized Appreciation   161

Part Three

Estate Planning: It Is Never Too Early to Start   167

Overview   169

10. Eddie and Emily: A Retirement and Estate Planning Case Study   171

11. How to Reduce Your Federal Estate Tax Burden   181

13. Laying the Foundation for Estate Planning: Using the Minimum Required Distribution Rules after Death

14. Using Disclaimers in Estate Planning

Foreword

I can't remember a time when people were more worried about their economic future. The potholes on Wall Street and Main Street are big enough to swallow a car, and people are anxiously looking for a safe route to protect what they have. If you are looking for a guidance system that will help you take control of your financial future and protect your family, this book is it. Think of *Retire Secure!* as a GPS for your money. You may know where you are and where you want to go, but you don't know how to get there. Jim offers the best routes.

Welcome to the second edition of *Retire Secure!* by James Lange.

When the first edition of *Retire Secure!* was released in 2006, I called it, "One of the best books about saving taxes I've ever read." Economic conditions have changed greatly since the release of the first edition, and I am even more confident that Jim's updated strategies in the second edition will guide you to a secure retirement. Jim's work has been time tested and vetted by the best in the business. He doesn't just speculate, he "runs the numbers," and all of his recommendations are backed up by real world results.

If you follow Jim's strategies, you are sure to get the most out of your IRAs and retirement plans. Whether you are still working, preparing to retire, or have already retired, this book will point you in the right direction. Jim also helps you chart a course for your family, after you are gone, with an estate plan that offers great flexibility. The advice and recommendations in *Retire Secure!* will be particularly beneficial for those approaching retirement or already retired. Those individuals have the least amount of time to make up market losses, and strategic planning is critical. If you are among that constituency, this book is definitely for you.

But what about short-term planning? Wouldn't you like to save taxes and keep more money for yourself right now? What about taking advantage of Roth IRA conversions now or in 2010? Have you even heard about this opportunity? A Roth IRA conversion could save you tens of thousands of dollars and could provide an additional million dollars or more to your children and grandchildren. If this piques your curiosity, the answers are inside this book.

Read *Retire Secure!* and learn how Jim's strategies can work for you. Then get additional advice if you think you need it. As Jim points out, too many people go it alone and miss out on many opportunities. The information in this book will help you recognize a good advisor, and you will definitely bring great ideas to the table.

So don't just try to avoid the potholes. Take control, and find a really good route to follow. Use Jim's advice to minimize wrong turns and detours as you travel the road to a comfortable and secure retirement.

—Larry King

Acknowledgments

The first and second editions of *Retire Secure!* could not have been written without the work and dedication of many others. I am indebted to a few individuals whose contributions were invaluable.

Steven T. Kohman, Certified Public Accountant, Certified Valuation Analyst, Certified Specialist in Estate Planning, has worked for me for over 13 years and has co-authored many articles with me. Steve is a skilled number cruncher and combines his extensive tax background with his superb quantitative and computer skills. Steve's quantitative analysis, evidenced in the graphs and charts throughout the book, presents compelling proof of the fundamental concepts that make up the backbone of *Retire Secure!* Steve's help in the second edition was also invaluable. His extensive writing and analysis in the area of IRAs, Roth IRA conversions, and life insurance make the second edition of this book even more valuable than the first.

Matt Schwartz, Esq., is an exceptionally bright and gifted IRA and estate attorney who has worked with me for eight years. I am proud to have him as a colleague. Matt has made many original contributions to the book, as well as many corrections. He works closely with my clients and me to complete the documentation necessary to implement our recommended planning solutions. Matt's review and update of this second edition was thorough and comprehensive. His contributions to the "What's New" section as well as the chapter on charitable giving stand out as examples of his excellent work.

Cynthia Nelson has been working with me for over 10 years. During this period, she has had full editing and writing responsibilities for virtually all my published works. She is a rare find. She cuts through some of the technical and legal jargon that I sometimes fall into and expresses complex thoughts in a way the lay reader can understand. She also allows me to express my humanity, and she adds touches of her own that make reading the book a better experience.

To Jillian Manus, my "rock-star agent," thank you for your patience with a difficult client. To Debra Englander, my Wiley editor, thank you for selecting *Retire Secure!* for publication and all your subsequent help with both editions.

Special thanks to Larry King. Your Foreword adds sizzle.

I also want to thank all the prerelease readers and reviewers of *Retire Secure!* Special thanks go to Charles Schwab and Ed Slott, both of whom provided insight and suggestions for the original manuscript. Many more of my colleagues and peers offered thoughtful testimonials. I have included as many as I could. Your support means more to me than I can adequately express.

I also want to thank Ed Slott for writing such a thoughtful Introduction.

I must also convey my gratitude to my full-time coworkers (in addition to Steve and Matt) who provide so much help in my practice that without them the book could never have been written: Glenn Venturino, CPA (how can I properly thank you for 23 years of superb service to our clients); Sandy Proto, our office manager (without Sandy the office would cease to function); Alice Davis, who is so wonderful and personable with our clients and is the first to jump on board when anything needs to be done; Donna Master, who keeps my books, which would certainly be a shambles without her dedicated precision; and Daryl Ross, our legal administrative assistant/master tax return compiler who rolls up her sleeves and gets it done year after year. Special thanks to my new marketing director, Beth Bershok, who has helped with the legwork needed to get this book in your hands.

There are two special subcontractors who work on my behalf whom I want to thank. Steve May, my webmaster for 10 years! How can I properly thank you? And Rich Davis who has been invaluable helping me produce fabulous CDs and DVDs of some of my best information.

Finally, to matters of the heart, a special thanks to my mother, Barnetta Lange, Ph.D., Professor Emeritus of Journalism. Out of her love for the English language, she tried to keep me from too many clichés and "ize" words, and she also improved the language and corrected grammatical errors. Forever the teacher.

And closest to my heart I want to thank my beloved wife, Cindy Lange, who surely is one of the few women alive who could put up with me. Her imprint is on every page of the book. Cindy has been enormously resourceful in many areas and has made both significant direct and indirect contributions to the book. This book would never have happened without her help, support, and love. Finally, thank you to my 14-year-old daughter, Erica, whom I love dearly, even though she now beats me in Boggle and many other board games. Thank you for not complaining when I went back to the office after dinner to work on the book.

Thank you all.

How to Read This Book

I recommend that you start with "The Big Retirement Question" and "A Summary of Tax Reduction Strategies" so you can begin to think about the underlying theme of "Pay taxes later" with respect to your personal situation. Then, please look at the detailed table of contents and pick out the chapters that grab your attention.

Virtually every chapter contains proof that my recommendations have been tested and proven worthy. You may want to skip over portions of the proof and just read the advice. Sometimes, when I am looking for information or advice, I want to scream, "Don't tell me *why*, just tell me *what* to do." If you feel similarly, or you find yourself moving in that direction after realizing there is enormous support for virtually every recommendation I make, the book's sidebars and summaries at the end of the chapters will serve you well.

Obviously, you would benefit greatly if you read the book cover to cover, and then took action on the recommendations appropriate for you and your family. I do, however, live in the real world and recognize that you may only read or even skim portions you know are personally relevant. But, no matter how you read the book, the important point is: Take action to make your retirement and estate planning the best it can be for you and your family.

I have tried to spice up the content by including some true stories (modified for confidentiality), an occasional sarcastic comment, at least one witty quote per chapter, and perhaps the most fun, the cartoons. I hope you enjoy them.

What *Retire Secure!* Doesn't Cover

Retire Secure! does not provide direct investment advice nor do I recommend any specific stocks, bonds, mutual funds, or even asset allocation models. Obviously choosing appropriate investments is critical, but this book is not the place for direct investment advice.

I also do not address the issue of determining an appropriate withdrawal rate for retirement.

Finally, though there is important analysis on Roth IRAs and Roth IRA conversions, the coverage is not as detailed as some readers might prefer. But don't despair; I am preparing a new book dedicated to Roth IRAs, Roth 401(k)s, Roth 403(b)s, and Roth IRA conversions that will offer an in-depth analysis of investing in the Roth environment. Please see www.retiresecure.com for details.

Additional Resources for the Reader

My goal is to provide you with the best information I have, and establish a continuing dialogue with you that reaches beyond the pages of this book. I offer a plethora of other information and services—much of it at no additional cost! It is my sincere hope that this book will serve as an introduction to a long and lasting relationship. Much of that information will be free in the form of an e-mail newsletter, the audio MP3, my radio show that streams, and the offer of numerous free reports throughout the book.

Of course as time goes on, the tax code will change, creating new opportunities and pitfalls. One wonderful source of free information is my *e-mail newsletter*. It will keep you up to date on the best ways to secure a comfortable retirement and the latest tax planning strategies. I highly recommend you sign up to receive it. Please go to www.retiresecure.com to sign up and receive a number of free reports that will update and supplement *Retire Secure!*

In addition, I would recommend you sign up for my blog. To do so, please go to www.retiresecure.com to find a link to my blog.

Feel free to use my blog to send comments, questions, and/or ideas you would like to relay to me. I will try to post questions and answers on a regular basis. Your thoughts are most appreciated. In addition to tax updates, I expect to continue improving this book for the next edition, and many of the improvements will be spurred by your comments.

When you purchased this book, you qualified for a free audio MP3. To receive your free audio MP3 visit www.retiresecure.com or refer to the back of the book for ordering information. This MP3 will supplement and reinforce many of the most important points in the book as well as provide some new material. Listen to it in your car and make good use of that downtime!

Thank you for purchasing *Retire Secure!* I have given everything I have to make this book worthy of your valuable time, and I truly believe that the strategies and ideas put forth will help you achieve a more secure retirement.

A Note Specifically for Financial Professionals

If you are a financial professional (financial planner, CPA, attorney, banker, stockbroker, insurance professional, CFP, money manager, and so on) and want to elevate the level of your service and significantly increase your income, this book will go a long way towards helping you achieve your goals. I would encourage you to actually read this book. I don't say this lightly. I fully realize that your time is a precious commodity. If you choose to do some strategic skipping of material because you understand the concepts and don't need to have the concepts proved, then strategic skipping is fine. If, after reading the book, you see the potential for Roth IRA conversions and the cascading beneficiary plan, then I strongly encourage you to go to www.therothirainstitute.com to see how you can use this information to attract high net worth clients and better serve your existing clients.

I think we have a sacred trust as advisors to give our clients the best advice we can. Taking the time to read this book is a critical step toward fulfilling that trust. After all, isn't becoming your clients' most trusted advisor the absolute best way to secure referrals and recommendations that will expand your business? The entire direction of the industry is to distinguish ourselves by the quality of our advice and service, and to provide our clients with added value. The information in this book is likely to radically improve the scope and quality of the advice you give your clients regarding IRA and retirement plans.

Before reading this book, I urge you to print out a list of your clients and keep it with the book. As you read, please think about how the different strategies could be used by individual clients to significantly improve their financial picture. I would hazard a guess that every one of your clients could benefit from at least one of the tax-saving strategies I talk about. Make notes next to your clients' names and then schedule meetings to discuss your latest personalized recommendations. There isn't a client who doesn't appreciate the personalized touch. By the time you are finished reading the book, chances are you will have a good reason to call and schedule a meeting with the majority, if not all, of your clients.

Then, please don't stop there.

I have created a product for financial professionals that will give you the exact language I use when I present this information in my workshops and when I am talking to clients. The product also contains a turnkey seminar system, one that I consistently get excellent results with despite the fact that most planners have not had good results with seminars or workshops lately. I have also founded the Roth IRA Institute to prepare advisors for the unlimited Roth IRA conversion opportunities for 2010 and beyond. If the content of the book resonates with you, I urge you to go to www.retiresecure.com and sign up for my e-mail newsletter specifically written for financial professionals, and for more information about how you can learn to present this information to your clients and prospects as well as opportunities in the Roth IRA Institute.

Every financial professional who has clients with significant IRAs and/or retirement plans should have a copy of *Retire Secure!* My publisher, Wiley & Sons, made a great deal with a company that wanted 1,000 books for its advisors. If you are a department manager or you oversee other financial professionals, I urge you to read this book with an eye to purchasing a copy for each of the financial professionals in your organization, as well as purchasing copies to offer as premiums for your clients. The chapter on survivorship life insurance alone should give you at least a 100 to 1 return on your investment.

I hope you will enjoy great benefits from reading and implementing the ideas in *Retire Secure!*

The Big Retirement Question

"Do I have enough money to last for the rest of my life?"

That's the $64,000 question.

While you can never answer that question with 100 percent certainty, you can take action on two fronts which will dramatically improve your odds.

1. *Develop an appropriate portfolio.* With the exception of several observations interspersed throughout, I leave the discussion of building a portfolio to another day.

2. *Take action to drastically reduce your taxes.* This is easier than you may think. With this book in hand you have the tools to significantly reduce your and your family's tax burden. Reducing your taxes will dramatically increase your chances of financial success.

The U.S. tax structure rewards certain actions and punishes others. The difference can mean, literally, millions of dollars.

Retire Secure! explains how you can use IRAs, retirement plans, and other tax-favored investments to let Uncle Sam subsidize your life style and increase the odds that you will have sufficient income for the rest of your and your spouse's life.

Retire Secure! is a summation of my best advice garnered from 30 years as a practicing CPA and 25 years as an estate attorney. Though the optimal treatment of IRAs and retirement plans is the focus of this book, even readers with IRAs and retirement plans as their primary assets, have other concerns besides planning for their retirement assets. Therefore, this book isn't limited to IRA and retirement plan advice but contains my best advice in many related areas as well. *Retire Secure!* provides critical advice for all stages of IRA and retirement plan saving and spending. We cover the best strategies for accumulating wealth while you are working, and distributing IRAs and retirement plans when you are retired.

In addition, *Retire Secure!* gives you a *uniquely flexible* solution for disbursing the IRA or retirement plan after the death of the IRA owner. The inherent flexibility of Lange's Cascading Beneficiary Plan™ provides the maximum flexibility for your survivors. We think it is highly likely you will prefer this plan to the more traditional, fixed-in-stone type of estate planning. Flexibility is important because we can't predict the future; changes in investments and in the tax environment are likely to affect the best plans. If we provide flexibility in our estate planning, we will often get a better result for the family.

Retire Secure! is supported with peer-reviewed mathematical proofs that these strategies result in more dollars—sometimes millions of additional dollars—to you and your family.

A Summary of Tax Reduction Strategies

For the reader who wants to take what I have to say on faith and wants several of the most important strategies in two pages or less, here you go.

The Clear Advantage of IRA and Retirement Plan Savings during the Accumulation Stage

If you are working or self-employed, to the extent you can afford to, please contribute the maximum to your retirement plans.

Mr. Pay Taxes Later and Mr. Pay Taxes Now had identical salaries, investment choices, and spending patterns, but there was one big difference. Mr. Pay Taxes Later invested as much as he could afford in his tax-deferred retirement plans—even though his employer did not match his contributions. Mr. Pay Taxes Now contributed nothing to his retirement account at work but invested his "savings" in an account outside of his retirement plan.

Please look at Figure 1. Mr. Pay Taxes Later's investment is represented by the black curve, and Mr. Pay Taxes Now's, by the gray curve. Look at the dramatic difference in the accumulations over time—nearly $2 million.

There you have it. Two people in the same tax bracket who earn and spend an identical amount of money and have identical investment rates of return. But, based on the simple application of the "Pay Taxes Later" rule, the difference is poverty in old age versus affluence and a $2 million estate. (Details are spelled out in Chapter 1.)

> "Pay taxes later" is a concept to embrace for a lifetime of earning, living, and estate planning

Figure 1

Retirement Assets, IRAs vs. After-Tax Accumulations

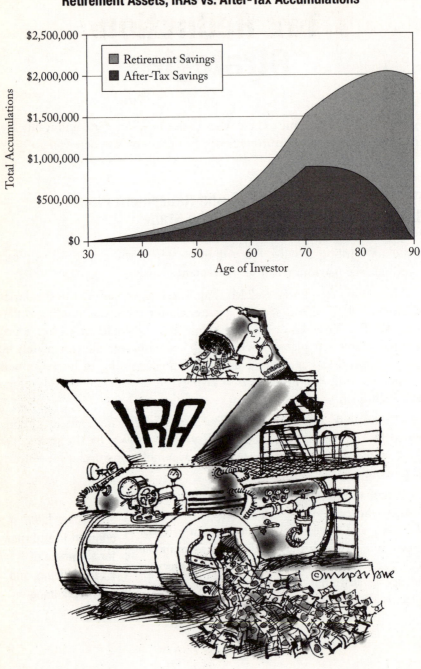

Spend Your After-Tax (Nonretirement or Non-IRA) Money First during the Distribution Stage

Mr. Tax-Efficient and Mr. Tax-Inefficient, both aged 65, begin at the same place with identical investments inside and outside of their IRAs and retirement plans.

Mr. Tax-Inefficient refuses to spend any of his after-tax funds (non-IRA and non-retirement plan funds) until all his IRA and retirement funds are depleted. Each withdrawal of his IRA and retirement plan triggers income taxes. Because he is spending the IRA and retirement plan money first, he is *paying tax now*. (See Figure 2.)

Mr. Tax-Efficient does the opposite. He spends nothing of his IRA or retirement plan until he runs out of money from his nonretirement sources or until he is required to take minimum required distributions when he reaches 70½. In the accompanying graph, Mr. Tax-Efficient is represented by the upper curve and the unfortunate Mr. Tax-Inefficient by the lower curve.

Which scenario looks better to you? The principle of "don't pay taxes now—pay taxes later" also applies to retirees' spending decisions.

Figure 2

Benefits of Spending After-Tax Savings before Tax-Deferred Retirement Accounts

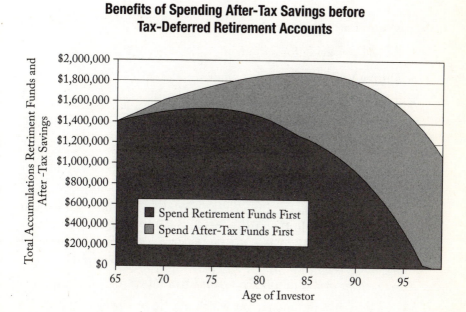

Making the correct decisions will have a dramatic impact on your life style and your ability to provide for your family. (Details are spelled out in Chapter 1.)

Finally, the concept of "Pay Taxes Later" also applies when you are planning for the disposition of your IRAs and retirement plans after your death. Paying taxes later is an important strategy for your heirs as well, and will help them accumulate more money.

My Best Advice—Read This Book

Whether you do it on your own or hire a professional advisor, pay attention to your investments and develop an appropriate portfolio. Also please determine a safe spending or withdrawal rate.

To discover tax-efficient strategies for retirement planning, read this book. Then act on my suggestions, finding professional help when necessary. Subject to a couple of exceptions, which I will identify and explain, don't pay taxes now—pay taxes later and reap the rewards of a richer life. Under most circumstances, you and your family will be better off, potentially by millions.

An Outline Overview of the Whole Process

Don't pay taxes now—pay taxes later:

- As you are saving for retirement
- During your retirement
- Through the estate planning process

Here is the lifetime outline:

While still working, that is, during the accumulation stage:

1. Contribute the maximum amount to your retirement plan or plans. (Chapter 1)
2. If you have a choice, choose the right plans including Roth IRAs, Roth 401(k)s, Roth 403(b)s, traditional 401(k)s, and even non-deductible IRAs. Allow the tax favored accounts to accumulate, while continuing to make new contributions. (Chapter 1)

At retirement, that is, during the accumulation stage:

3. First, spend the money on which you have already paid income tax. (Chapter 4)

4. After the first pool of money is spent, then spend any retirement plan or IRA money (tax-deferred or tax-free). (Only make withdrawals from your IRA, etc., after you have exhausted your non–retirement plan assets.) (Chapter 4)

5. At 70½, you will have to begin taking minimum required distributions (MRDs). If you can afford to, limit your annual distribution to the minimum required distribution and allow the rest of the account to continue to accumulate tax-deferred. (Chapter 5)

When you are planning for your heirs:

6. Develop an estate plan that continues the tax-deferred status of your IRA or retirement plan long after your death. Some variation of Lange's Cascading Beneficiary Plan™ is probably the best solution for the IRA beneficiary form for most readers. (Chapter 15)

Finally, know when to make an exception to the "pay taxes later" rule. Notable exceptions include:

7. Roth IRAs and Roth 401(k)s (better than nonmatched 401(k) or 403(b) or traditional IRAs). (Chapters 2 and 3)

8. Roth IRA Conversions (often the best move, but violate the spirit of don't pay taxes now—pay taxes later). (Chapter 7)

9. Distributions of IRA and retirement plan money at targeted income tax brackets. (Chapter 4)

10. In large estates, sometimes it does pay to withdraw money from IRAs prematurely to avoid the dreaded combination of estate tax and income tax on the IRA within the estate. (Chapter 11)

That's it in a nutshell, but there is so much more. So, jump on board and enjoy the ride.

What's New!

The biggest change since the first edition is the stock market meltdown. Retirees looking for specific guidance on how to respond should pay special attention to Chapters 4, 7, and 8. In addition, there have been several important new laws passed over the last few years that offer new planning opportunities. Each of the new strategies that we mention in *What's New!* are covered in more detail in the book. This section, however, offers an overview for readers who may want to jump to the sections of the book that give the details supporting our most recent recommendations.

Consider Establishing a One-Person 401(k) Plan

In response to several new tax laws, I have developed a new favorite strategy that will work for many IRA and retirement plan owners. I am now encouraging IRA and retirement plan owners to set up their own one-person 401(k) plan. The one-person 401(k) plan could become your primary plan, and potentially even the preferred holding place for both your old 401(k) plan and your IRA. If you are retired and still have money in your former employer's 401(k) plan, subject to exceptions mentioned in Chapter 6, I would consider rolling at least a portion, if not all of your existing 401(k) plan from your former job into your new one-person 401(k) plan. I would even suggest that you consider rolling your IRA to your new one-person 401(k) plan. This offers the following benefits:

- Expanded Roth IRA conversion possibilities of after-tax dollars in a retirement plan or non-deductible IRA (new)

- Better protection from creditors than traditional IRAs

- Extremely flexible investment choices

- Eliminates problems with the potential acceleration of income of the inherited 401(k)

- Upon your death your nonspouse beneficiaries would still be able to make a Roth IRA conversion of the inherited IRA (new, see Chapter 6)

There are two drawbacks to this strategy. The first is that to set up a one-person 401(k) plan you must have self-employment income—taking a job with an outside employer will not meet the criteria; you must be independently self-employed. Without self-employment income the strategy of transferring your company 401(k) or your IRA to your one person 401(k) doesn't work because you need self-employment income to set up a one person 401(k) plan. Therefore, one of the things I love to see my "retired" clients do is earn a little self-employment income. Perhaps they do some consulting in their field, or perhaps they get paid independently for services they provide—such as working at the golf course or teaching a part-time course. Some retirees will even charge people for services they used to perform for free. For example, a retiree could consult with his self-employed child and the self-employed child could pay the parent for consulting. That income could provide the earned income and the basis for setting up and making a new 401(k) contribution. The second drawback of the one person 401(k) is administrative. There are some fees to set it up, but often the holding company of your money (Vanguard, Charles Schwab, etc.) will offer the plan documents for little or no money as an accommodation for their clients. At some point, you may be required to file a simple tax information form (Form 5500-EZ) every year.

It is not that having a lot of money in a company 401(k) or even an IRA is bad, but having it in a one-person 401(k) plan that is completely under your control is, for many retirees, a better strategy.

In the spirit of full disclosure, using a one-person 401(k) to house the majority of your retirement assets is not the standard advice. It is my original idea and if you bring it up in conversation or even go to an advisor and discuss it, it is likely to be a new concept to them. I have mentioned this idea to many financial and tax experts and though some of them identified the downsides that I included above, none of them pointed out any significant downsides or danger, and they all saw its benefits.

Roth IRA Conversions Available to Everyone in 2010

The most dramatic opportunity for many IRA and retirement plan owners will come as a result of the new law allowing all taxpayers, without regard to income, to make a Roth IRA conversion in tax year 2010 and thereafter. We have expanded our analysis of Roth IRA conversions and I would encourage all readers to read the new chapter on Roth IRA conversions. I believe that most IRA and retirement plan owners would benefit from developing and implementing a long-term Roth IRA conversion strategy and reading this book and Chapter 7 in particular, will help you determine an appropriate Roth IRA conversion strategy.

Roth IRA conversions are favorable because long-term income tax-free growth on the Roth funds ultimately more than compensates for the taxes you have to pay on whatever amount of money you convert from your IRA or 401(k). With a sufficient investment time line, it isn't unusual for families to be better off by well over $1,000,000 with a $100,000 Roth IRA conversion.

Here are some additional considerations if you are contemplating a Roth IRA conversion in 2010:

- If an IRA owner makes a Roth conversion in 2010 he or she will be able to spread the taxable income over two years: 2011 and 2012.

- The Roth IRA conversion will reduce future minimum required distributions for the IRA owner because there are no minimum required distributions (MRDs) from Roth IRAs for the original owner or the spouse of the original owner.

- Roth IRA conversions will be especially advantageous to wealthy IRA owners who have sufficient after-tax funds to pay the income taxes due on the conversion.

- For those subject to death taxes, the Roth IRA conversion gives the taxpayer an opportunity to reduce the size of their estates by the income taxes paid on the conversion.

So what can wealthy IRA owners do now to lay the groundwork for Roth IRA conversions beginning in 2010?

- IRA owners who still have earned income should consider contributing to nondeductible IRAs now so that they can convert those nondeductible IRAs to Roth IRAs. Only the earnings on those nondeductible IRAs from now until 2010 will be subject to income tax when you make the Roth IRA conversion.

- You can also try to control the timing of income to maximize the Roth IRA conversion.

- Finally, if you are going to have to come up with the money to pay the tax on the conversion, it is better to know that ahead of time and plan your investments and cash accordingly. (See Chapter 7 for more details.)

The New Roth 401(k) and Roth 403(b)

With the introduction of the new Roth 401(k) and Roth 403(b) more and more companies are offering their employees the option of making contributions to a traditional 401(k)/403(b) or the new Roth 401(k)/Roth 403(b). For people who are working for companies that offer the new Roth plans, this is a great opportunity to move into the savings environment that offers tax-free growth. Accordingly, we have included a new chapter on Roth 401(k)s and Roth 403(b)s.

All Non-Spouse Beneficiaries of an IRA May Be Entitled to the "Stretch" Benefits of an Inherited IRA, 401(k), and 403(b)

The Pension Protection Technical Corrections Act of 2008 (which may or may not be passed either by the time this book is published or over the next several years) will make it mandatory for all employer retirement plans to offer a non-spouse beneficiary the ability to transfer his or her inherited retirement account balance to an inherited IRA, inherited 401(k) or inherited 403(b). This change will prevent the draconian income tax consequences that non-spouse beneficiaries had to endure when the employer plan required a lump-sum distribution or a five year payout.

This law change will put non-spouse beneficiaries of employer retirement plans on equal footing with non-spouse beneficiaries of inherited IRAs who already qualified for stretch IRA treatment. If this law is passed, 401(k) plan beneficiaries will be able to retain the inherited 401(k) in the tax-deferred account and opt to stretch the distributions over their life expectancies. Now, retirees with balances in their 401(k) accounts who have a portion of their account invested in very good guaranteed investment contracts (GIC) and/or fixed income investment options, may opt to keep a portion of the money in their existing 401(k) rather than feeling compelled to roll their entire 401(k) into an IRA.

Unexpected Roth IRA Conversion Opportunities for Non-Spouse Beneficiaries of Inherited Retirement Plans

Another reason for retirement plan owners to consider opening their own one-person 401(k) plan during their lifetimes is IRS Notice 2008-30 which now permits non-spouse beneficiaries of inherited retirement plan accounts to make a Roth IRA conversion of the inherited 401(k). Until now, inherited IRAs and inherited 401(k)s were treated similarly for the purposes of a Roth IRA conversion of the inherited IRA or retirement plan—neither the inherited IRA nor the inherited 401(k) permitted non-spouse beneficiaries to make a Roth conversion. You would think if Congress decided it was okay to allow non-spouse beneficiaries to do a Roth IRA conversion of an inherited retirement plan (including inherited 401(k)s), they would also offer non-spouse beneficiaries of an inherited IRA the same option.

But they didn't. So at least for now, there are more options for an heir of an inherited 401(k) than an inherited IRA. This change will make it more advantageous for retirees to have their retirement funds in their own controlled one-person 401(k) plan than in an IRA.

Although minimum required distributions would be required from the inherited Roth IRA accounts during the non-spouse beneficiary's lifetime, this unexpected Roth IRA conversion opportunity will provide certain non-spouse beneficiaries with significant income tax benefits. It is anticipated that the IRS or Congress will announce a change in the law in the next few years that will allow inherited IRA to Roth IRA conversions for non-spouse beneficiaries.

Direct Roth IRA Conversion from 401(k) and 403(b) Plans

The final new development is related to a provision in the Pension Protection Technical Corrections Act. Beginning in 2008, you will be able to make a direct conversion from a qualified plan account to a Roth IRA. In the past, you had to transfer your 401(k) balance into a traditional IRA and then convert that traditional IRA to a Roth IRA. The new law makes it possible to transfer your 401(k) account directly to a Roth IRA. But the good news doesn't stop there. There is an additional—and likely unanticipated by Congress—tax benefit with respect to a direct Roth IRA conversion from a 401(k) account. This development relates to the potential opportunity to transfer after-tax contributions (basis) from your qualified plan account into a Roth IRA without having to pay the tax. For a detailed example of what this could mean for you, please see the section in Chapter 6 called *Additional Advantages of Retaining a 401(k) Rather Than Rolling into an IRA*.

As we mentioned at the beginning of this section you will find more details on all of these topics in the book. But we also offer a few other resources for more information.

Please see the back of the book or go to www.retiresecure.com to order your free audio MP3 as well as receive numerous free special reports and updates.

Introduction

The fear of running out of money has grown from a lingering, nagging concern to widespread dread. People ask themselves, "Will we have enough to live comfortably for the rest of our lives? What kind of legacy will we leave our children and grandchildren? Are we proactively taking the right steps to get the most out of what we've got?"

Unfortunately, many people spend too much time worrying about the day-to-day fluctuations in the market and lose sight of the big picture. They need long-term effective tax-savvy strategies and good advice to implement now. Effective strategies are even more important for IRA and retirement plan owners because of the heavy tax burden on these plans. The difference between effective and ineffective tax planning for IRA and retirement plans can be the difference between prosperity and financial ruin.

To provide direction in the IRA and retirement plan field, I have authored several books, and write a monthly IRA and retirement planning newsletter that goes to over 4,000 professional advisors. I also deliver more than 150 presentations each year—all in an effort to provide much-needed advice to both consumers and professional advisors on how to build, preserve, and protect their retirement savings.

Jim Lange shares my passion and vision in this area. He is making a powerful impact by providing cutting-edge advice for IRA and retirement plan owners and their advisors. Jim's valuable analysis and recommendations are unique to *Retire Secure!* You won't find his combination of information and analysis anywhere else—not even in my published work.

But don't think for a minute that Jim's recommendations are new and untested. In 1998, Jim wrote a groundbreaking, peer-reviewed article on Roth IRA conversions for the American Institute of CPAs. In that same article, Jim outlined his comprehensive and now-famous cascading beneficiary plan; an estate plan that many IRA and retirement plan owners should consider. Fortunately for you, the details are all in this book. Jim's advice has stood the test of time and has been thoroughly vetted.

Retire Secure! covers many of the classic directives for sound retirement and estate planning, but the book evaluates them in light of the most recent tax laws. Thankfully, it is also spiced with humor. There are numerous cartoons, fun quotes, and flashes of Jim's good sense of humor.

Jim's overarching recommendation to "Pay Taxes Later" is as valid today as it was when the first edition of *Retire Secure!* was published. This simple phrase applies to all three stages of retirement planning: accumulating retirement assets, spending your assets in retirement, and planning for your heirs.

But let's not forget whose book this is. Jim is a champion of Roth IRAs, Roth 401(k)s, and Roth IRA conversions, and those investments reflect the one place where Jim makes an important exception to his "Pay Taxes Later" mantra. Fortunately for us, Jim succeeds in untangling the myriad of complexities of IRAs and Roth IRAs that can derail even the best of intentions. Jim also delves into an area that deserves much more attention than it's getting—Roth IRA conversions for high-income taxpayers. Due to changes in the 2010 tax laws, Jim and I agree that Roth IRA conversions are going to become a game changer for many families.

I highly recommend that you do yourself and your family a big favor and read *Retire Secure!* Planning for the future is not something to leave to chance. Knowledge is the first defense against mistakes, and taking action is what wins the game. Use *Retire Secure!* to effectively plan for your future.

—Ed Slott, CPA,
Author and Speaker,
www.irahelp.com

Part One

THE ACCUMULATION YEARS

The Best Way to Save for Retirement

1

Fund Retirement Plans to the Maximum

The most powerful force in the universe is compound interest.
—Albert Einstein

Main Topics

- Why contributing the maximum to a retirement plan is so valuable
- The clear advantage of pretax IRA and retirement plan savings
- Why you *must* always contribute to plans with employer-matching
- The two principal categories of retirement plans
- Eight major types of retirement plans and their contribution limits
- Running the numbers for an employer-matching program
- Nonmatched contributions
- Tax-deferred accumulations versus after-tax accumulations
- Options for contributing to more than one plan
- Minimize your life insurance costs to maximize your retirement contributions
- Making contributions when you think you can't afford it

KEY IDEA

Every employee who has access to a retirement plan should contribute the maximum his or her employer is willing to match or even partially match. If you can afford more, make nonmatched contributions.

Why Contributing the Maximum to a Retirement Plan Is So Valuable

A trusted client of mine recently referred to me as her "guardian angel." At first I was totally taken aback—no one had ever called me a guardian angel before. She continued, "Twenty years ago you advised me to put the maximum into my retirement plan. I didn't know if it was a good idea or not, but I trusted you and did what you recommended. Now I have a million dollars in my retirement plan. What should I do now?"

Her question is ultimately answered in this book. But her comment also compelled me to complete a comprehensive analysis of why it was such good advice. I wanted to be able to persuasively convince anyone who harbored the least little doubt about the advantages of saving money in a retirement plan over saving money outside of a retirement plan.

I set myself the challenge of evaluating the outcomes of two different scenarios:

1. You earn the money, you pay the tax, you invest the money you earned, and you pay tax on the dividends, interest, and capital gains.

2. You put money in your retirement plan and you get a tax deduction. Looked at another way, you don't pay income taxes on that money when you invest it. The money grows tax-deferred. You don't have to pay taxes on that money until you take it out.

The first question is, "Is it better to save inside the retirement plan or outside the retirement plan?" The answer: "It is better to save within the retirement plan." Why? This isn't a touchy-feely issue. It comes down to numbers. Let's take a look.

MINI CASE STUDY 1.1

The Clear Advantage of Pretax IRA and Retirement Plan Savings

Mr. Pay Taxes Later and Mr. Pay Taxes Now are neighbors. Looking at them from the outside, you wouldn't be able to tell them apart. They own the same type of car; their salaries are the same; they are in the same tax bracket. Their savings have the same investment rate of return. They even save the same percentage of their gross wages every year.

They have one big difference. Mr. Pay Taxes Later invests as much as he can afford in his tax-deferred retirement plan—his 401(k)—even though his employer does not match his contributions. Mr. Pay Taxes Now feels that putting money in a retirement account makes it "not really his money," as he puts it. He doesn't want to have to pay taxes to take out his own money, or put up with the other limits to his access of "his money." Thus he contributes nothing to his retirement account at work but invests his savings in an account outside of his retirement plan. Mr. Pay Taxes Now invests the old-fashioned way: earn the money, pay the tax, invest the money, and pay the tax on the income that the invested money generates (dividends, capital gains, etc.).

Both men begin investing at age 30.

- In 2008, they start saving $5,000 per year, indexed for inflation.

- Mr. Pay Taxes Later has his entire $5,000 withheld from his paycheck and deposited to his tax-deferred 401(k). (The analysis would be identical if he contributed the money to a traditional deductible IRA.)

- Mr. Pay Taxes Now chooses not to have any retirement funds withheld but rather to be paid in full. He has to pay income taxes on his full wages, including the $5,000 he chose not to contribute to his retirement plan. He has to pay income tax immediately on the $5,000. After the 25 percent income tax is paid, he has only 75 percent of the $5,000, or $3,750, left to invest.

Now look at Figure 1.1. Mr. Pay Taxes Later's investment is represented by the gray curve, and Mr. Pay Taxes Now's by the black. Look at the dramatic difference in the accumulations over time.

Figure 1.1

Retirement Assets, IRAs, etc., vs. After-Tax Accumulations

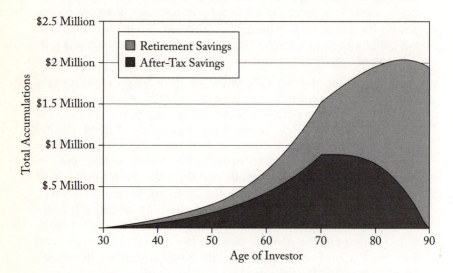

The assumptions for this graph include the following:

1. Investment rate of return is 7 percent including 70 percent capital appreciation, with 15 percent portfolio turnover rate, 15 percent dividend income, and 15 percent interest income.

2. Mr. Pay Taxes Later makes retirement savings contributions of $5,000 per year. Mr. Pay Taxes Now invests 25 percent less due to taxes. Both amounts are indexed for 2.5 percent annual raises, starting at age 30 until age 70.

3. Starting at age 71, spending from both investors' accounts is equal to the minimum required distributions (MRDs) from Mr. Pay Taxes Later's retirement plan less related income taxes.

4. Mr. Pay Taxes Later withdraws only the minimum required distribution (MRD), pays the 25 percent income tax due on his distribution, and spends the rest. Mr. Pay Taxes Now spends the same amount plus he pays income taxes due on his interest, dividends, and realized capital gains.

5. Ordinary tax rates are 25 percent.

6. Capital gains tax rates are 15 percent for 2008 to 2010 and 19 percent thereafter.

7. Dividends are taxed as capital gains during 2008 to 2010 and as ordinary income thereafter.

Now, to be fair, Mr. Pay Taxes Later will have to pay the taxes eventually. When he is retired, for every dollar he wants to withdraw, he has to take out $1.33. He pockets the dollar and pays $0.33 in taxes (25 percent of $1.33). If Mr. Pay Taxes Now withdraws a dollar, subject to some capital gains taxes, it's all his, just as he wanted. At age 90, however, Mr. Pay Taxes Now has depleted his funds entirely whereas Mr. Pay Taxes Later has $1,946,949 left in his retirement plan.

> **All things being equal, following the adage "Don't pay taxes now—pay taxes later" can be worth almost $2 million over a lifetime.**

Given reasonable assumptions and all things being equal, following the adage "Don't pay taxes now—pay taxes later" can be worth almost $2 million over a lifetime.

After spending your life working hard, paying the mortgage, paying the bills, raising a family, and putting your kids through college, you may never have expected to have such a substantial IRA or retirement plan and be so well off in retirement. To many of my clients, it seems like a fantasy.

A realistic and common emotional reaction is fear. It could be fear of the unknown or fear because you're not sure what to do next. Many readers are scared they will make costly mistakes and/or mismanage their retirement money. The fear is paralyzing, so they do nothing—literally, nothing. They procrastinate and avoid doing important planning for their IRA and retirement plan. That may have been you until now.

You have already made a great start by buying this book. Now, please read it and know that I have done everything in my power to provide you with the best information available on planning for your IRA and/or retirement plan. After all, your future and your financial security depend on your handling your retirement finances properly. After reading this book, *don't do nothing*. Promise yourself that reading this book will be more than an academic exercise. Promise yourself that it will motivate you to take action—take the critical steps that will put you and your family in a much more secure position than you are in today.

Make Those Nonmatched Contributions to Retirement

What conclusion can we draw from Mini Case Study 1.1? Don't pay taxes now—pay taxes later. Even putting aside the additional advantage of matching contributions, you should contribute the maximum to your retirement plan, assuming you can afford it. Money contributed to a retirement plan, whether a 401(k), 403(b), SEP, SIMPLE, 457, deductible IRA, or another type of retirement plan, is a pretax investment that grows tax-deferred. There are no federal income taxes on the wages contributed.

Some taxpayers look at it as a deduction. Whichever way you look at it, you are getting a tax break for the amount of the contribution multiplied by the tax rate for your tax bracket. Furthermore, once the contribution is made, you do not pay income taxes on the interest, dividends, and appreciation *until you take a distribution* (i.e., withdrawal) from the retirement plan. In other words, you pay taxes later.

By not paying the taxes up front on the wages earned, you reap the harvest of compounding interest, dividends, and capital gains on the money that would have gone to paying taxes—both on the amount contributed and on the growth had the money been invested outside of the retirement plan.

In the real world, not only is there a tax advantage to saving in a retirement plan but it builds in the discipline of contributing to your retirement plan with every paycheck. The example above is assuming that if you don't put the money in your retirement plan, you are saving and investing an amount that would be equivalent to your contribution. But can you trust yourself to be a disciplined saver? Will the temptation to put it off till the next paycheck undermine your resolve? Even if it is put away for savings, knowing you have unrestricted access to the money, can you be confident that you would never invade that fund until you retire?

In my practice, the clients who usually have the most money saved at retirement are the ones who religiously contributed to a retirement plan during their long career.

> In my practice, the clients who usually have the most money saved at retirement are the ones who religiously contributed to a retirement plan during their long career.

The idea of paying taxes later and contributing the maximum to your retirement plan(s) is something that I have preached in my practice for over 20 years. Many of my long-standing clients took my advice 20 years ago—even if they didn't completely understand why—and now they are thanking me.

The Employer Matching Retirement Plan

With all due respect, broadly speaking, you have to be pretty "simple" (that's a nice word for "stupid") not to take advantage of a retirement plan where the employer is making a matching contribution.

The Cardinal Rule of Saving for Retirement

Money won is twice as sweet as money earned.
— Paul Newman, *The Color of Money*

If your employer offers a matching contribution to your retirement plan, the cardinal rule is: Contribute whatever the employer is willing to match—even if it is only a percentage of your contribution and not a dollar-for-dollar match.

Imagine depositing $1,000 of your money in a bank, but instead of getting a crummy toaster, you receive an extra $1,000 to go along with your deposit. To add to the fun, imagine getting a tax deduction for your deposit and not having to pay tax on your gift. Furthermore, both your $1,000 and the gift $1,000 grow (it is to be hoped), and you don't have to pay income tax on the interest, dividends, capital gains, or the appreciation until you withdraw the money. When you withdraw the money, you will have to pay taxes, but you will have gained interest, dividends, and appreciation in the meantime. That is what employer-matching contributions to retirement plans are all about. If the employer matches the employee contribution on a dollar-for-dollar basis, it offers a *100 percent return on the investment in one day* (assuming no early withdrawal penalties apply and the matched funds are fully vested).

Over the years, I have heard hundreds of excuses for not taking advantage of an employer-matching plan. With few exceptions, all those reasons come down to two words: *ignorance* and *neglect*. If you didn't know that before, you know it now. If you are not currently taking advantage of your employer-matching plan, run—don't walk—to your plan administrator and begin the paperwork to take advantage of the employer match. Matching contributions are most commonly found within 401(k), 403(b), and 457 plans. Many eligible 403(b) plan participants also may have access to a 457. You can, in effect, enjoy double the ability to tax-defer earnings through participation in both the 403(b) and 457 plans. Even if your employer is only willing to make a partial-match up to a cap, you should still take advantage of this opportunity. For example, a fairly common retirement plan agreement may provide that the employer contribute 50 cents for every dollar up to the first 6 percent of salary you contribute. Keep in mind: This is free money!

> **Many eligible 403(b) plan participants also may have access to a 457. You can, in effect, enjoy double the ability to tax-defer earnings through participation in both the 403(b) and 457 plans.**

Again, this isn't touchy-feely stuff. It is backed by hard numbers.

MINI CASE STUDY 1.2
Running the Numbers for Employer-Matched Retirement Plans

Scenario 1

- Bill earns $75,000 per year and is subject to a flat 25 percent federal income tax (for simplicity, I ignore other taxes and assume a flat federal income tax). (25% × $75,000 = $18,750 tax)

- He spends $50,000 per year.

- He doesn't use his retirement plan at work, so he has $6,250 available for investment: ($75,000 income – [$18,750 tax and $50,000 spending] = $6,250 available cash).

Scenario 2

Bill's dad is very wise. He bought *Retire Secure!* After reading this chapter, he advises his son Bill to contribute the maximum amount that Bill's employer is willing to match. Uncharacteristically, Bill listens to his dad and contributes $5,000 to his retirement account. Bill is fortunate because his employer matches his contribution 100 percent. Thus $10,000 goes into his retirement account.

Under current tax laws, Bill will not have to pay federal income tax on his retirement plan contribution or on the amount his employer is willing to match.

By using his employer's retirement plan, Bill's picture changes for the better as follows:

- Bill pays tax on only $70,000.

  ($75,000 income – $5,000 tax-deferred)

  (25% × $70,000 = $17,500 tax)

- He now has $57,500 ($75,000 income – $17,500 taxes).

- He makes his plan contribution of $5,000, leaving him with $52,500 outside the plan.

- His employer matches the $5,000 (also tax-deferred).

- He now has $10,000 in his retirement plan (growing tax-deferred).

- He spends $50,000 per year.

- He is left with $2,500 in cash.

Which scenario strikes you as more favorable: Scenario 2 with $10,000 in a retirement plan and $2,500 in cash, or Scenario 1 with no retirement plan and $6,250 in cash? The extreme cynic can figure out situations when he may prefer a little extra cash and no retirement plan. For the rest of us, we will take advantage of any employer-matching retirement plan.

Please remember that the money in the retirement plan will continue to grow, and you will not have to pay income taxes on the earnings, dividends, interest, or accumulations until you or your heirs withdraw your money. Even without the future deferral, at the end of the first year, assuming the employer-matched funds are fully vested, the comparative values of these two scenarios are measured by after-tax purchasing power as follows:

	Scenario 1	Scenario 2
After-tax cash available	$6,250	$2,500
Retirement plan balance	0	$10,000
Tax on retirement plan balance	0	($2,500)
Early withdrawal penalty	0	($1,000)
Total purchasing power	$6,250	$9,000

Obviously, it is better to take advantage of the retirement plan and the employer's matching contributions. Let's hope you can afford to do this and maintain the tax-deferred growth for many years, thus avoiding early withdrawal penalties altogether.

There is an interesting option if you want to see your child's retirement plan grow, but your child claims not to have sufficient cash flow to contribute to his retirement plan, even though his employer is matching 100 percent. You may consider making a gift to your child in the amount that your child would be out of pocket by making a contribution to his retirement plan. In this example, you could make a gift of $3,750 ($6,250 − $2,500).

For your $3,750 gift, your adult child would end up with $10,000 in his retirement plan. That is an example of a leveraged gift. Lots of bang for your gifted buck.

The long-term advantages of the employer match are even more dramatic. Using the same facts and circumstances as in Mini Case Study 1.1 with the addition of a 100 percent employer match of annual contributions, Figure 1.2 compares stubborn Bill who refuses to use the retirement plan versus compliant Bob who contributes to his retirement plan:

Figure 1.2 reflects higher spending from both accounts since the retirement plan's larger balance requires larger distributions. The higher distributions deplete stubborn Bill's unmatched funds even faster. He would run out at age 80 instead of 90 (in Mini Case Study 1.1), while compliant Bob's matched retirement savings has $3,908,093 remaining, and despite the

Figure 1.2

Retirement Assets Plus an Employer Match vs. After-Tax Accumulations

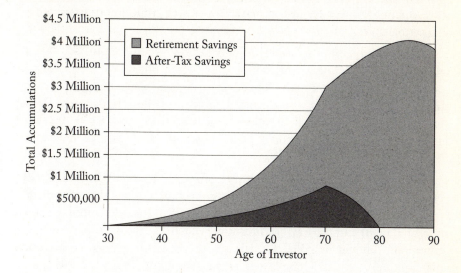

large distributions being made after age 80, compliant Bob's savings are still growing when he reaches 80. The obvious conclusion again is, if you are not already taking advantage of this, run—don't walk—to your plan administrator and begin the paperwork to take advantage of the employer match.

Occasionally, clients moan that they literally can't afford to make the contribution, even though their employer is willing to match it. I am not sympathetic. I would rather see you borrow the money to make matching contributions. Beg, borrow, or steal to find the money to contribute to an employer-matching plan.

Two Categories of Retirement Plans

Generally all retirement plans in the workplace fall into two categories: defined-contribution plans and defined-benefit plans. The plan in the previous example is a defined-contribution plan.

Defined-Contribution Plans

In a defined-contribution plan, each individual employee has an account that can be funded by the employee or the employer or both. At retirement or termination of employment, subject to a few minor exceptions, the account balance represents the funds available to the employee. In a defined-contribution plan, the employee bears the investment risks. In other words, if the market takes a downturn, so does the value of your investments. Conversely, if the market does well, you are rewarded with a higher balance.

The most common defined-contribution plans are 401(k), 403(b), and 457 plans. Defined-contribution plans often offer a wide array of tax-favored investment options. Defined-contribution plans are relatively easy to understand. Most employees with defined-contribution plans usually can tell you the balance in their account—at least to the nearest $100,000. Most employees with defined-benefit plans, however, have no idea how much their plan is worth.

A growing number of employers offer the Roth 401(k) and 403(b) plans. Both are new options for defined-contribution plans that provide tax-free growth. The Simplified Employee Pension plan (more commonly known as a SEP plan) and the Savings Incentive Match Plans for Employees (more commonly known as SIMPLE plans) are attractive defined-contribution plan options for small employers or self-employed individuals. For self-employed individuals with higher incomes (or even my new idea for the "self-employed formerly retired"), consider the relatively new, one-man Super-K, which is basically a one-person 401(k) plan on steroids. More detailed descriptions of these plans appear below.

At retirement or service termination, my most frequent recommendation for retirees used to be "Transfer your funds from defined-contribution plans to an individual retirement account (IRA)." Now, however, since the new law permits beneficiaries of an inherited 401(k) to make a Roth IRA conversion, but (at least while this book was being written) it does not permit nonspouse beneficiaries of IRAs to make a Roth IRA conversion of an inherited IRA, the advice becomes more complicated.

My favorite new strategy is for retirees to set up a personal 401(k) plan. Then retirees should consider rolling their 401(k) plan from their primary place of employment, and even their IRA, to their new personal 401(k) plan. This offers the following benefits:

- There are extremely flexible investment choices.
- Upon the retiree's death, his or her beneficiaries would still be able to make a Roth IRA conversion of the inherited 401(k).
- New Roth IRA conversions are possible.
- There is better protection from creditors than with traditional IRAs.

The flaw of this strategy is that to set up your one-person 401(k) plan, you must have earned income. If you don't have earned income or the possibility of having earned income, then the strategy doesn't work. Therefore, one of the things I love to see my retired clients do is earn a little self-employment income. Perhaps they do a little consulting in their field, or perhaps they take a postretirement job working at the golf course or doing some part-time teaching. Some retirees will even charge people for services they used to perform for free. For example, a retiree could consult with his self-employed child and the self-employed child could pay the parent for consulting. That earned income could be the basis of the new 401(k). On the downside there may be some administrative expenses in setting up and maintaining the plan, but this might amount to only several hundred dollars a year, at the most.

That is not to say that having a lot of money in a company 401(k) or even an IRA is bad, but having it in a one-person 401(k) plan that is completely under the retiree's control is a better strategy for many.

Common Defined-Contribution Plans

Defined-contribution plan accounts often become substantial and are frequently the largest asset in the estate. Typically they are rolled into an IRA at retirement (although, as mentioned above, this strategy must now be evaluated on a case-by-case basis). Therefore the planning for the defined-contribution plan, or the IRA that the defined-contribution plan is eventually rolled into, becomes the most important part of the retirement and estate planning process. The following paragraphs discuss some of the more common defined-contribution plans.

401(k) Plans: This type of plan usually includes both employee and employer tax-deferred contributions. No federal income taxes are paid until the money is withdrawn. Some states, such as Pennsylvania, however, will tax the employee's contribution in the year that the contribution is made. Employer contributions to 401(k)s are usually determined as a percentage of earnings, and the deductible employee contribution is usually limited to a prescribed amount which is $22,000 in 2009 for someone 50 or older and $16,500 under age 50, (it was $20,500 in 2008 for someone 50 or older, $15,500 under 50) with higher inflation adjusted amounts in future years. The company—that is, the employer—is responsible for providing the employee with investment choices, typically six to ten choices in either one or two families of mutual funds. The employer is also responsible for the investments and administration of a 401(k) plan.

403(b) Plans: This plan is similar to a 401(k) plan but is commonly used by certain charitable organizations and public educational institutions, such as universities, colleges, and hospitals. One of the biggest differences between a 401(k) plan and a 403(b) plan is that 403(b) plans can only invest in annuities and mutual funds. TIAA-CREF is the best known and most common 403(b) provider. The new Roth 403(b) combines the features of a Roth IRA and a 403(b). When given a choice, I usually prefer the Roth 403(b) over the traditional 403(b).

457 Plans: After the Economic Growth and Tax Relief Reconciliation Act of 2001 (EGTRRA), 457 plans have become more similar to 401(k) plans. They are commonly used by state and local governmental employers and certain tax-exempt organizations. Typical 457 employees are police officers, firefighters, teachers, and other municipal workers.

An interesting side note is that many eligible 457 plan participants don't even know they are eligible to make a 457 plan contribution. They may have a 403(b) plan and don't know they can in effect enjoy "double" the ability to tax defer earnings through participation in both the 403(b) and 457 plans. A perfect candidate for using both plans would be a married teacher whose spouse has income and the two of them have more than sufficient income for their needs. If they have substantial savings and if they are aged 50 or older in 2009, the teacher could contribute $22,000 to her 403(b) and $22,000 to her 457 plan. By doing that, the couple reduced their taxable income by $44,000.

Roth 401(k) and 403(b) Plans: These plans are discussed more fully in Chapter 3. If your company adopts one of these plans, you will have the option of contributing either into your traditional deductible 401(k) or 403(b) or your nondeductible but tax-free Roth 401(k) or Roth 403(b). Many employers began implementing Roth 401(k) plans beginning in 2006. The new Roth 401(k) combines the features of a Roth IRA and a 401(k). When given a choice, I usually prefer the Roth option for the same reasons that I prefer a Roth IRA to a traditional IRA. At retirement, the Roth 401(k) and 403(b) accounts can be rolled into a Roth IRA. The Roth 401(k) and 403(b) options apply only to the employee's contribution. Any contributions made by the employer are put into a traditional 401(k) or 403(b) account.

SEP: SEP is an acronym for Simplified Employee Pension. These plans are commonly used by employers with very few employees and self-employed individuals. Under a SEP, an employer makes contributions to IRAs, which are not taxable for federal income tax purposes, on behalf of employees. Contribution limits are higher with SEPs than with IRAs. Maximum contributions equal 25 percent of compensation. (You must be careful to look at how *compensation* is defined. After you go through the technical hoops, the contribution actually works out to about 20 percent of what most self-employed people think is compensation.)

Super-K or One-Person 401(k): The Super-K is commonly used by self-employed individuals (with no employees) who want to contribute the most money possible to their own retirement plan. You can contribute a deferral portion up to $22,000 in 2009 (it was $20,500 in 2008) for someone 50 or older with higher inflation-adjusted amounts for later years plus the 25 percent contribution amount subject to limitations. (As with a SEP plan, be careful to define compensation accurately.) For an example of the power of the Super-K and a calculation, please see Judy's example in Mini Case Study 1.3. Please note this is the type of plan I like for the new self-employed retiree. These Super-K plans can also contain the Roth option as mentioned above under Roth 401(k) and 403(b) plans. Again, when given a choice, I usually prefer the Roth feature for the deferral portion.

Deferral Contribution Limits

As a result of a series of tax law changes starting with the Economic Growth and Tax Relief Reconciliation Act of 2001 (EGTRRA), the new deferral contribution limits for employees and owners of many of these individual and defined-contribution plans have grown substantially more generous. The government now allows us to put more money in our retirement plans and provides greater tax benefits. I recommend that we take the government up on its offer to fund our own retirement plans to the extent we can afford it.

The maximum deferral contribution limits for 2008 and 2009 (and methods for changes in 2010) are shown in Table 1.1. (The maximum contributions for individuals younger than 50 are in the regular font and the maximum contributions for those 50 and older are in italics.)

Table 1.1: Maximum Deferral Contribution Limits for 2008–2010

	2008	2009	2010*
SIMPLE Plans[b]	$10,500	$11,500	$11,500[a]
50 and older	*13,000*	*14,000*	*14,000*[a]
401(k), 403(b), 457[c]	$15,500	$16,500	$16,500[a]
50 and older	*20,500*	*22,000*	*22,000*[a]
Roth 401(k) + Roth 403(b)	$15,500	$16,500	$16,500[a]
50 and older	*20,500*	*22,000*	*22,000*[a]
SEP, Super-K[d]	$46,000	$49,000	$49,000[e]
50 and older	*51,000*	*54,500*	*54,500*[e]

*At the time of publication, we did not have conclusive numbers for 2010. As soon as we have the information, which should be in late 2009, we will post it to www.retiresecure.com. Please visit the web site for updates and additional information.

[a] Plus inflation adjustment in $500 increments.

[b] SIMPLE plans are for enterprises with 100 or fewer workers.

[c] 403(b) plans are for nonprofits; 457 plans are for governments and nonprofits. In the last three years before retirement, workers in 457 plans can save double the "under age 50" contribution limit.

[d] Overall plan limits for business owners include total of all contributions by the employer (self-owned business), employee (self), and any forfeitures.

[e] Plus amounts for inflation-related adjustments.

Please note that with the exception of the Roth 401(k) and Roth 403(b) discussed more fully in Chapter 3, every one of the listed retirement plans works basically the same way. Subject to limitations, the participant in each plan receives a tax deduction on the contribution to the plan. The employer's contribution is not subject to federal income taxes nor is the employee's deferral contribution. The employee pays no federal income tax until the funds are withdrawn; funds can only be withdrawn according to specific rules and regulations. Ultimately, the distributions are taxed at ordinary income tax rates. These plans offer tax-deferred growth because as the assets appreciate, taxes on the dividends, interest, and capital gains are deferred—or delayed—until there is a withdrawal or a distribution.

Please note that the taxation of retirement plans differs for state income tax purposes. Some states, such as Pennsylvania, will not give employees a tax deduction for the contribution to their retirement plan. On the other hand, Pennsylvania doesn't tax IRA or retirement plan distributions. Other states, such as California and New York, will give you a state income tax deduction for a contribution, but will require you to pay income tax on the distribution, which presumably over time would mean more revenue for the state because the distributions would include appreciation.

In many respects, an employee's contributions to Roth 401(k) or Roth 403(b) plans are treated similarly to Roth IRA contributions. Just as with a Roth IRA, the participant does not receive a tax deduction on his or her contributions to the plan. Instead, the employee pays the federal and state taxes up front and all investments grow tax-free. As long as the employee does not make a withdrawal during the first five years and until age 59½, there will be no taxes to pay when the money, including growth, is withdrawn. Unlike a Roth IRA, there are MRDs for the Roth 401(k)s and Roth 403(b)s, but transferring the money to a Roth IRA upon retirement could help you avoid these required distributions. Any matching contributions made by the employer would be made with pretax dollars (the traditional 401[k], etc.), and the federal taxes would not be paid until those funds are withdrawn.

Timing and Vesting of Defined-Contribution Plans

It is important to understand when employers are required to make their contribution and when your interest becomes vested.

Employers must make their contributions to an employee's retirement plan by the due date of the employer's federal tax return. As a result, if your employer is on a calendar-year-end, you might not see the match portion of your 401(k) until well after year-end. Other employers match immediately when a contribution is made.

Also, just because the money is credited to your account doesn't necessarily mean it is all yours immediately. The portion you contribute will always be yours, and if you quit tomorrow, the contribution remains your money. The employer's contribution will often become available to you only after working a certain number of years. A common vesting schedule is 20 percent per year that an employee remains with the company until five years have passed. At that point, the employee is 100 percent vested. This is called *graded vesting*. Other plans allow no vesting until the employee has worked for a certain number of years. Then, when he or she reaches that threshold, there is a 100 percent vesting in the employer's contributions. This is called *cliff vesting*.

Defined-Benefit Plans

With a defined-benefit plan, the employer contributes money according to a formula described in the company plan to provide a monthly benefit to the employee at retirement. Many people refer to these types of plans as "my pension." The amount of the benefit is determined based on a formula that considers the number of years of service, salary (perhaps an average of the highest three years), and age. Defined-benefit plans usually do not allow the employee to contribute his or her own funds into the plan, and the employer bears all of the investment risk. When it is time for the employee to collect his monthly benefit, the employer is responsible for paying the benefit—regardless of how the investments have done from the time of the employer's contribution to the time of the employee's distribution.

At retirement, the employee is often given a wide range of choices of how to collect his or her pension. Distribution options generally involve receiving a certain amount of money every month for the rest of one's life. Receiving regular payments for a specified period, usually a lifetime, is called an *annuity*. (Please don't confuse this type of annuity with a tax-deferred annuity or a 403(b) plan, which is also often called an annuity.) The annuity period often runs for your lifetime and that of your spouse. Or it might be defined with a guaranteed period for successor beneficiaries; maybe it is guaranteed for the life of the longest living spouse, or perhaps for a 10-year term regardless of when you die or your wife dies. (A further discussion of annuities can be found in Chapter 8.)

The failure of companies to make their promised payments and announcements of reduced payments has reached crisis proportions and is getting worse. For example, retirees in the airline industries and many other industries suffered serious reductions in their pension income. Many other plans have been frozen, meaning that you will get the benefit accrued up to the frozen date, but you don't get credit for more years of service or increases in pay.

If you are a participant in such a plan, you have some important options to consider at the time of your retirement. For example, let's assume that you are in good health and want the highest annuity income for your life. That often seems like the best option. However, when you die, your surviving spouse is out of luck. It might make more sense to receive reduced payments, but guarantee the payments over the lives of both the husband and wife.

Sometimes owners choose a lower monthly payment because it will last through their life and their spouse's life. Sometimes the owner will take a large annual payment and his or her surviving spouse will receive a fraction, perhaps half or two-thirds throughout his or her life.

But there is another option to consider. The most prudent course might be to take a one-life (not two-life) annuity and use some of the income to purchase life insurance on the owner's life. Should the owner die, the life insurance death benefit can go toward the surviving spouse's support. This is an important decision to be made at your retirement. In these situations, "running the numbers," that is, comparing different potential scenarios, can provide guidance in making a decision. Please note that if you have already retired and already decided to take the highest pension without a survivorship feature, it is not too late to get insurance, if you are still insurable. In other words, if you are retired and are now concerned that by taking a one-life annuity with the highest monthly payment you did not sufficiently provide for your surviving spouse, you could still purchase life insurance.

In many, if not most, situations it is often simplest and best to choose a two-life option ensuring full income to you and your spouse.

Defined-benefit plans were far more popular 20 years ago than they are today. For people with defined-benefit plans, there are limited opportunities to make strategic decisions during the working years to increase retirement benefits. It might be possible to increase the retirement benefit by deferring salary or bonuses into the final years, or working overtime to increase the calculation wage base. These opportunities, however, depend on the plan's formula, and they are often inflexible and insignificant.

Cash Balance Plan

A relatively new and unique version of a defined-benefit plan is known as a *cash balance plan*. Technically, this is a defined-benefit plan, but it has features similar to a defined-contribution plan. Though on the rise, this type of plan is not common. Each employee is given an account to which the employer provides contributions or pay credits, which may be a percentage of pay and an interest credit on the balance in the account. The account's investment earnings to be credited are usually defined by the plan, and the employer bears all downside risk for actual investment earning shortfalls. The increase in popularity of the cash balance plan has been spurred by the increasingly mobile workforce in the United States. Employees may take their cash balance plans with them to a new employer when they change jobs or roll them into an IRA.

How Many Plans Are Available to You?

There is a good possibility that you have the opportunity to invest more money in your retirement plan or plans than you realize. For

There is a good possibility that you have the opportunity to invest more money in your retirement plan or plans than you realize.

many readers who are still working, applying the lessons of this mini case study could save you thousands of dollars every year.

MINI CASE STUDY 1.3
Contributing the Maximum to Multiple Retirement Plans*

Tom and his wife, Judy, both 55, want to make the maximum retirement plan contributions allowable. Tom earns $46,000 per year as a secretary for a school district that has both a 403(b) plan and a Section 457 plan. Judy is self-employed, has no employees, and shows a profit on her Schedule C, Form U.S. 1040, of $80,000 per year. Tom and Judy have a 16-year-old computer-whiz child, Bill, who works weekends and summers doing computer programming for Judy's company. Bill is a legitimate subcontractor, not an employee of Judy's company. Judy pays Bill $17,200 per year. What is the maximum that Tom and Judy and Bill can contribute to their retirement plans for calendar year 2008?

Tom: Calculating Maximum Contributions to Multiple Plans

Under EGTRRA, Tom could contribute $20,500 to his 403(b) plan in 2008 ($15,500 normal limit plus another $5,000 because he is over 50). Please note that under EGTRRA, Tom's retirement plan contribution is not limited to 15 percent of his earnings as it would have been under prior law. Under a special rule specifically relating to 457 plans, he could also contribute another $20,500 to the plan in 2008 (same $15,500 plus $5,000). In addition, he could also contribute $6,000 in 2008 to a Roth IRA ($5,000 per year limit plus $1,000 because he is over age 50) by using the remaining $5,000 of his income (his income is $46,000 less $20,500 for the 403(b) less $20,500 for the 457, which leaves $5,000) and using $1,000 of Judy's income. (Roth IRAs are discussed in more detail in Chapter 2.) Please note the new law allows contributions to all three plans—something not previously permitted. Tom was able to contribute

---

*We have used 2008 amounts for this example. As shown in Table 1.1, the retirement plan contribution limits for 2009 are even higher. It is likely that the contribution amounts will increase in future years as well. As soon as we have the information we will post it to www.retiresecure.com. Please visit www.retiresecure.com for updates and additional information.

the entire amount of his income into retirement plans. In addition, he could use $1,000 of Judy's income to maximize his Roth IRA contribution for 2008.

Judy: Calculating Maximum Contribution to a Super-K

After rejecting a more complicated and more expensive defined-benefit plan, Judy chooses the newly introduced one-person 401(k) plan, or the Super-K plan. Judy could contribute as much as $35,370 into her 401(k) plan. This amount comes from two components. If you were an employee with a 401(k) plan, there would be an employer share and an employee share. Since you are self employed, the plan for self employed taxpayers has the equivalent of an employee and employer share. The first component is the 401(k) elective deferral amount that is limited to $20,500 (the same limits as Tom's 403[b] plan). This $20,500 is the equivalent of the employee's share. Most Super Ks are set up so that you can deduct this $20,500 on your tax return and have this portion taxed like a regular 401(k). If you want this portion to be taxed like a Roth IRA, like we generally recommend, you can set up a Roth Super K, and elect to put this $20,500 into the Roth Super 401(k). Please note this $20,500 could be invested in a traditional Super 401(k) or in the new Roth Super 401(k). Please see Chapter 3 for a detailed comparison of a Roth 401(k) vs. a traditional 401(k).

The second component is a $14,870 discretionary profit-sharing contribution. This is like the employer contribution. Please note that just like a traditional 401(k) plan, the employer portion may not be a Roth. To arrive at the $14,870, Judy's net self-employed income of $80,000 must be reduced by half of her computed self-employment tax, which is $80,000 × 92.35% × 15.3% = $11,304 × 50%, or $5,652. The $74,348 ($80,000 − $5,652) is multiplied by the 20 percent contribution rate limit (for self-employed individuals, and equal to 25 percent of earnings net of the contribution itself) to compute the maximum profit-sharing contribution amount of $14,870. Judy also can make an additional $6,000 contribution to her Roth IRA.

Bill: For Parents Who Are Considering Funding Retirement Plans for Their Children

Although Bill is young, if he can afford it, he should use his $17,200 income to begin making contributions to his retirement plan. Bill will owe $2,430 of self-employment tax, half of which is deductible, so his net earned income for the purposes of retirement plan contributions is $15,985.

Bill could open up a SIMPLE plan and contribute $10,500, plus a 3 percent SIMPLE matching contribution, which is $477 (3% of $17,200 × .9235). The net earned income less these amounts is $5,008, which is enough to fully fund his Roth IRA with $5,000. If he already spent some of the $5,000, his parents could make him a gift of the money.

The tax-free benefit of the Roth IRA and the tax-deferred benefit of the SIMPLE plan are so important to a child during his or her lifetime that some parents who have sufficient funds are willing to fund their child's retirement plan. This is a wonderful idea. However, in order to fund a retirement plan or IRA, the child must have earned income. Some parents will be tempted to create a sham business for their child or even put their child on the payroll as a sham transaction. I do not recommend this approach. I advocate that the child do legitimate work, complying with all child labor laws. All retirement plan contributions should stem from legitimate businesses and, if based on self-employed earnings, be a real business. (I had to say that in case the IRS reads this. In all seriousness, however, there are also nonfinancial benefits in having a child do legitimate work to receive money.)

I have seen parents paying infants to model, characterizing the payment to the infant as self-employed income and making a retirement plan contribution for the infant. I think that goes too far. Any situation where a child younger than 11 years old receives employment compensation is highly suspect. Even at age 11, legitimate compensation should not be too high.

Let's assume that Tom, Judy, and Bill max out their retirement plan contributions. Even though Tom and Judy earned only $126,000 and Bill earned only $17,200, the family could contribute over $104,000 into their retirement plans and Roth IRAs. For subsequent years, the contribution limits are even more generous. Is this a great country or what?

This example intentionally exaggerates the family's likely contributions. The point is to show maximum contribution limits and the variety of plan options. In this particular case, Tom and Judy and Bill may choose not to maximize their contributions because they may not receive any income tax benefits beyond a certain level of contribution. It is worthwhile, however, to review this case study to help with choosing and implementing a new plan.

How to Minimize Your Life Insurance Costs to Maximize Your Retirement Contributions

Often, our younger clients will complain that they cannot maximize their retirement plan contributions because of the cost of their life insurance. Although whole life or guaranteed universal life can be a great vehicle for high income earners to save more money, term insurance is often a better solution for individuals whose budgets don't stretch to afford both the high whole life insurance premiums and maximized retirement plan contributions.

The objective of term life insurance is to protect a family from the financial devastation that can ensue from the untimely death of the primary bread winner(s). It is also important to insure the value of the services of a stay-at-home parent. It is critically important insurance, but it is also to your advantage to try to get the appropriate level of coverage for the most reasonable price. The following section, though by no means complete, presents my favorite idea for many young families to protect themselves in the event of an early, unexpected death, but to do so relatively cheaply. I am working from the premise that I do not like to see people underinsured, but I also want everyone to be thinking ahead to retirement.

One of the most common mistakes my younger clients make is not having sufficient term insurance. Most healthy young people survive until retirement and paying for term insurance is not something anyone really wants to do. In my practice, however, I have known young healthy people who died much too early. In my experience, it is rarely the result of a catastrophic car or plane accident, but more frequently because of the sudden onset of cancer or some other fatal disease.

Most people, however, also have this vague sense that the responsible thing to do is to purchase insurance to protect their families. Some people seek out an insurance provider and initiate a policy; others do something when they are approached by a life insurance professional. In either case they usually end up with some kind of policy. The key is to find a policy that balances adequate insurance and minimum premiums. I don't like to see people, especially younger people, who are working on a limited budget pay high life insurance premiums.

It isn't my intention to present a detailed prescription for determining your life insurance needs. For my purposes here, I will ask you to think about "How much income will your survivors require to live comfortably?" Let's say that after some analysis you decide that an appropriate income is

$60,000 per year in today's dollars. Please note I did not derive this number as a multiple of current salary; it is based purely on projected need.

I am not going to delve into the intricacies of calculating a safe withdrawal rate—that is to say, how much as a percentage of principal you can withdraw and have the money last for a lifetime—but I would say for young people with a long life expectancy, 4 percent would probably be on the high side for a safe withdrawal rate. This means if there is no other source of income, an individual will need at least $1,500,000 of life insurance ($1,500,000 $\times$ 4% = $60,000).

First, I hope I didn't just bum you out and make you realize you are vastly underinsured because $60,000 of income doesn't sound that high and you don't have anywhere near $1,500,000 of insurance.

Admittedly, whatever resources you have can be used to reduce the need for life insurance. If both spouses work, the income of the survivor can certainly be factored in. If you have significant investments or savings, they can also be used to reduce the need.

But to keep things simple, let's assume there aren't significant additional resources and the need is $1,500,000. Also, in this basic example I am not factoring in the additional money that would be required for living expenses and education if there were young children involved.

Let's also assume that at least one member of the couple is working and he or she receives some life insurance as a job benefit. For discussion's sake, we will assume the salary is $100,000 and the insurance benefit is equal to three times the salary. You might say, "Well, that's a start. Now I only need $1,200,000 more."

Sorry, that's the wrong answer. What if you get sick and can't perform your job? You lose your job, you lose your insurance, and because you are sick, you can't get life insurance. (Hopefully, you either have disability insurance through work or you have your own policy, but that is something I don't cover in this book). Whereas group insurance at work is a blessing for people who are uninsurable and can't get life insurance on the open market for a reasonable rate, there are two problems with group life insurance. The first, I just mentioned: If you lose your job, you lose your insurance. The second is that if you are healthy, you can almost always get insurance more economically on the open market.

For young people with cash flow problems, keeping the premiums affordable is critical. Many insurance professionals make a convincing case for permanent insurance, which is a type of policy that ultimately has a cash value. There is a payout when you die, or sometimes upon reaching a certain age. Term insurance, on the other hand, is not designed to pay out if you reach a normal life expectancy. It is designed to pay if you don't survive to a normal life expectancy.

Permanent insurance is expensive. The insurance company will ultimately have to write a check to your beneficiaries, so it costs more. Many of my young working clients come in with some measure of permanent insurance—in some ways it feels better to them. They are paying money into insurance, but they know there will be a payback. However, since it is so much more expensive, many of these same young people are significantly underinsured. If you have permanent insurance of even $500,000, you are still $1,000,000 underinsured even though you have a big premium every year. I would rather see the money going toward sufficient term insurance so the surviving spouse and other family members are protected.

Let's assume that you have a good job and marketable skills. You are prudent and thrifty, putting money into your retirement plan at work and maxing out your Roth IRAs. You do projections and determine that you will have sufficient money to retire at 60 (assuming you are 30 now). You might logically think "Okay, I need a 30-year level term policy (premiums are guaranteed never to go up) for $1,500,000."

Well, that is a reasonable start, but you are likely to find that the guaranteed premium for a level term policy for 30 years for $1,500,000 is more than you want to pay for insurance. Well, are you really going to need that much coverage for the whole time? Perhaps not. If you work and save for 10 years, you may only need $1,000,000 at that point in time. Perhaps in the 10 years beyond that, your need may drop to $500,000. I am trying to keep it simple to make a point. As you change, your insurance needs will change, and thinking within this more flexible framework offers some new options.

Since I am being frugal with your insurance budget, consider the following set of policies, assuming the above situation.

- Get a 30-year term policy for $500,000 coverage
- Get a 20-year term policy for $500,000 coverage
- Get a 10-year term policy for $500,000 coverage

If you die between the date the policy is issued and year 10, your heirs get $1,500,000, which is what we determined was the needed amount. At the end of 10 years, the first policy ends and you will only have $1,000,000 of coverage. That is okay. By this point you should have $500,000 in retirement plans and savings. In addition, the need for insurance will be down a little bit because your heirs will have a shorter life expectancy.

After 20 years the second policy ends and you will only have $500,000 of coverage remaining. That is okay because by this time you should have $1,000,000 of retirement and savings, and your need will only be $500,000. At the end of 30 years, you will have no coverage, but again, that is okay because hopefully by then you will have accrued sufficient resources for your surviving spouse.

Of course in the above example I have kept things really simple. I have not included relevant factors like inflation, children's needs, the ability of the surviving spouse to work, and so forth.

But you get the idea. We have helped a number of our clients reach their goal of adequate coverage through this layered system. Frequently, a 30-year level term policy costs more than individuals might want to pay or can afford, so they compromise by not getting the insurance coverage they really need. I would prefer to see you get the coverage you need using some variation of the layered approach that I have suggested. Remember, the goal was sufficient coverage for a reasonable cost.

In all fairness, I didn't invent this layered approach. I learned it from Tom Hall, an excellent broker I work with in Pittsburgh. This brings up another point. After you decide to get the insurance you need, I recommend purchasing your insurance through an ethical insurance broker (someone who can purchase insurance from many different companies). In our experience, working with a broker is the way to get the best policies at the best rates. (For more on working with brokers and qualifying for the best insurance rates, read Chapter 12.) If you don't have or know an appropriate insurance broker, please see the back of the book.

When You Think You Can't Afford to Make the Maximum Contributions

Maybe now I have helped you rethink your insurance-retirement savings quandary. But you still feel you cannot afford to save for retirement. The truth is you may very well be able to afford to save, but you don't realize it. That's right. I am going to present a rationale to persuade you to contribute more than you think you can afford.

Let's assume you have been limiting your contributing to the portion that your employer is willing to match and yet you barely have enough money to get by week to week. Does it still make sense to make nonmatched contributions assuming you do not want to reduce your spending? Maybe.

If you have substantial savings and maximizing your retirement plan contributions causes your net payroll check to be insufficient to meet your expenses, I still recommend maximizing retirement plan contributions. The shortfall for your living expenses from making increased pretax retirement plan contributions should be withdrawn from your savings (money that has already been taxed). Over time this process, that is, saving the most in a retirement plan and funding the shortfall by making after-tax withdrawals from an after-tax account, transfers money from the after-tax environment to the pretax environment. Ultimately it results in more money for you and your heirs.

Maybe now I have helped you rethink your insurance-retirement savings quandary. But you still feel you cannot afford to save for retirement. The truth is you may very well be able to afford to save, but you don't realize it.

MINI CASE STUDY 1.4
Changing Your IRA and Retirement-Plan Strategy after a Windfall or an Inheritance

Joe always had trouble making ends meet. He did, however, know enough to always contribute to his retirement plan the amount his employer was willing to match. Because he was barely making ends meet and had no savings in the after-tax environment, he never made a nonmatching retirement plan contribution. Tragedy then struck Joe's family. Joe's mother died, leaving Joe $100,000. Should Joe change his retirement plan strategy?

Yes. Joe should not blow the $100,000. If his housing situation is reasonable, he should not use the inherited money for a house—or even a down payment on a house. Instead, Joe should increase his retirement plan contribution to the maximum. In addition, he should start making Roth IRA contributions (see Chapter 2). (This solid advice freaked out a real estate investor after he read it in the first edition. He thought the money should have been used to invest in real estate. Being that aggressive, however, is a risky strategy, unsuitable for many, if not most, investors.)

Assuming Joe maintains his preinheritance lifestyle, between his Roth IRA contribution and the increase in his retirement plan contribution, Joe will not have enough to make ends meet without eating into his inheritance. That's okay. He should cover the shortfall by making withdrawals from the inherited money. True, if that pattern continues long enough, Joe will eventually deplete his inheritance in its current form. But his retirement plan and Roth IRA will be so much better financed that in the long run, the tax-deferred and tax-free growth of these accounts will make Joe better off by thousands, possibly hundreds of thousands, of dollars. The only time this strategy would not make sense is if Joe needed the liquidity of the inherited money, or he preferred to use the inherited funds to pay personal expenses or even to liquidate debt.

A Key Lesson from This Chapter

You should contribute the maximum you can afford to all the retirement plans to which you have access.

2

Traditional IRAs versus Roth IRAs

All days are not [the] same. Save for a rainy day.
When you don't work, savings will work for you.

—M. K. Soni

Main Topics

- How traditional IRAs and Roth IRAs differ
- The principal advantages and disadvantages of a Roth IRA
- Eligibility rules for both Roth and traditional IRAs
- Contribution limits for both Roth and traditional IRAs
- Choosing between opening a Roth IRA and a traditional IRA
- Distribution regulations for Roth IRAs and traditional IRAs

---

KEY IDEA

The Roth IRA is always preferable to a nondeductible traditional IRA and usually better than a deductible traditional IRA contribution.

What Is the Difference between an IRA and a Roth IRA?

IRAs allow individuals who earn income to make contributions to their own retirement accounts. IRA owners can deduct IRA contributions if they meet either of these two requirements:

- They (and their spouse, if married) do not have a retirement plan at work.

- They earn less income than the adjusted gross income (AGI) limit for deducting IRA contributions. (Please see discussion following regarding traditional IRA eligibility rules.)

If IRA owners have income above the limit for which they are permitted to deduct the contribution, they may still contribute to an IRA, but without the benefit of a tax deduction. These are commonly referred to as *nondeductible IRA contributions*.

Within limits, the IRA owner deducts the contribution to the IRA and the IRA grows tax-deferred. That is to say, no income taxes are due until money is withdrawn, at which point the distribution will be subject to federal income taxes. With the exception of the Roth and the defined benefit plan, all the other plans mentioned in Chapter 1 can usually be rolled into an IRA, income tax-free, at retirement or service termination.

> The main characteristic of the Roth IRA is that the investment grows tax-free, and is not taxed when qualified withdrawals are made.

The main characteristic of the Roth IRA is that the investment grows tax-free, and is not taxed when qualified withdrawals are made. However, unlike the traditional IRA, there is no income tax deduction up front.

Roth IRAs differ from traditional IRAs in the following ways:

	Roth IRA	**IRA**
Investment	Grows tax-free	Grows tax-deferred
Withdrawals (qualified)	Tax-free	Taxed as ordinary income
Contributions	Not deductible	Deductible (if qualified)
Income limits	Much higher than for a deductible IRA	Much lower (for deduction) than for a Roth IRA
Contribution limits	Same as IRA	Same as Roth IRA
Required distributions at 70½	No	Yes

The Roth IRA income limit on contributions is much higher than the traditional deductible IRA income limit on contributions. This allows many higher income earners who are not eligible for a deductible IRA to participate in a Roth IRA. Individuals who earn less than the maximum Roth IRA income limit (please see discussion below regarding Roth IRA eligibility rules) can make annual Roth IRA contributions, bearing in mind that there is no tax deduction for Roth IRA contributions.

Nondeductible IRA Contributions

People with earned income who are ineligible to make traditional deductible IRA or Roth IRA contributions because their income is above the limits, can still make contributions to their IRAs, but without the deduction. These nondeductible IRAs are also available for people who are above the income limits to make Roth IRA contributions.

It is important to recognize that if you are eligible to make Roth IRA contributions, the Roth is a much better choice than the nondeductible IRA. Remember, the Roth IRA will be tax-free when the money is withdrawn, and the nondeductible IRAs will be taxable to the extent of growth in the account. Roth IRAs can provide a much better result over the long term. Many people make the mistake of contributing to the nondeductible IRA instead of the Roth IRA when they have a choice. Although the mistake can be mitigated if caught in time, this mistake results in needless taxes in the future.

> It is important to recognize that if you are eligible to make Roth IRA contributions, the Roth is a much better choice than the nondeductible IRA. Remember, the Roth IRA will be tax-free when the money is withdrawn, and the nondeductible IRAs will be taxable to the extent of growth in the account.

Nondeductible IRA contributions that provide tax-deferred growth, however, are still of great benefit for many high income people who do not qualify for Roth IRAs and deductible IRAs. Furthermore, in 2010, high income individuals will be eligible to convert their nondeductible IRA accounts into Roth IRAs with little or no tax cost. This is opportunity knocking, given a little forethought.

What Makes a Roth IRA So Great When Compared with a Traditional IRA?

The advantages of compounding on both tax-deferred investments and on tax-free investments outweigh paying yearly taxes on the capital gains, dividends, and interest of after-tax investments. Generally, you are better off putting more money in the tax-deferred and tax-free accounts than the less efficient after-tax investments. Remember that with a regular after-tax investment you have to pay income taxes on annual dividends, interest, and, if you make a sale, a capital gains tax.

The advantage that the Roth IRA holds over a traditional IRA builds over time with an increase in purchasing power. Let's assume you make a $6,000 Roth IRA contribution. Purchasing power of $6,000 will be added to your Roth IRA and that money will grow income tax-free. Let's assume you contribute $6,000 to a deductible traditional IRA and you are in the 25 percent tax bracket. In that case, you will receive a tax deduction of $6,000 and get a $1,500 tax break (25% × $6,000). This $1,500 in tax savings is neither tax-free nor tax-deferred. If it is saved in an investment account, you will be taxed each year on realized interest, dividends, and capital gains. This is inefficient investment growth. The $6,000 of total dollars added to the traditional IRA offers only $4,500 of purchasing power ($6,000 total dollars less $1,500 that represents your tax savings). The $1,500 of tax savings initially has $1,500 of purchasing power, so initially the purchasing power is the same as for the Roth that is equal to $6,000. However, going into the future, the growth on the $6,000 of purchasing power is all tax-free in the Roth and only partially tax-deferred and partially taxable on an annual basis in the traditional IRA scenario. And remember, tax-free growth has a significant advantage over taxable growth.

One of the few things in life better than tax-deferred compounding is tax-free compounding. If you are eligible and can afford it, after making your employer-matched contribution to a retirement plan and the appropriate nonmatched contributions as well, I generally recommend making additional annual contributions to a Roth IRA. Although you don't get an income tax deduction for your contribution to a Roth IRA, as you might with a traditional IRA, the tax savings are neither tax-free nor tax-deferred. When you eventually do make a withdrawal from your Roth IRA (or even when your heirs make a withdrawal), the distribution is income tax-free. The distribution from a traditional IRA will be taxable.

> **One of the few things in life better than tax-deferred compounding is tax-free compounding.**

The essence of a Roth IRA (in contrast to a traditional IRA) is that you pay tax on the seed (the contribution because you don't get a deduction) but reap the harvest tax-free (the distribution). With a traditional IRA, you deduct the seed, but pay tax on the harvest.

The principal advantages of Roth IRAs are:

> **The essence of a Roth IRA (in contrast to a traditional IRA) is that you pay tax on the seed (the contribution because you don't get a deduction) but reap the harvest tax-free (the distribution).**

- With limited exceptions, they grow income tax-free.

- They are not subject to the minimum required distribution rules requiring withdrawals at age 70½. You will never be required to take distributions during your lifetime. You may choose to, but you don't have to. When you die and if you leave your Roth IRA to your spouse, your spouse will not have to take minimum required distributions either.

- More liberal contribution rules are in place.

- If needed, all of your after-tax annual contributions are always eligible for withdrawal at any time without tax consequences.

- If you have earned income after age 70½, you can keep contributing money to your Roth IRA (and so can your spouse, based on your income). This is not an option for a traditional IRA; contributions must stop at 70½.

- In cases where maximum retirement contributions are made and there are also after-tax-savings, forgoing a tax deduction helps to lower the amount of after-tax savings while putting more value in the tax-free environment. Keep in mind that after-tax savings have inefficient tax consequences on their investment returns.

The result of the many advantages of the Roth IRA in many cases is that the heirs receive income tax-free distributions for their entire lives.

The principal disadvantages of Roth IRAs are:

- You do not receive a tax deduction when you make a contribution. You will then have less money to invest in after-tax funds or to spend. But remember, after-tax funds are not tax efficient due to taxes on income. And if you simply spend the tax savings, the Roth alternative will look even better because it forces you to save and build a more valuable IRA.

- If you drop into a lower tax bracket once you begin taking your IRA distributions, you may sometimes do better with a traditional IRA. In this case, the tax savings from the deductible contribution would exceed the taxes paid upon withdrawal. Sometimes this disadvantage can be offset by a longer period of tax-free growth.

- The Roth IRA account may go down in value. In that case, if the decline becomes large enough, you would have been better off with a deductible IRA. At least you would have received a tax deduction on your contributions. If you have lost a lot of money in a Roth IRA, there is some relief. If you liquidate all your Roth IRAs and you recognize a loss, this loss can be claimed as a miscellaneous itemized deduction, subject to phase outs, on schedule A. As always, prudent investment strategies should be used to reduce this possibility.

- If Congress ever eliminates the income tax in favor of a sales tax or value-added tax, you will have given up your tax deduction on the traditional IRA. And since the distribution will be tax-free anyway, in retrospect, the choice of a Roth IRA would have been a mistake. This situation is similar to the extreme example of having lower tax brackets in retirement.

What follows is a primer comparing traditional IRAs or nonmatched retirement plan contributions versus Roth IRAs. This section covers eligibility rules, limitations, and analysis.

Roth IRA Eligibility Rules

1. As with any IRA, an individual must have earned income in order to contribute to a Roth IRA. Earned income includes wages, commissions, self-employment income, and other amounts received for personal services, as well as taxable alimony and separate maintenance payments received under a decree of divorce or separate maintenance.

2. Individuals must meet the income tests, which exclude higher income taxpayers from contributing to Roth IRAs.

3. A married individual filing a joint return may make a Roth IRA contribution for the nonworking spouse by treating his compensation as his spouse's, but must exclude any of his own IRA contributions from the income treated as his spouse's. (Total contributions cannot exceed your income. For example, if you make $7,000, you can contribute $5,000 to your Roth, but only $2,000 to your spouse's Roth.) (See Table 2.1.)

Table 2.1: 2008 and 2009 Eligibility Rules for Roth IRAs

		Full Contribution	Reduced Contribution	No Contribution
Single & Head of Household	2008	Up to $101,000	$101,001–$115,999	$116,000+
	2009	Up to $105,000	$105,001–$119,999	$120,000+
Married Filing Jointly	2008	Up to $159,000	$159,001–$168,999	$169,000+
	2009	Up to $166,000	$166,001–$175,999	$176,000+

Traditional IRA Eligibility Rules

1. All taxpayers with earned income are allowed to contribute to a traditional IRA without regard to income level.

2. If neither you nor your spouse participates in an employee-sponsored retirement plan, you can deduct the full amount of the traditional IRA contributions.

3. If you are covered by a retirement plan at work, there are adjusted gross income (AGI) limits for allowing full deductions, partial deductions, and limits above which no deductions are permitted. They are shown in Table 2.2.

Table 2.2: 2008 and 2009 AGI Limitations for Deducting a Traditional IRA if There Is a Retirement Plan at Work

		Fully Deductible	Partially Deductible	Not Deductible
Single & Head of Household	2008	Up to $53,000	$ 53,001–$62,999	$ 63,000+
	2009	Up to $55,000	$ 55,001–$64,999	$ 65,000+
Married Filing Jointly	2008	Up to $85,000	$85,001–$104,999	$105,000+
	2009	Up to $89,000	$89,001–$108,999	$109,000+
Married Filing Separately	2008 and 2009	n/a	Up to $10,000	$ 10,000+

4. A spousal contribution can also be made for a nonworking spouse when the other spouse has earned income and a joint tax return is filed. The nonworking spouse's contributions are limited when the working spouse participates in an employee-sponsored retirement plan:

   a. Fully Deductible—Up to $159,000 of AGI for 2008; $116,000 for 2009

b.   Partially Deductible—$159,001 to $168,999 of AGI for 2008; $166,001 to $175,999 for 2009

c.   Not Deductible—$169,000 + of AGI for 2008; $176,000 for 2009

If you are not eligible to deduct a traditional IRA contribution, but you are eligible and choose to make a nondeductible IRA contribution, you will still gain the advantage of tax-deferred growth, but you won't get the income tax deduction up front.

The choice between a nondeductible IRA that grows tax-deferred and a Roth IRA that grows income tax-free is a no-brainer: Choose the Roth. Neither one offers a deduction, but the Roth grows tax-free, whereas the nondeductible IRA only grows tax-deferred.

Contribution Limits for Both Roth and Traditional IRAs

The permitted contribution amounts are the same for both Roth IRAs and traditional IRAs. Note that the total permitted contribution amount applies both to IRAs and Roth IRAs, which means that for 2008 and 2009, you can only contribute a total of $5,000 ($6,000 if you are 50 or older) to IRAs and Roth IRAs. The total IRA and/or Roth IRA contributions cannot exceed earned income, but other than that, the contribution limits for 2008 and 2009 and beyond are shown in Table 2.3.

Table 2.3: Contribution Limits for 2008, 2009, and Beyond

Year	Annual IRA/Roth IRA Contribution Limits	Catch-Up Contribution Limits for Individuals 50 and Older
2008, 2009 and beyond*	$5,000	$1,000

*At the time of publication, we did not have conclusive numbers for 2010. As soon as we have the information, we will post it to www.retiresecure.com. Please visit the site for updates and additional information.

As with traditional IRAs, a married individual filing a joint return may make a Roth IRA contribution for the nonworking spouse by treating his compensation as his spouse's.

Should I Contribute to a Traditional Deductible IRA or a Roth IRA?

As stated earlier, a Roth versus a nondeductible IRA is a no-brainer: Always go for the Roth. But for those individuals with a choice between a Roth IRA and a fully deductible IRA, how should you save? The conclusion is, in most cases, the Roth IRA is superior to the deductible IRA (and nonmatched retirement plan contributions like 401[k]s).

To determine whether a Roth IRA would be better than a traditional IRA, you must take into account:

The conclusion is, in most cases, the Roth IRA is superior to the deductible IRA (and nonmatched retirement plan contributions like 401[k]s).

- The value of the tax-free growth of the Roth versus the tax-deferred growth of the traditional IRA including the future tax effects of withdrawals

- The tax deduction you lost by contributing to a Roth IRA rather than to a fully deductible IRA

- The growth, net of taxes, on savings from the tax deduction from choosing a deductible traditional IRA

In most circumstances, the Roth IRA is significantly more favorable than a regular IRA. (In May 1998, I published an article in *The Tax Adviser*, a publication of the American Institute of Certified Public Accountants, that offered the mathematical proof that the Roth IRA was often a more favorable investment than a regular IRA.) The Jobs and Growth Tax Relief Reconciliation Act of 2003 (JGTRRA) and subsequent tax legislation changed tax rates for all brackets and reduced tax rates for dividends and capital gains to 15 percent for years through 2010. After these tax laws changed, I incorporated the changes into the analysis of Roth versus traditional IRA. The Roth was still preferable in most situations, although the advantage of the Roth was not quite as great as before JGTRRA. Now, with anticipated future increases in dividend and capital gains rates, and potentially ordinary tax rates, the Roth's advantage is increasing.

Figure 2.1 shows the value to the owner of contributing to a Roth IRA versus a regular deductible IRA measured in purchasing power.

Figure 2.1 reflects the following assumptions:

1. Contributions to the Roth IRA are made in the amount of $6,000 per year, beginning in 2008, for a 55-year-old investor, for 11 years until age 65.

2. Contributions to the regular deductible IRA savings are made in the amount of $6,000 per year for the same time period, but because this creates an income tax deduction, 25 percent of this amount, or $1,500, is also contributed into an after-tax savings account.

3. The investment rate of return is 8 percent per year.

Figure 2.1

Roth IRA Savings vs. Traditional IRA Savings

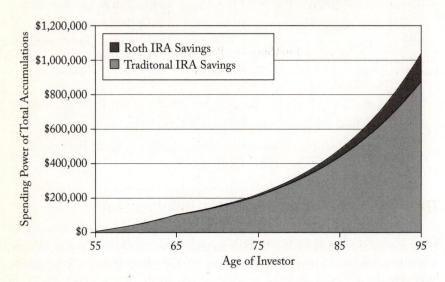

4. For the after-tax monies, the rate of return includes 70 percent capital appreciation, a 15 percent portfolio turnover rate (such that much of the appreciation is not immediately taxed), 15 percent dividends (taxed as capital gains from 2008 to 2010), and 15 percent ordinary interest income.

5. Ordinary income tax rates are 25 percent for all years.

6. Tax rates on realized capital gains are 15 percent through 2010 and 19 percent thereafter.

7. Beginning at age 71, the required minimum distributions from the traditional IRA are reinvested into the after-tax savings account.

8. The balances reflected in the graphs reflect spending power, which is net of an income tax allowance of 25 percent on the remaining traditional IRA balance. If the full amount was actually withdrawn in one year, however, the tax bracket may be even higher and make the Roth IRA appear more favorable.

The amounts reflected in the graph always show that saving in the Roth IRA is more favorable than saving in the traditional IRA. If tax rates become higher in the future, as they were before the 2003 changes, the overall Roth IRA advantage will appear larger. Given a long enough time horizon (such as when monies are passed to succeeding generations), however, the Roth IRA advantage becomes even bigger. The spending power of these methods at selected times is shown in Table 2.4.

Table 2.4: Total Spending Power of Savings Methods

End of Year Age	Traditional IRA	Roth IRA
55	$ 6,236	$ 6,240
65	102,516	103,868
75	215,179	224,243
85	442,042	484,124
95	882,166	1,045,186

The Effect of Lower Tax Brackets in Retirement

I will recommend the traditional IRA over a Roth IRA when you drop to a lower tax bracket after retiring and have a relatively short investment time horizon.

Under those circumstances, the value of a deductible IRA could exceed the benefits of the Roth IRA. It will be to your advantage to take the high tax deduction for your contribution and then, upon retirement, withdraw that money at a much lower tax rate.

> **I will recommend the traditional IRA over a Roth IRA when you drop to a lower tax bracket after retiring and have a relatively short investment time horizon.**

For example, if you are in the 25 percent tax bracket, and you make a $6,000 tax-deductible IRA contribution, you save $1,500 in taxes. Then, when you retire, your tax bracket drops to 15 percent. Assuming no investment growth, when you withdraw the traditional IRA of $6,000, you pay $900 in tax; you have just saved yourself $600.

$1,500	(Initial tax savings)
−900	(Tax payment)
$ 600	(Final tax savings)

With that caveat, however, my analysis shows that the Roth can become more favorable when a longer investment period is considered. The tax-bracket advantage diminishes over time. So I ran the analysis again, starting with the same assumptions as in the previous example, except that beginning in retirement, at age 66, the ordinary income tax bracket is reduced from 25 to 15 percent, and the capital gains tax rate is reduced from 19 to 9 percent.

The spending power of these methods at selected times is shown in Table 2.5.

Table 2.5: Total Spending Power of Savings Methods

End of Year Age	Traditional IRA	Roth IRA
55	$ 6,236	$ 6,240
65	102,516	103,868
(Lower Tax Brackets)		
75	240,357	224,243
85	505,444	484,124
95	1,046,149	1,045,186
105	2,136,475	2,256,479

Of course, most people will not survive until 105, but we show the analysis to point out that even facing a lowered tax bracket, the Roth IRA will become more valuable with time—an advantage for your heirs.

I usually recommend the deductible traditional IRA over the Roth IRA if you anticipate that your retirement tax bracket will always remain lower than your current tax rate and that the IRA will be depleted during your lifetime. Unfortunately, once the minimum required distribution (MRD) rules take effect, at age 70½ for tax-deferred IRAs and retirement plans, individuals may find that the distribution rules require them to withdraw so much money that their tax rate is just as high as their preretirement tax rate, or sometimes, when the MRD is added to Social Security income, a higher rate than when they were working. For these people, a Roth IRA contribution is usually preferable to a traditional IRA.

These numbers demonstrate that even with a significant tax-bracket disadvantage, the Roth IRA can become preferable with a long enough time horizon. Furthermore, when you consider the additional estate planning advantages, the relative worth of the Roth IRA becomes more significant. (Please see www.retiresecure.com for a free report on Roth IRAs and Roth IRA conversions that includes information on the tax law change that will eliminate $100,000 AGI limit for converting IRAs to Roth IRAs in 2010.)

Comments on Your Actual Tax Brackets: A Subtle Point for the Advanced Reader

The above analyses reflect simple assumptions of 25 percent income tax savings on your deductible IRA or retirement plan contributions. This is in essence the cost of the Roth IRA or Roth 401(k)/Roth 403(b) in these comparisons to deductible amounts. However, the U.S. tax code has several complications that create actual incremental tax brackets that are much higher than the tax brackets listed on the federal tax tables based on your taxable income. These items must be considered in the context of measuring the advantages of Roth IRAs to deductible IRA contributions.

These tax code complications can have extreme effects on the actual tax bracket for some people including retirees with Social Security income and itemized deductions that involve medical expenses. For example, consider Fred Jones, a single 65-year-old retiree who in 2007 had pension income of $32,000, Social Security income of $25,000, and part-time wage income of $5,000. He also has itemized deductions of $15,000, including $10,000 of medical expenses. After looking at Table 2.4, Fred is considering the potential advantages of making a $5,000 Roth IRA contribution rather than a deductible IRA contribution of $5,000. If he makes the traditional deductible IRA contribution, he pays $4,173 of tax. If he chooses the Roth IRA, his tax is $6,518, or $2,345 more. This is nearly 47 percent of the IRA contribution amount. This means his actual tax bracket is almost 47 percent even though the IRS tables indicate he is in the 25 percent tax bracket! The reasons, in Fred's situation, are that the additional income from losing the IRA deduction also caused much more of his Social Security income to be taxable, as well as losing out on some of the medical expense deduction, due to its 7.5 percent of AGI limitation. Thus, Fred felt the cost of choosing the Roth IRA was too high that year and wisely chose the deductible IRA.

Although Fred's future situation may not always be so extreme, his numbers did not appear to be that unusual. Fred's example illustrates why careful tax planning is so important. There are many things in the tax code that result in a different actual tax bracket than the IRS tables would indicate. Before finalizing Roth contribution or conversion decisions, it is best to run the numbers or see a competent tax advisor to determine the actual effects.

In our analyses of Roth IRA advantages and disadvantages when compared to deductible contributions, we keep referring to the marginal tax rates to help us decide if the conversion makes sense in the long term. For most people, the current actual marginal tax rate is not hard to determine, and similar to what the IRS tables would indicate. Therefore, we will continue to use these references to a simply calculated tax bracket rate in our analyses of Roth accounts. But please keep in mind that it is prudent to calculate the actual current year tax cost of the Roth.

In addition, our analyses do not reflect any additional advantages of the Roth IRAs when held in retirement due to these actual tax bracket variances. For example, Fred's situation can be turned around to result in an extreme advantage if instead of considering a Roth IRA contribution, Fred is in need of an additional $5,000 in income for December and he is comparing the effects of a withdrawal from either a taxable traditional IRA account or a Roth IRA account. Being able to get his money tax-free will then save him from paying an additional 47 percent tax when he files his return. This kind of situation gives the Roth IRA a potential advantage that our analyses in this book do not reflect. Instead we refer to a simple measure of the tax bracket, both when the Roth account is established and during retirement.

Distribution Rules for Roth IRAs

1. To make completely tax-free or qualified withdrawals from a Roth IRA that has grown in value, five years must have elapsed since opening the account. There is a separate five-year holding period for each Roth IRA conversion as well (conversions are discussed in more detail in Chapter 7).

2. This restriction also applies to the beneficiary of a Roth IRA whose owner dies before the five-year period has ended. The beneficiary may withdraw funds tax-free as long as they do not exceed the contribution amount, but he or she must wait until the five-year period has passed before being able to enjoy tax-free withdrawal of the Roth IRA's earnings.

3. Withdrawals prior to age 59½ may be taken without tax or penalties to the extent of previous annual contributions.

4. All withdrawals after the five-year holding period is met, including those in excess of previous contributions, are tax-free in the following circumstances:

    • Made to a beneficiary (or the individual's estate) on or after the individual's death

    • Attributable to the individual's being disabled

    • For qualified first-time home purchase expenses

5. Withdrawals in excess of previous contributions made before the five-year holding period is met are taxable, but penalty-free in the following circumstances:

   - For qualified college expenses

   - For qualified medical expenses that exceed 7.5 percent of adjusted gross income

   - For health insurance premiums paid for certain unemployed individuals

   - If withdrawals are part of substantially equal periodic payments over the life of the participant

   - If the distribution is part of an IRS levy

6. All other withdrawals prior to age 59½ that are in excess of previous contributions are taxable and subject to a 10 percent penalty.

7. Roth IRA amounts are not subject to minimum required distributions during the original owner's lifetime.

Furthermore, a Roth IRA owner can designate his or her spouse as the beneficiary who, upon the Roth IRA owner's death, would have the option of postponing minimum distributions until death. After the surviving spouse's death, the subsequent beneficiary (usually a child) would be required to take nontaxable minimum distributions of the inherited Roth IRA based on her own long life expectancy. (Please see Chapter 13 for distribution rules for inherited IRAs and inherited Roth IRAs.)

The five-year holding requirement for Roth IRAs is to promote long-term savings. The five-year clock starts ticking on January 1 of the tax year associated with the first contribution or conversion, which results in making the five-year period actually less than five years. The period begins on the first day of the tax year for which a contribution is made. If you open a Roth IRA account for the 2008 tax year by making a contribution on April 15, 2009 (the last day you can make your Roth IRA contributions for 2008), the five-year period is from January 1, 2008, to December 31, 2012. To achieve the same five-year period start date when opening a Roth IRA account using a Roth IRA conversion, you must make the conversion by December 31, 2008 (the last day you can make your Roth IRA conversions for 2008). Pursuant to these Roth IRA rules, if you suddenly need the money the day after or at any time after you make the contribution, you can take the contributed amount out free of tax.

Wealthy clients and readers raise a lot of questions about the five-year holding period. What I really want to do when I hear that question is yell, "Why do you care?"

Wealthy clients and readers raise a lot of questions about the five-year holding period. What I really want to do when I hear that question is yell, "Why do you care?"

Most people who have a Roth IRA as part of their significant retirement accumulations have at least some after-tax money and some traditional IRA or retirement plan funds. Because the Roth IRA is the last money I want people to spend, it should not matter that there is a five-year waiting period to achieve tax-free growth. The important features described below almost always more than make up for any lack of liquidity resulting from the five-year rule.

The fact that individuals can continue to contribute to a Roth IRA if they continue working past age 70½ is a great opportunity to continue saving, especially since more and more people continue to earn income well after the traditional age of retirement.

The no-minimum required distributions rule gives rise to significant estate planning opportunities to stretch savings for those willing to leave the money in the tax-free account for a long time. As with traditional IRAs, heirs must take minimum required distributions, but they generally are extended over a lifetime. Depending on the lifespan of the beneficiary, the funds can grow tax-free to great advantage.

Advanced Distribution Rules for Traditional IRAs

1. Traditional IRA withdrawals are generally taxable. For traditional IRAs with basis (after-tax amounts in an IRA are referred to as its *basis*), the basis comes out tax-free but is determined in prorated amounts based on the ratio of the basis to total value. Basis is created by making nondeductible contributions to the account. In other words, if you received a tax deduction for your retirement plan contribution, you have no basis. If, for some reason, you made an IRA or a retirement plan contribution for which you did not receive an income tax deduction, you have basis to the extent of your nondeductible contribution. I hope you filed a Form 8606 to keep track of the basis of the IRA. This form should be filed every year as an attachment to your tax return once you have any basis in your IRA. It will make things a lot easier once you begin to take distributions and reduce your taxes, too. My forthcoming book on Roth Retirement Plans and IRAs, including Roth conversions, will reveal a great technique for

converting after-tax or nondeductible IRAs or after-tax dollars inside a traditional 401(k) to Roth IRAs without paying any tax. Please visit www.retiresecure.com to be put on the list of people who will receive first notice of the new Roth IRA book.

2. All traditional IRA withdrawals prior to age 59½ are subject to a 10 percent penalty (for amounts exceeding basis) unless the withdrawal falls under one of the following exemptions:

- Made to a beneficiary (or the individual's estate) on or after the individual's death
- Attributable to the individual's being disabled
- Qualified first-time home purchase expenses
- Qualified college expenses
- Qualified medical expenses that exceed 7.5 percent of adjusted gross income
- Health insurance premiums paid for certain unemployed individuals
- Part of substantially equal periodic payments over the life of the participant—that is, distributions qualifying under Section 72(t) (which we do not cover in this book) for exemption from the premature distribution penalty
- Due to an IRS levy

3. All traditional IRAs are subject to minimum required distributions for years after age 70½.

Please note that as of press time, it appears that this penalty is likely to be at least temporarily suspended in limited amounts to enable taxpayers to reach their retirement plans without incurring a penalty during tough economic times.

A Key Lesson from This Chapter

Roth IRAs have significant benefits over traditional deductible IRAs:
1. No taxes are due upon the eventual distributions.
2. No required distributions are necessary during the owner's lifetime.
3. Withdrawals prior to age 59½ are free from any tax and penalties to the extent of previous annual contributions.

3

Traditional 401(k)s and 403(b)s versus Roth 401(k)s and Roth 403(b)s

The question isn't at what age I want to retire, it's at what income.

—George Foreman

Main Topics

- What are Roth 401(k)s and 403(b)s?
- How do Roth 401(k)/403(b) accounts differ from a Roth IRA?
- Advantages and disadvantages of Roth 401(k)/403(b) contributions
- Availability of the Roth 401(k)/403(b)
- Contribution limits for both Roth and traditional 401(k)s/403(b)s
- Choosing between the Roth and traditional 401(k)/403(b)
- Additional advantages for higher income taxpayers
- Effects of a higher liquidation tax rate
- What if tax rates drop in retirement?
- A higher liquidation rate may be appropriate
- Extremely lower tax brackets in retirement
- What if you need the money . . . not your heirs: Spending down the Roth 401(k)

- Conclusion
- Making it happen

KEY IDEA

The Roth 401(k) and Roth 403(b) plan options offer high income participants an entrée to the world of tax-free wealth accumulation that was previously unavailable to them via traditional plans.

What Are Roth 401(k)s and Roth 403(b)s?

In Chapter 1 we touched on some of the basic differences between traditional and Roth 401(k)s/403(b)s. The Roth 401(k) and Roth 403(b) combine the features of a traditional 401(k) and traditional 403(b) and a Roth IRA. Employees are permitted to treat part or all of their own contribution, which is the amount deducted from their paychecks, as a contribution to a Roth account, meaning it will receive tax treatment similar to a Roth IRA. The laws governing retirement plan contributions, however, require that the employee always have the option to defer money into the traditional deductible account when the Roth account is offered as an option. No one is forced to use the new Roth account if they prefer to get the tax deduction.

Unlike traditional contributions to a 401(k)/403(b) plan, employee contributions to a Roth 401(k)/403(b) account do not receive a federal tax deduction. But the growth on these contributions will not be subject to taxes when it is withdrawn.

Unlike traditional contributions to a 401(k)/403(b) plan, employee contributions to a Roth 401(k)/403(b) account do not receive a federal tax deduction. But the growth on these contributions will not be subject to taxes when it is withdrawn. The Roth account grows tax-free. In short, if you have two plans, one a traditional 401(k) and the other a Roth 401(k) with the same amount of money in each, the Roth 401(k) plan will be of greater value since the income taxes imposed on withdrawals from the traditional 401(k) greatly reduce its overall value. By this we do not mean to imply that these new Roth retirement plans are better than the traditional plans for everyone, but they are for many. The choice is similar to deciding whether to make a Roth IRA contribution or a *deductible* contribution to a traditional IRA as discussed in Chapter 2.

These plans were first offered in 2006, but under temporary rules. Many employers did not offer the Roth feature to their existing plan because of the additional paperwork, plan amendments, reporting, and recordkeeping involved. More recently, the law has become permanent and more employers are offering Roth 401(k) and 403(b) features. These significant additions to the retirement planning landscape offer many more individuals an extraordinary opportunity to expand, and, in many cases, to begin saving for retirement in the Roth environment where their investment grows *tax-free*. Coupled with the increased contribution limits for the traditional 401(k) and 403(b) plans, employees and even self-employed individuals will be able to establish and grow their retirement savings at a rate greater than ever before.

> These significant additions to the retirement planning landscape offer many more individuals an extraordinary opportunity to expand, and, in many cases, to begin saving for retirement in the Roth environment where their investment grows *tax-free*.

How Do Roth 401(k)/403(b) Accounts Differ from a Roth IRA?

One of the most significant advantages of the Roth 401(k)/403(b), and the one that distinguishes it from a Roth IRA, is that the new Roth 401(k) and Roth 403(b) plans are available to a much larger group of people. Roth IRA contributions are only available to taxpayers who fall within certain modified adjusted gross incomes (MAGI) ranges. The 2008 income limits are, for married couples filing jointly, less than $169,000 ($176,000 in 2009) and for single individuals and heads of household, less than $116,000 ($120,000 in 2009). These restrictive MAGI limitations *do not apply* to the new Roth 401(k) or 403(b) plans providing higher income individuals and couples with their first entrée into the tax-free Roth environment.

This increased accessibility is really big news. Roth IRAs have always appeared to be ideal savings vehicles for wealthier individuals, but up until January 1, 2006, or more recently if their employers just began offering the Roth 401(k) and 403(b) options, wealthier individuals had been precluded from establishing Roth accounts due to the income limits.

> The longer the funds are kept in the tax-free Roth environment, the greater the advantage to both the Roth IRA owner and his or her heirs.

In Chapter 2 we demonstrated how Roth IRAs can be of great advantage as part of the long-term retirement and estate plan, and these wealthier individuals are the folks who can generally afford to let money sit in a Roth account and gather tax-free growth. The longer the funds are kept in the tax-free Roth environment, the greater the advantage to both the Roth IRA owner and his or her heirs.

Advantages and Disadvantages of Roth 401(k)/403(b) Contributions

The 401(k)/403(b) plan option offers advantages and disadvantages similar to those of Roth IRAs discussed in Chapter 2, but they are worth repeating and expanding upon here:

Advantages of the Roth Plans

1. By choosing the Roth, you pay the taxes up front. While you might have taken the tax savings from your traditional plan contribution and invested the money in after-tax investments, over time, you will receive greater value from the tax-free growth.

2. If your tax bracket in retirement stays the same as it was when you contributed to the plan, you will be better off (assuming the Roth account grows and possibly even if it goes down in value somewhat).

3. If your tax bracket in retirement is higher than when you contributed to the plan, you will be much better off. (Please note that we will look more closely at the effect of higher and lower tax brackets in retirement later.) There are many reasons why you could move into a higher tax bracket after you retire. Here are a few examples:

   a. The federal government could decide to raise tax rates.

   b. You need to increase your income with taxable withdrawals from your traditional plan.

   c. You own or inherit income-producing property or investments that begin to give you taxable income.

   d. You own annuities or have other lucrative pension plans that begin paying you income.

   e. The combination of your pension, Social Security, and minimum required distributions are higher than your former taxable income from wages.

4. While you are alive, there are no MRDs from the Roth IRA accounts. The Roth 401(k)/403(b) is subject to MRDs, but the accounts can easily be rolled into a Roth IRA upon retirement. Traditional plans have MRDs beginning at age 70½ for retirees. The Roth IRA provides a much better long-term tax-advantaged savings horizon as shown in Chapter 2.

5. Your heirs will benefit from tax-free growth if the Roth is left in your estate. They can extend the tax-free growth by taking the required withdrawals over their lifetime. Whatever advantage you achieved with the Roth can be magnified by your heirs over their lifetimes.

6. The Roth provides greater value for the same number of dollars in retirement savings. This may lower federal estate and state inheritance taxes in an estate with the same after-tax spending power.

7. If you are in a low tax bracket now or even if you have no taxable income now (possibly because of credits and deductions), contributing to the Roth plan instead of the traditional plan will not cost you anything or perhaps a minimal amount now, but will have enormous benefits later.

8. If you were previously unable to consider Roth IRAs because your income exceeded the income caps, you are now eligible to consider the use of Roth accounts.

9. If you need to spend a large amount of your retirement savings all at once, withdrawals from a traditional plan would increase your marginal income tax rate. The Roths have a significant advantage in these high spending situations. The marginal tax rate never goes up. Roth withdrawals are tax-free.

10. Having a pool of both traditional plan money (funded by the employer contributions and taxable upon withdrawal) and Roth plan money (funded by the employee and tax-free) to choose from, can give you an opportunity for effective tax planning in retirement. With both types of plans, the Roth portion can be used in high income years and the traditional plan can be used in lower income years when you are in a reduced tax bracket. These low tax brackets may occur during years after retirement but before the MRDs from the employer's contributions begin.

Disadvantages of the Roth Plans

1. Your paycheck contributions into the Roth 401(k)/403(b) are no longer tax deductible. You will get smaller paychecks if you

contribute the same amount because of increased federal income tax withholding. Losing the tax-deferred status means that by the time you file your tax return, you will have less cash in the bank, that is, after-tax investments. (Keep in mind, however, that after-tax investments are the most inefficient savings tools when compared with retirement savings.)

2. The retirement investments may go down in value. If the decline becomes large enough, you would have been better off in a traditional tax-deferred plan, because, at the very least, you would have received a tax deduction on your contributions.

3. If Congress ever eliminates the income tax in favor of a sales tax or value-added tax, you will have already paid your income taxes. However, it seems unlikely that such a system would be adopted without grandfathering the rules for plans in place to prevent such inequities.

4. Your tax bracket in retirement drops, you withdraw funds from your retirement assets before sufficient tax-free growth, and the taxes you save on your Roth 401(k) plan withdrawals are less than the taxes you would have saved using a traditional plan. This can be the case if you earn an unusually high amount of money from your employer in one year, maybe from earning a large bonus that puts you in a very high tax bracket, but ultimately you do not end up with such high income after retirement. If that were the case, a better approach might be to use the traditional account for deferrals in that year or other years where your income is unusually large. (Please note that later we will look more closely at the effect of lower tax brackets in retirement.)

Availability of the Roth 401(k)/403(b)

Employers that now offer a 401(k) plan or a 403(b) plan *may* choose to expand their retirement plan options to include the Roth 401(k) or Roth 403(b), but they are not required to do so.

Employers that now offer a 401(k) plan or a 403(b) plan *may* choose to expand their retirement plan options to include the Roth 401(k) or Roth 403(b), but they are not required to do so. Some companies will be early adopters; others may take more time to incorporate the new plans into their offerings; still others may never offer them.

Contribution Limits for Roth and Traditional 401(k)s/403(b)s

In 2008, the traditional and Roth 401(k)/403(b) employee contribution limits are $15,500 per year ($20,500 if you are 50 or older). Just as we went to press, we have received the 2009 limits, which are $16,500 per year ($22,000 if you are 50 or older). For subsequent years, the limits will increase in $500 increments for inflation.

The limits apply to the *total* employee contributions. That is to say, in 2008, a 50-year-old employee *cannot* make a $20,500 contribution to a traditional 401(k) account and a $20,500 contribution to a Roth 401(k) account; the combined amounts cannot exceed $20,500. The Roth 401(k)/403(b) contributions will be treated like a Roth IRA for tax purposes.

Perhaps an example would help.

Joe, a prudent 50-year-old employee, participates in his company's 401(k) plan. He has dutifully contributed the maximum allowable contribution to his 401(k) plan since he started working. Until his employer adopted the new Roth 401(k) option, his expectation was to continue contributing the maximum into his 401(k) for 2008 and beyond.

Now Joe has a choice. He could either continue making his regular deductible 401(k) contribution ($20,500 for 2008); he could elect to make a $20,500 contribution to the new Roth 401(k); or he could split his $20,500 contribution between the regular 401(k) portion and the Roth 401(k) portion of the plan. His decision will not have an impact on his employer's contribution—the employer's matching contribution remains unchanged and goes into a traditional tax-deferred account.

With Joe's $20,500 contribution, however, there is a fundamental difference in the way his traditional 401(k) is taxed and the way his new Roth 401(k) is taxed. With the traditional 401(k), Joe gets an income tax deduction for his contribution to the 401(k). After Joe retires, however, and takes a distribution from his traditional 401(k), he will have to pay income taxes on that distribution. If Joe contributes to the Roth 401(k), he will not get a tax deduction for making the contribution but the money will grow income tax-free. When Joe takes a distribution from his Roth 401(k), he will not have to pay income taxes, provided other technical requirements are met. These other requirements are usually easy to meet, and include such things as waiting until age 59½ before making income withdrawals and waiting at least five years from the time the account is opened before the first withdrawal.

Because Joe has some after-tax savings already and does not really need more from income tax deductions, he is advised to contribute to the Roth portion of his 401(k). Assuming Joe takes the advice and switches his annual contributions to the Roth 401(k), he will have three components to his 401(k) plan at work. He will have the employer's portion of the plan, which remains unchanged. He will have his own (the employee's) traditional portion of the plan, which consists of all the contributions plus the interest, dividends, and appreciation on those contributions. Then, starting in 2009, he will have a Roth 401(k) portion.

If Joe is married filing a joint tax return and his 2008 adjusted gross income is less than $169,000, he may have already been making contributions to a Roth IRA outside of his employer's retirement plan. He would have been able to make the maximum Roth IRA contribution of $6,000 ($5,000 for people under age 50) to the plan. As long as Joe is working, the Roth 401(k) at work will remain separate from any Roth IRA he may have outside of his employer's plan.

If his 2008 adjusted gross income was more than $169,000, he would not have had a Roth IRA (the phase-out range is between $159,000 and $169,000). What is much different for Joe, as there is no income limit for the Roth 401(k)/403(b), is that the amount of money he will be allowed to contribute into the income tax-free world of the Roth will see a dramatic increase.

Choosing between the Roth and Traditional 401(k)/403(b)

The following analysis is equally important for individuals considering a Roth IRA conversion. I do not repeat this analysis in Chapter 7, but people who are considering a Roth IRA conversion, or interested in learning more about them should read this material with the Roth conversion in mind.

Many clients come to us wondering whether they would be better off making contributions to a Roth account or to a traditional retirement account. If the comparison is between using a Roth versus a nondeductible traditional IRA, it is pretty easy to make the case for the Roth. However, because of the nature of the Roth's advantages and disadvantages which are contingent on your current and future income tax brackets, it is necessary to formulate a scenario based on specific assumptions to provide an objective answer. We have made calculations and graphs showing how the Roth accounts become advantageous using the following assumptions:

1. The investor is 55 years old. He or she will retire at age 66.

2. Annual contributions are made to either the traditional 401(k) or the Roth 401(k) for 11 years until he retires. The contributions are initially $20,500 and increase for inflation each subsequent year.

3. By age 70, the Roth 401(k) part of the plan is rolled over to a Roth IRA to avoid MRDs.

4. For contributions to the traditional 401(k) plan, the tax savings are invested in the after-tax environment.

5. Income tax rates are as follows:

    a. Ordinary incremental tax rate during working years is 25 percent.

    b. Ordinary incremental tax rate during retirement years is 25 percent.

    c. Capital gains tax rates are 15 percent for the years through 2010 and 19 percent for the years thereafter (the average of 20 percent for less than five-year gains and 18 percent for gains held over five years).

6. The minimum required distributions from the traditional 401(k) plan begin at age 70, ordinary income taxes are paid on it, and the rest is spent. The Roth account has tax-free spending withdrawals taken in the same amount.

7. Overall investment rates of return are 8 percent annually for all funds. For after-tax fund investments, this consists of:

    a. Interest income of 15 percent of the total return.

    b. Dividend income of 15 percent (taxed as capital gains through 2010).

    c. Capital appreciation of 70 percent. This is not all taxed as capital gains immediately. A portfolio turnover rate of 15 percent per year is used to determine how much accumulated appreciation is taxed.

8. At the end of each year, we measure the spending power for each scenario. To measure the spending power of pretax traditional 401(k) plan balances, an allowance is made for income taxes. The tax rate of this allowance or liquidation rate is, initially, 25 percent, comparable to the ordinary tax rate.

Figure 3.1

Roth 401(k) Savings vs. Traditional 401(k) Savings
MRD Is Spent Annually

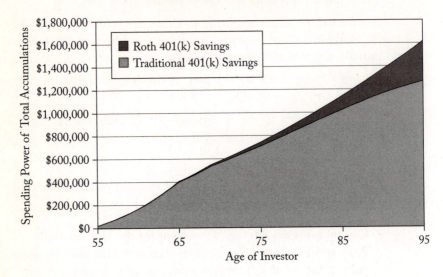

Now we are able to run the numbers and graph the resulting spending power of remaining assets as shown in Figure 3.1.

Figure 3.1 shows that there is an increasing advantage from investing in the Roth 401(k) instead of the traditional 401(k) plan. In fact, with our assumptions, the advantage is manifest in the first year. As of retirement age, the advantage has grown to $4,869, or 1.25 percent. By age 75, after MRDs have begun, the advantage is 4.68 percent; by age 85, it is 11.57 percent; and by age 95, it is a 27.17 percent advantage of $334,966.

For people whose circumstances match the assumptions, the cumulative advantage over the 40-year projection period should provide the incentive to use the Roth 401(k). If the owner should pass away, the non-spouse heir who is willing to let the money grow can extend the period of the tax-free growth, and extend the advantage over a period as long as his or her normal life expectancy. If the heir is the surviving spouse, the Roth IRA can be treated as his or her own, thereby avoiding MRDs for the surviving spouse's lifetime.

Even though we are not talking about Roth IRA conversions at this point in the book, the reasoning that goes into deciding to put money in a Roth 401(k) versus a traditional 401(k) is conceptually similar to the reasoning that goes into deciding to make a Roth IRA conversion. So, although you may be retired, the following analysis is relevant for retirees thinking about a Roth IRA conversion.

Additional Advantages for Higher Income Taxpayers

One great feature of the new Roth 401(k)/403(b) plan is that it allows higher income taxpayers to save money in the Roth environment. How does the advantage change in their situation? Figure 3.2 uses similar assumptions as noted above, except that the ordinary income tax rate is always 35 percent, including the liquidation tax rate used for measurement.

Figure 3.2

**Roth 401(k) Savings vs. Traditional 401(k) Savings
35 Percent Ordinary Tax Rates**

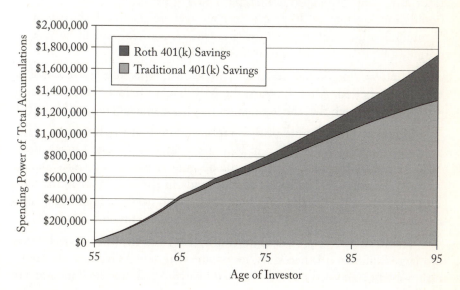

In Figure 3.2 we discover that the Roth 401(k) advantage for a higher income taxpayer is greater than for the lower income taxpayer in the 25 percent tax bracket (Figure 3.1). The advantage has now become a huge 40.23 percent, or $541,557, after 40 years. And guess what. The higher income taxpayer is more likely not to need to spend the Roth investments, thus making the long-term benefits more achievable. The bottom line is that the Roth 401(k) is dollar for dollar more valuable for the higher income retirement plan owner than a middle income retirement plan owner. The counterargument is that the amount of savings to middle income taxpayers, though smaller, is more meaningful in terms of the impact on their lives.

Effects of a Higher Liquidation Tax Rate

Let's further consider the liquidation tax rate. This is a tax rate applied to remaining amounts in your traditional pretax retirement accounts if you were to liquidate your account. By applying the liquidation tax rate you get a measure of what the account would be worth in after-tax dollars. You can think of it as a measure of the total amount you could spend out of the traditional 401(k) as of each year end. If you needed to spend the total balance, what would that do to your income tax rate? Wouldn't all this extra income from cashing out the plan put you in a higher tax bracket? What if the federal government raised income tax rates after you retired? What happens to Figure 3.1 if we use a higher liquidation tax rate of 30 percent for an average income level taxpayer? Figure 3.3 still reflects ordinary withdrawal rates of 25 percent but incorporates a liquidation withdrawal taxed at 30 percent.

What we find is that the graphs are similar, especially near the end of the 40-year period. After 40 years, the MRDs have reduced the traditional 401(k) balance such that the liquidation rate has a smaller comparable effect.

However, in the center of the graph, we find that the Roth has a bigger comparable advantage than in Figure 3.1. This shows that using a Roth 401(k) protects our nest egg from the additional income tax costs should we unexpectedly need to spend all the funds in the middle of retirement. This might be a typical situation for a retiree who needs to liquidate a large amount of retirement funds in order to move into a retirement home.

The Roth 401(k) provides a level of safety from the income tax burden if a large liquidation is necessary, for whatever reason. Whatever the financial problem is, it need not be worsened by extra-high marginal income tax brackets.

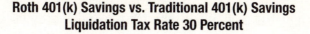

Figure 3.3

Roth 401(k) Savings vs. Traditional 401(k) Savings
Liquidation Tax Rate 30 Percent

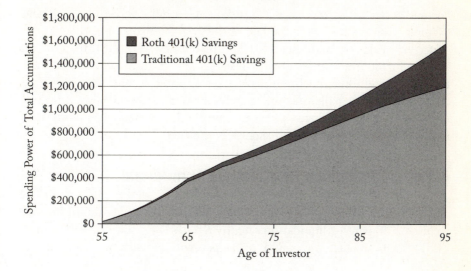

What if Your Tax Rates Drop in Retirement?

A situation that makes a Roth 401(k) less appealing is when the employee earns a high income and is in a high tax bracket while working, but when she retires, she is in a lower tax bracket. The employee has accumulated enough after-tax funds from paychecks to survive on spending Social Security and MRDs from the traditional 401(k), beginning at age 70.

If we now make a graph similar to Figure 3.2, but instead of continuing the 35 percent ordinary tax bracket throughout retirement, we use a lower 28 percent tax bracket, and we also use a liquidation rate equal to the ordinary tax rate of 28 percent in retirement, we find the graph looks like Figure 3.4.

Figure 3.4 illustrates that there is still a long-term advantage for the Roth 401(k), although the advantage is smaller when the income tax rates are lower in retirement. The numbers show the Roth has an advantage until the liquidation rate is dropped from 35 percent at age 65 to 28 percent at age 66. Then the traditional 401(k) has the advantage of 4.35 percent or $19,357 (hidden in this graph). This slight advantage decreases until age 79 when the Roth 401(k) again has the advantage. The advantage builds until age 95 when the advantage is 15.27 percent, or $220,386. Again, when the long-term plan is to keep the money in the tax-free Roth environment for a long time, possibly leaving it to heirs who will do the same, the Roth is the preferred vehicle.

Figure 3.4 is hard for many people to believe. How can the Roth become better with lower taxes in retirement—a full 7 percent lower in this example? The answer lies in the fate of the original income tax savings generated by using the traditional 401(k). This money went into the after-tax investment pool where its growth became subject to income taxes. These taxes don't seem like much: ordinary taxes on interest (and dividends after 2010), and much smaller income tax rates applied to capital gains. But these taxes, even at their reduced rates, are fiercely disadvantaged in contrast to the Roth 401(k) where growth is entirely *tax-free*.

A Higher Liquidation Rate May Be Appropriate

An objective analysis of Figure 3.4 would cause some skepticism because we used a 28 percent liquidation rate. By *liquidation rate* we mean the marginal tax rate the taxpayer would incur upon withdrawing, or cashing in, his

Figure 3.4

**Roth 401(k) Savings vs. Traditional 401(k) Savings
35 Percent Taxes While Working and 28 Percent
Taxes in Retirement and Liquidation**

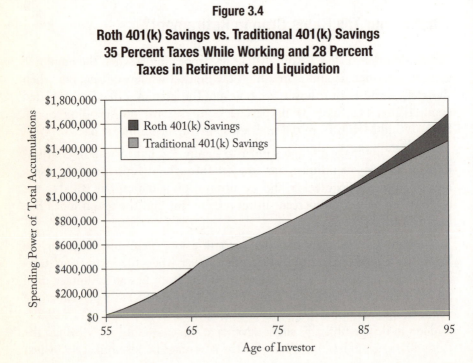

or her IRA or retirement plan. We should probably apply a higher marginal rate to traditional plan balances to allow for higher marginal rates if the entire IRA or retirement plan is cashed in at once, because the additional income from the IRA withdrawals will push the taxpayer into a rate even higher than 28 percent.

Also a higher rate could be used to allow for the potential advantage the heirs would realize after death from the continued tax-free growth of the inherited Roth IRA. The advantage to the heirs can be more than a few percent if the maximum tax-free growth is maintained over their life expectancy. Three-generation calculations have illustrated that a Roth inheritance can be worth over 50 percent more than a comparable pretax fund inheritance. Suffice it to say that an heir would be better off inheriting a Roth account than a larger amount of pretax money.

In any case, the use of a 35 percent liquidation tax rate on Figure 3.4 may be more appropriate. This assumption is used in Figure 3.5.

Again, as with Figure 3.3, there is not much difference after 40 years. However, during the buildup, there is no disadvantage to a Roth 401(k) as Figure 3.4 would indicate!

Figure 3.5

Roth 401(k) Savings vs. Traditional 401(k) Savings
35 Percent Taxes While Working and in Liquidation
and 28 Percent Taxes in Retirement

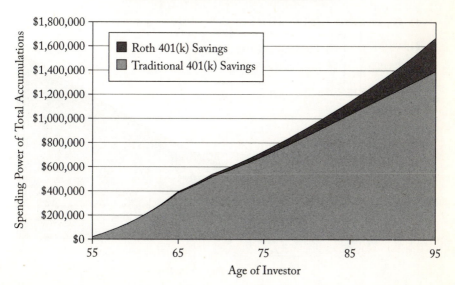

The bottom line here is that even with somewhat lower tax rates in retirement, the Roth 401(k) is better.

Extremely Lower Tax Brackets in Retirement

In a sobering illustration, however, we can see where the Roth 401(k) is not advantageous. Figure 3.6 assumes an individual in the 35 percent tax bracket while working and the 15 percent tax bracket in retirement. Maybe they were extravagant spenders during their early working years and neglected to save much in traditional retirement accounts. Maybe most of what they have is Roth IRAs and little else, for whatever reason. Figure 3.6 shows a different story.

Here the Roth 401(k) contributor went too far. The Roth has its usual advantages (hidden in this graph) as long as all tax rates are 35 percent, but when we drop the liquidation and subsequent tax rates to 15 percent (and consequently lower the capital gains rates), the traditional plan proves to be more advantageous. By age 95, the Roth 401(k) is *disadvantaged* by 37.93 percent, or $473,430.

Figure 3.6

**Roth 401(k) Savings vs. Traditional 401(k) Savings
35 Percent Taxes While Working and 15 Percent
Taxes in Retirement and Liquidation**

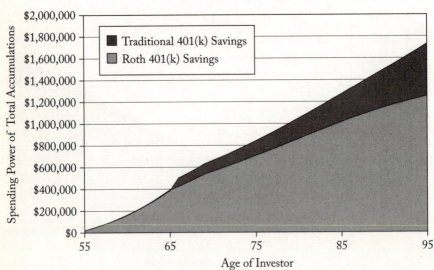

The bottom line here is that in order to get the tax advantages from the Roth, you should ensure that you will still have a tax rate in retirement that is not too much less than your rate while working. Otherwise, the tax deduction from traditional 401(k) contributions is too good to pass up. Typically, the Roth is used after a decent taxable retirement income is ensured.

Higher Liquidation Rates Should Again Be Considered

Even if you do fall into the 15 percent bracket, your heirs may not. And, if they were to inherit the Roth, they could potentially reap continued tax-free advantages from the Roth 401(k). So perhaps using the 35 percent liquidation rate in Figure 3.6 may be appropriate (see Figure 3.7).

Figure 3.7 and related calculations show the Roth 401(k) retains an advantage of up to 3 percent until age 76, when the traditional plan has the advantage due to lower taxes upon withdrawals. Again if these substantially lower income tax rates persist for long enough after retirement, the traditional plan ends up better as shown in Figure 3.6.

Figure 3.7

**Roth 401(k) Savings vs. Traditional 401(k) Savings
35 Percent Taxes While Working and in Liquidation
and 15 Percent Taxes in Retirement**

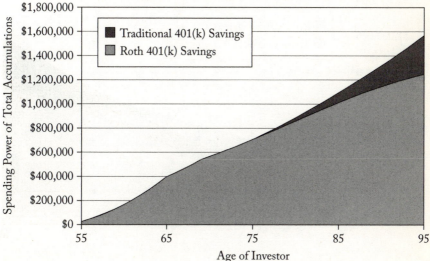

What if You Need the Money, Not Your Heirs: Spending Down the Roth 401(k)

All the above figures may indicate that the Roth 401(k) is a good idea and can eventually result in huge gains for the family. But what if you need to spend it? As a quick answer, if that is all you have to spend, without any other taxable income, as in Figure 3.6, you may be better off taking the original tax deductions on the traditional 401(k).

But what about a more balanced situation, where you have a pension income as well as Social Security, and your tax rate is 25 percent all along, as in Figure 3.1, but you need to tap into your nest egg, taking more than the MRD. Will it have been a mistake if you systematically deplete the Roth 401(k) over time?

To answer this question, we prepared the graph in Figure 3.8, which is similar to Figure 3.1, but instead of taking only the MRDs from retirement accounts, we take $20,000 from the traditional 401(k) during ages 66 to 69 and $20,000 more than the resulting MRDs thereafter.

Figure 3.8

Roth 401(k) Savings vs. Traditional 401(k) Savings
Moderate Additional Spending

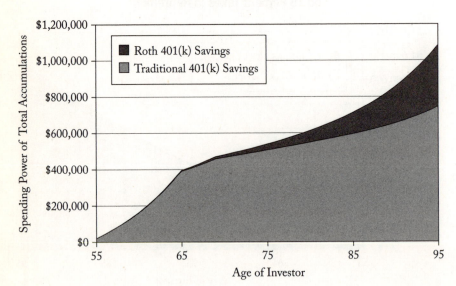

Figure 3.8 still indicates a significant advantage to the Roth 401(k) due to the tax savings which began in Year 1. The level of spending is higher in the first years, but actually becomes lower in future years because of a much reduced MRD from the lower accumulated balance compared to the MRD-only scenario in Figure 3.1.

The result of this sooner-than-expected withdrawal rate is not significant to the decision of which is better. The Roth still grows its advantage to 45.19 percent, or $334,966, by age 95.

Let's try again. This time we will begin to take $40,000 at age 66 and increase the withdrawal every year for inflation: This creates the graph shown in Figure 3.9.

Now the Roth advantage is less apparent. The traditional 401(k) plan runs out of money at age 86, but the Roth 401(k) plan runs out at age 88—a period of slightly over two years. This graph does not make the Roth 401(k) look quite as favorable as some of the other graphs, but two years really is a significant advantage. The bottom line is that despite the excessive spending in retirement, the Roth 401(k) is still better than the traditional 401(k) plan.

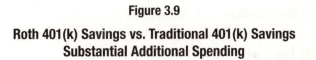

Figure 3.9

Roth 401(k) Savings vs. Traditional 401(k) Savings
Substantial Additional Spending

Conclusion

Of course it is unlikely that the assumptions made in the above analyses will reflect your exact personal situation. In addition, there will always be an uncertainty regarding future investment rates, tax rates, and even your own spending. However, there is value in seeing objective numbers in different scenarios. Hopefully, the information can help you make decisions regarding your own retirement and estate plan. Seeing an appropriate financial advisor who will personalize the advice for you would be the recommended course of action. Also, please keep in mind this analysis is also quite valuable for someone interested in Roth IRA conversions because there are a lot of similarities in the calculation and the sensitivity of tax brackets.

> **The Roth 401(k)s/403(b)s can change people's lives for the better. Subject to a few exceptions discussed above, if you have access to a Roth 401(k) or Roth 403(b), I highly recommend you take advantage of that option, and if you can afford it, contribute the maximum.**

The Roth 401(k)s/403(b)s can change people's lives for the better. Subject to a few exceptions discussed above, if you have access to a Roth 401(k) or Roth 403(b), I highly recommend you take advantage of that option, and if you can afford it, contribute the maximum.

Making It Happen

Notice, however, there is a caveat. I said "If you have access." Though Congress has now created these Roth 401(k)s and Roth 403(b)s, that doesn't mean your employer has adopted these features or made plans to do so. The additional paperwork seems insignificant to me. I suspect the biggest reason more companies haven't added a Roth 401(k) component is inertia. Locally, in Pittsburgh, a few of the big companies and the two major universities have just come on board to offer the Roth options. If you are an employee who is not given the option of a Roth 401(k) or Roth 403(b), you should gently (or not so gently depending on your personality and the office politics) suggest that your employer adopt the Roth 401(k) or Roth 403(b) plan and allow you to participate.

The IRS has provided in Notice 2006–44 a sample amendment for Roth elective deferrals, which should ease the burden for plan sponsors. If you are a retirement plan administrator or owner of a small business and if you have not already considered implementing a Roth 401(k) or Roth

403(b), you should strongly consider it. We did it in our own business and now in addition to what I contribute to my employees' retirement plan, each employee has the option of a Roth 401(k) or a traditional 401(k). The cost was minimal.

A Key Lesson from This Chapter

For most readers, however, the expansion or entrée into the tax-free world of Roth 401(k)s and Roth 403(b)s is well advised and over the long term will be one of the best things you can do for yourself and your family.

Part Two

THE
DISTRIBUTION
YEARS

Spend the Right Funds First and Other Critical Decisions You Face in Retirement

4

Optimal Spending Strategies for Retirees

I am having an out-of-money experience.

—Author Unknown

Main Topics

- The optimal order for spending assets
- Four mini case studies:
  - Spend Your After-Tax Money First
  - A Note for Those Who Fear Capital Gains Tax
  - The Optimal Order for Spending Classes of Assets
  - Figuring Your Tax Bracket Advantage into the Spending Order

---

KEY IDEA

Spend after-tax dollars first, tax-deferred dollars second, then Roth.

Which Assets Should I Spend First?

With retirement an individual moves into distribution mode—that is, he or she begins to spend retirement savings. This is not to say that accumulation stops. Income and appreciation on the investments, Social Security funds, and any pension plan proceeds might still be exceeding your expenses.

You may be fortunate enough to find that your Social Security, pension, minimum required distributions from your IRA (if any), and dividends and interest on your after-tax investments provide enough funds for your living expenses. Let's assume, however, that isn't the case, and you are required to either tap into your after-tax funds (your nest egg) or make (additional) taxable withdrawals from your IRA or retirement account to make ends meet.

In general, it is preferable to spend principal from your after-tax investments rather than taking taxable distributions from your IRA and/or retirement plan.

> In general, it is preferable to spend principal from your after-tax investments rather than taking taxable distributions from your IRA and/or retirement plan.

I've been in business for 30 years. Most of my clients actually listen to me, but I always have a few who don't. Instead of following my recommendations, they choose to spend their IRAs first. It drives me crazy. When I review their tax return, I see it. You can't hide it because it's an IRA distribution and you have to pay taxes on it. With this one particular client, every year, when I delivered his tax return, I would include a personal note saying, "I really hate to see you pay income taxes on this." I would also call him. He said his stockbroker wanted to maintain a balance between IRA and after-tax dollars. Now, I'm all for an appropriate and well-balanced portfolio. I agree that you don't want to have all your eggs in one basket. But I'm not into this allocation between IRA and non-IRA dollars. Particularly if you're past 59½, you don't have to worry about maintaining the liquidity of your after-tax dollars because you can take money out of an IRA whenever you want without a penalty. I would much rather that subject to some exceptions, most taxpayers follow the "pay taxes later" rule.

Mini Case Study 4.1 and Figure 4.1 provide a comparison of the benefits of spending after-tax savings before pretax accumulations.

MINI CASE STUDY 4.1

Spend Your After-Tax Money First

Figure 4.1

Benefits of Spending After-Tax Savings before
Tax-Deferred Retirement Accounts

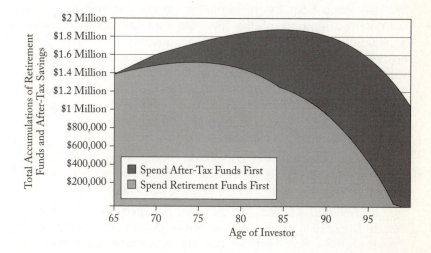

Both Mr. Pay Taxes Now and Mr. Pay Taxes Later start from an identical position in 2008. They are both 66 years old and both have $300,000 in after-tax funds, with a cost basis of $255,000, and $1,100,000 in retirement funds. They both receive $25,000 per year in Social Security income. They want to spend $8,000 per month, or $96,000 per year, after paying income taxes. Their investment return is 8 percent, consisting of 70 percent capital appreciation with a 15 percent portfolio turnover rate, 15 percent dividend income, and 15 percent interest income. Income-tax assumptions include the lower rates on ordinary income and capital gains established by Jobs and Growth Tax Relief Reconciliation Act of 2003 (JGTRRA) and subsequent tax laws. State income taxes are ignored.

Mr. Pay Taxes Now does not spend any of his after-tax funds until all the retirement funds are depleted. By spending his retirement funds first, he triggers income taxes on the withdrawals, reducing the tax-deferral period, and his balance goes down. He also subjects a larger share of his after-tax funds to income taxes on the dividends, interest, and potential capital gains. All income taxes due on the retirement funds and the after-tax funds cause a greater amount to be withdrawn from his retirement account. In 32 years, by paying taxes prematurely, he has sacrificed a fortune in tax-deferred growth. When he is 98 years old, Mr. Pay Tax Now is out of funds.

Mr. Pay Taxes Later first uses his after-tax funds to meet expenses. Only when the after-tax funds are depleted are withdrawals made from the retirement accounts. He fully uses the tax-deferred features of the IRA. Mr. Pay Tax Later has over $1,400,000, when he is 98. Both he and Mr. Pay Taxes Now enjoyed an identical lifestyle, investments, and so forth, but there was a $1,400,000 difference in the remaining amounts. In states such as Pennsylvania that do not tax retirement income but do tax after-tax investment income, the benefits of spending the after-tax money first is even greater. The principle stands: Don't pay taxes now—pay taxes later!

Please note that the conclusion would most likely be the same for any reasonable set of assumptions in terms of how much money there is and what interest rate you assume.

I have read scholarly articles that disagree with my recommended spending order—first after-tax dollars, then IRAs, and then Roth IRAs. Some articles cite the importance of different tax rates and I address that concern later in this chapter. What I would say to anyone who disagrees is "Please show me a flaw with my math or logic." For me, an argument based on general notions without mathematical proof will not hold water. Of course everyone has their own circumstances and, yes, some taxpayers have unique circumstances where my general advice would not optimize their estate.

It should be noted that in late stages of spending and certain other circumstances it does not hold true that no Roth dollars should be spent while traditional IRA dollars remain. If you live long enough to fully deplete your traditional IRAs and are left with only Roth dollars and little taxable income other than Social Security, you will be in the zero percent tax bracket. From that point on, you will be missing out on what could have been tax-free traditional IRA withdrawals. It would be a mistake to have completely wiped out the traditional IRA before spending the Roth. Before the traditional IRA is all gone, it makes sense to spend a combination of traditional and Roth IRAs so that zero percent tax brackets never get wasted.

Also, there are strategic times when spending Roth dollars can save more in taxes than the 15 percent tax bracket you expect to be in. Your actual taxes on incremental additional IRA withdrawals may be 27 percent or more because of the phase-in rules on the taxability of Social Security. There may be other situations where spending some Roth dollars before traditional IRA dollars could benefit you in retirement.

For the most part, however, the advice spend your after-tax dollars first, your IRA second and your Roth IRA last carries the day.

The Big Picture

MINI CASE STUDY 4.2

A Note to Those Who Fear Capital Gains Tax

One of the primary reasons people think it may be better not to spend the after-tax money first is because of capital gains. For example, if instead of having a basis of $255,000 on the $300,000 of after-tax funds, which was one of the assumptions in the last mini case study, let us assume the basis is zero. All spending of these after-tax funds will be taxed as capital gains. If we use the same assumptions as above, the graph now looks like the one shown in Figure 4.2.

Figure 4.2

Benefits of Spending After-Tax Savings with No Tax Cost Basis before Tax-Deferred Accounts

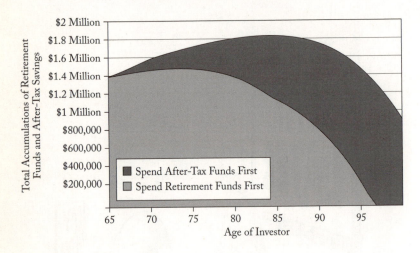

You may have a hard time telling the difference. These results show that Mr. Pay Tax Now is out of funds at age 97 rather than age 98 as in Mini Case Study 4.1, while Mr. Pay Tax Later still has about $1,200,000 left, which will last him another seven years. The bottom line is that spending after-tax money first is still wise, even when capital gains are involved. The step-up in basis rules, however, may provide planning scenarios that contradict this conclusion. The step-up in basis rule states that inherited property assumes a basis equivalent to its fair market value at the date of the decedent's death. It is referred to as a step-up because frequently the fair market value of the property at the date of death is greater than the decedent's basis—that is, its cost when it was first acquired.

For example, in estate situations where only a short remaining lifetime is anticipated, it may be advantageous to not spend highly appreciated investments. If you anticipate being in a situation like this, consult with a qualified advisor who will run some numbers for you. Most of the numbers we have run indicate that unless you are going to die in a few years, you are usually better off spending your after-tax dollars first, even if you will incur capital gains tax and give up your step-up in basis.

MINI CASE STUDY 4.3
The Optimal Order for Spending Classes of Assets

Phyllis Planner is 65 years old and widowed (though the conclusion would be basically the same for a married taxpayer). She is thinking ahead. She wants her money to provide her with a comfortable standard of living, and she also wants to leave some money to her three children. How should Phyllis evaluate which pool of money to spend first and which to save for as long as possible?

There are four general categories of money to support her retirement. They are ranked in order of how I recommend Phyllis spend her money, exhausting each asset category before breaking into the next asset category.

1. After-Tax Assets Generated by Income Sources:

   • Pension distributions

   • Dividends, interest, and capital gains

   • Social Security

   Of course when Phyllis is 70½, she will be required to take minimum distributions from her IRA. Since she will have to pay income taxes on the distributions, the proceeds that remain after she pays taxes on the IRA distributions could also be spent before any of the following assets or sources of income.

2. After-Tax Assets (Investments that are not part of a qualified pretax retirement plan that would generate income subject to taxes annually):

   • Investments that will either sell at a loss or break even

   • Then, more highly appreciated investments

3. IRA and Retirement Plan Assets (Assets subject to ordinary income tax):

- IRA, 403(b), 401(k), and so forth, dollars over and above minimum required distributions

4. Roth IRA:

- Roth IRA dollars

The assets in the income category should be spent first, since she has to pay tax on that money anyway. But let's assume that Phyllis's Social Security and the pension, dividends, and interest are not sufficient to meet her spending needs. Then the question becomes, "Which pool of money should be spent next?" If we keep in mind the premise of "Don't pay taxes now—pay taxes later," the answer is obvious: the after-tax dollars. If we spend our after-tax dollars, except to the extent that a capital gain is triggered on a sale, those dollars will not be subject to income taxes and the money in the IRA can keep growing tax-deferred. Then, when Phyllis has exhausted her after-tax funds, she can delve into her IRA or pretax funds.

Whenever you make a withdrawal from an IRA, you are going to have to pay income taxes. To get an equivalent amount of spending money from the IRA assets and the after-tax assets, you have to take the taxes into consideration. Assuming a 25 percent tax bracket, you need $1.33 from the IRA assets to get $1.00 of spending money ($1.00 cash + $0.33 to pay the taxes). (We get $0.33 cents because $1.33 × 25% = .33.) On the other hand, the after-tax money is withdrawn tax-free, so to get $1.00, you withdraw $1.00 (with the exception of capital gains tax at 15 percent on the appreciation when you withdraw the money).

Finally, when she exhausts her IRA and pretax funds, she spends her Roth IRA. Why should she spend her traditional IRA before her Roth IRA? If tax-deferred growth is a good thing, then tax-free growth is even better. By spending taxable IRA money before Roth IRA money, she increases the time that the Roth IRA will provide income tax-free growth.

If your plan is to leave money to your heirs, their tax situations should be considered as well. If the heirs to the Roth have tax deferral/avoidance as a goal and their tax bracket is the same as yours or higher, then the Roth assets are the best to inherit. The opposite conclusion may be reached if the heirs plan on spending the money soon after they inherit it and are in a lower tax bracket.

If that is the case, you could be better off spending the Roth IRA yourself. The facts of each case should be considered. In general, however, I would stick to what I recommended for Phyllis.

> Determining a strategy for the distribution years is where the rubber meets the road. I've had clients who, while beginning their planning, get upset because they have not accumulated as much as they could have, or for mistakes made along the way. That's water under the bridge. If that's you, it's okay. Properly planning the optimal strategy for the distribution years will help you make up for mistakes made during the accumulation years.

I had a client who came in to see me nine years ago, and at the time we thought this was going to be his last chance to make a Roth IRA conversion. I recommended that he make a $500,000 Roth IRA conversion, which is much higher than I would normally recommend for anyone. When we were done with the conversion, he had three pots of money: He had after-tax dollars, his traditional IRA, and the $500,000 Roth IRA.

The plan that we worked out for him (and by the way he has stuck to that plan) was for him to start out by using only his after-tax dollars for spending purposes and for gifts to his children and grandchildren. He was planning to spend and give away all of his after-tax dollars, so that within a couple of years he would have no after-tax dollars left.

The next step of the plan was to eat up his IRA based on his spending pattern; it was going to take until he was 90 to exhaust his IRA. If he and his wife were still alive at age 90, then they would have the Roth IRA that, if it earned 7 percent interest, would be worth $2 million. So, he wasn't likely to run out of money. More likely what is going to happen is that when he dies, he will leave the entire Roth IRA to his heirs.

That was a terrific plan. We calculated that this plan will literally save his family millions of dollars. The spending order is critical to both your financial well-being and your family's.

One possible exception to spending after-tax dollars first is to prematurely make small IRA withdrawals, or small Roth IRA conversions, if your current tax bracket is lower than your tax bracket will be once you retire.

MINI CASE STUDY 4.4
Figuring the Tax Bracket Advantage into the Spending Order

One possible exception to spending after-tax dollars first is to prematurely make small IRA withdrawals, or small Roth IRA conversions, if your current tax bracket is lower than your tax bracket will be once you retire. This strategy saves some taxes since you are getting some money out of your IRA before you have to take minimum required distributions, which will be taxed at your higher postretirement rate. If you withdraw just enough to take you to the top of your current (low) tax bracket, then you get that money out at a lower tax rate without pushing yourself into a higher tax bracket. But first, let me clarify a common misunderstanding about taxes and tax brackets.

What many people don't understand is that the first sliver of income is taxed at a lower bracket (income up to $16,050 in 2008 is taxed at 10 percent for married filing jointly). Then the next layer of income is taxed at the next bracket (income from $16,050 to $65,100 is taxed at 15 percent for married filing jointly), then the next layer is taxed at the next bracket (income from $65,101 to $131,450 is taxed at 25 percent for married filing jointly for 2008). Some people are deathly afraid of getting one more dollar. They think, "Oh no! If I get one more dollar I'm going to be thrown into the 25 percent tax bracket and my taxes are going to explode." But that's not right. What happens is that just the one additional dollar would be in the 25 percent bracket.

Though Joe and Sally Retiree, aged 65, have an estate of $1.5 million, their taxable income is only $30,000. (Taxable income is arrived at after subtracting itemized deductions and personal exemptions and dependents.) When Joe reaches age 70½, his minimum distribution will push his income well into the 25 percent tax bracket. Joe decides to make voluntary withdrawals from his IRA every year until he reaches his minimum required distribution date as follows.

The top of the 15 percent bracket for married filing jointly (using 2008 tables) is $65,100. Joe and Sally already have $30,000 in taxable income before any IRA withdrawal. If Joe then makes an additional $35,100 IRA withdrawal, he still pays tax at the 15 percent rate. If he waits, much of the later distributions will be taxed at 25 percent. Depending on the circumstances, this might be a reasonable strategy. Calculations reveal that the higher distribution yields a slight long-term advantage, although not as much as you might think because of the simultaneous loss of some tax deferral.

For many clients, particularly frugal clients, I would prefer a variation of this strategy that provides better long-term benefits. Instead of making an IRA withdrawal of $35,100, paying tax on the funds, and then being left with after-tax dollars that will generate taxable income, I would recommend Joe make a $35,100 Roth IRA conversion. Many clients will resist this advice, but I urge you to at least consider it. This advice is perfectly consistent with Jonathan Clements's article in the *Wall Street Journal* dated February 23, 2005, in which Jonathan quoted me giving this identical analysis.

In Chapter 7 we will assess some of the implications of Roth IRA conversions. For now, suffice it to say that I am a big fan of Roth IRA conversions, and my wife and I have made a Roth IRA conversion well into the six figures of our own money and had an enormous tax bill.

If Joe doesn't want to make a Roth IRA conversion, he should at least consider making premature IRA distributions based on tax brackets. Please note that adding income in the form of extra IRA distributions and/or Roth IRA conversions may have an impact on the taxability of Social Security benefits and other items (refer back to "Comments on Your Actual Tax Brackets" in Chapter 2), which should be worked into the numbers for the amount to with-draw or convert.

A Key Lesson from This Chapter

Leaving money in the tax-deferred environment for as long as possible confers advantages that almost always outweigh concerns over paying capital gains on your after-tax assets. The optimal spending order is first your after-tax dollars, then your IRA dollars and then your Roth IRA dollars.

5

||||||||||||||||||||||

Minimum Required Distribution Rules

There was a time when a fool and his money were soon parted,
but now it happens to everybody.

—Adlai Stevenson

Main Topics

- An overview of the minimum required distribution rules
- How to calculate your MRD
- An explanation of the IRS tables

KEY IDEA

If you can afford it, take only the minimum the government requires you to withdraw from your retirement plan or IRA. This distribution pattern retains more money in the tax-deferred account and is consistent with our motto, "Don't pay taxes now—pay taxes later." Note that after taking the minimum required distribution, you can always withdraw more money should the need arise.

Eventually Everyone Must Draw from Retirement Savings

At press time, there was serious discussion by the federal government to suspend the minimum required distribution rules, at least temporarily. The reasoning was that older retirees shouldn't be forced to sell their investments when the value of the investments is low. That reasoning didn't make sense to me because investors are allowed to take their minimum required distribution in stock instead if they prefer. The only forced sale would be the sale of securities to pay the tax on the minimum required distribution. However, this is an area where the well established law could change.

Even if you stick to the game plan to spend your income and after-tax dollars first, eventually, by law, you will have to withdraw funds from your IRA (not your Roth IRA) or qualified retirement plan. You will usually be required to take annual MRDs by April 1 of the year following the year that you reach age 70½. The key word here is *minimum*. Keeping in mind the "Don't pay taxes now—pay taxes later" rule of thumb, I want you to continue to maintain the highest balance possible in the tax-deferred environment. If you take a minimum distribution the year you turn 70½ and a distribution the following year, you may remain in a lower tax bracket which would be advantageous. You can always take out more if you need it.

> ... eventually, by law, you will have to withdraw funds from your IRA (not your Roth IRA) or qualified retirement plan.

Calculating Your MRD after Age 70½

Currently, minimum required distributions are calculated by taking your projected distribution period, based on your age and the age of a beneficiary deemed to be 10 years younger than you, and dividing that factor into the balance of your IRA or qualified plan as of December 31 of the prior year. Bear in mind that your projected life expectancy factor or the projected distribution period is not based on your eating and exercise habits or even your genetic history! It is an actuarial calculation from the IRS determined solely by age.

The new tables that contain the factor are in the IRS's Supplement to the 590 Publication. Alternatively, you could go to www.PayTaxesLater.com/calculator, select the minimum required distribution calculator, enter your birth date and the balance of your IRA, and your minimum required distribution will appear. See the appendix at the end of this book.

The IRS provides three life expectancy tables. The most frequently used table is Table III, not Table I. I present them here in the reverse order.

Table III: Uniform Lifetime Table (*for use by unmarried IRA owners and married owners whose spouses are not more than 10 years younger*). The table is available at www.PayTaxesLater.com/mrd_table.htm, or from a link on the page www.PayTaxesLater.com/calculator or in the appendix of this book.

Table II: Joint Life and Last Survivor Expectancy Table (*for IRA owners with spouses 10 or more years younger*). Not covered on our web site nor in the appendix because it is too long. See IRS Publication 590.

Table I: Single Life Expectancy Table (*for IRA beneficiaries*). The table is available on the web page with the IRA Beneficiary Calculator at www.PayTaxesLater.com/calculator and in the appendix.

Table III: Uniform Lifetime Table for IRA Owners

Generally speaking, most IRA owners will use Table III. In effect, the age-dependent projected distribution periods in Table III are based on joint life expectancy projections of an IRA owner and a hypothetical beneficiary 10 years younger. Using a joint life expectancy is advantageous because the longer joint-life expectancy factor reduces the annual minimum required distribution. But rather than using the actual life expectancy of the beneficiary for the calculations, the IRS simplified the terms. Table III deems all beneficiaries—from children to grandmothers—to have a life expectancy 10 years longer than that of the owner. At age 71, the projected distribution period is 26.5 years (roughly the single life expectancy from Table I plus 10 years, although you must refer to the tables for the precise factor).

MINI CASE STUDY 5.1
MRD Calculation for IRA

Owners

Bob turns 75 in 2009. As of December 31, 2008, he has two IRAs worth $500,000. He names his son Phillip as the beneficiary for one IRA and his wife, Mary, for the other. To calculate his 2009 minimum required distribution for the IRA with his son as beneficiary, he takes the life expectancy from Table III, 22.9, and divides that into his balance, $500,000, to arrive at $21,834.

When Bob dies, Phillip will inherit the IRA, and he will then have to take minimum distributions on the inherited IRA. The minimum distribution for the inherited IRA will be based on Phillip's life expectancy as stipulated in Table I.

Table II: Joint Life and Last Survivor Expectancy Table for IRA Owners with Spouses 10 or More Years Younger

Because nothing is ever without complications, there is an exception for married individuals when the IRA owner is 10 or more years older than his or her spouse. Those individuals are permitted to use their actual joint life expectancy factor which will result in smaller minimum required distributions. One of the benefits of being older and having a wife 10 years younger is a reduced minimum required distribution.

MINI CASE STUDY 5.2

MRD Calculation with IRA Owner and Spouse More Than 10 Years Younger

Bob has to use a different calculation for the minimum required distribution for the IRA with Mary, his 63 year old wife, as beneficiary. According to Table II, Bob's and Mary's joint life expectancy factor is 24.3. Bob calculates his MRD by dividing 24.3 into his balance of $500,000 to arrive at $20,576. Bob's MRD for the account with his wife as the beneficiary is lower than for the account with his son as the beneficiary because Bob and his wife were permitted to use their actual joint life expectancy factor for his calculation.

Table I: Single Life Expectancy Table for IRA Beneficiaries

Nonspouse beneficiaries of inherited IRAs must take distributions based on their actual life expectancies as projected in Table I. The beneficiary finds his life expectancy factor in Table I as of the year following the year of the IRA owner's death. A spousal beneficiary of an IRA owner who dies before 70½ who does not wish to treat the IRA as his or her own can choose to defer distributions until the year that the IRA owner would have attained

70½ and then find his or her life expectancy factor in Table I as of that year. That is his divisor. For each subsequent year, the nonspouse beneficiary subtracts one (1) from the original number, because his life expectancy is diminished by one year for every year he survives.

Calculating Your Life Expectancy after the Initial Year

Notice in Table I that the life expectancy of the beneficiary is reduced by one full year as each year passes. Tables II and III, however, reduce the life expectancy of the IRA owner by less than one each year. This is analogous to the old double recalculation method. (Readers who remember those rules get bonus points.) The idea is that as we age, our life expectancy declines, but it does not decline by an entire year.

There is a unique exception for a surviving spouse who inherits an IRA but does not roll over the IRA to treat it as his or her own IRA. During the surviving spouse's lifetime, the life expectancy is recalculated each year based on his or her life expectancy under Table I. When the surviving spouse dies, the nonspouse heirs must use the life expectancy of the surviving spouse at the time of death, reduced by one for each subsequent year, for their MRD calculation. For a discussion on whether a spouse should treat an IRA as his or her own IRA, refer to Chapter 13.

Timing Your First Required Distribution

Participants born between July 1, 1937, and June 30, 1938, will have to take one distribution in 2008 and one in 2009, or two distributions in 2009 if they failed to take a distribution in 2008. If the participant failed to take a distribution in 2008, the first distribution in 2009 would have to be taken prior to April 1, 2009 (in effect, for what should have been taken in 2008), and the second distribution will have to be taken by December 31, 2009.

A participant born between July 1, 1938, and June 30, 1939, will reach 70½ during 2009. Technically, he or she could delay taking the first required minimum distribution until April 1, 2010. The rule was, and remains, that the required beginning date for taking minimum required distributions is April 1 of the year following the year the participant turns 70½. However, if a participant was born between July 1, 1938, and June 30, 1939, and he or she waits until 2010 to take the first distribution, then that person must take two distributions in 2010. The first distribution would be due before April 1, 2010, and the second distribution would be due by December 31,

2010. Annual minimum distributions would continue for the rest of the participant's life.

For participants born July 1, 1939, or afterward, there is no minimum required distribution for 2009. Unless the participant needs the money or is pursuing the early distribution of an IRA because of a lower income tax bracket or estate plan strategy, he or she is better off leaving the money in the IRA and taking the first minimum required distribution when required in 2010 or later.

So, if you have a choice, should you limit your distributions to one per year, or should you wait and then take two the following year? If you take a minimum distribution the year that you turn 70½ and only one distribution the following year, you may remain in a lower tax bracket, which would be advantageous. Taking two distributions in one year could push you into a higher tax bracket and possibly accelerate the phaseout of certain tax credits or deductions. If that is the case, you will likely be better off violating our "Pay taxes later" rule by taking one distribution and paying some tax before you have to. On the other hand, if it will not make a difference, in other words, if you will remain in the same tax bracket even with two distributions, then wait until you are required to begin distributions, and take advantage of the additional period of tax-deferred growth.

Special Rule for Qualified Plan Owners Who Are Still Working Past Age 70½

Minimum required distribution rules apply to traditional IRAs (not Roth IRAs) and qualified plans (401[k]s, 403[b]s, Roth 401[k]s, and Roth 401[b]s, etc.). However, the rules governing 401(k)s and 403(b)s are slightly different than for IRAs.

- If you are still working after age 70½, you do not have to take a distribution from the retirement plan connected to your current job as long as you do not own more than 5 percent of the company.

- If you have a plan such as a 401(k) plan associated with a job from which you have retired, you will have to take your initial minimum required distribution by April 1 of the year following the year in which you reached age 70½.

- If you had a 401(k) plan from a former job and rolled that 401(k) plan into a plan associated with the job at which you are still working, then you will have to check with the plan administrator of your current plan to see whether you will be forced to take MRDs from the portion of that 401(k) plan that is attributable to your former employment upon attaining age 70½. PLR 200453015, published in January 2005, states that the IRS permits deferral of the MRDs on all of the funds in the new employer's account including the rollover contributions from the former employer until April 1 of the year after the employee retires from the new employer. You must, however, make sure that the employer's plan will allow you to do what the IRS will allow you to do.

MINI CASE STUDY 5.3
MRD if Still Working Past Age 70½

Joan continues to work although she is older than 70½. She has a total of $1 million in her 401(k) plans: $500,000 associated with her current job and $500,000 from a former job. She has never consolidated the two plans. Her new plan has her and her employer's most recent contributions.

By April 1 of the year after she turns age 70½, she will be required to take minimum distributions from the $500,000 associated with the job she left but not from the account that is still active due to her employment. Whether she could take the money from the 401(k) from the job she retired from, roll it into her current plan (by trustee-to-trustee transfer), and avoid an MRD is not clear. The IRS will allow it, but her current employer may not.

There may be an incentive for someone still working after age 70½ to consider rolling money out of their IRA and into a retirement plan at work. Usually, I prefer money going the other way, which is from 401(k) to IRA, or my current preferred strategy, from a work 401(k) or IRA to a one-person 401(k) plan that you control.

I have a client who became really excited about the prospect of avoiding his minimum distribution. He wanted to start his own retirement plan (actually a one-person 401(k)) based on his small self-employment income. Then he wanted to roll his IRA into the a one-person 401(k) and suspend his minimum required distributions on his IRA. It was a good thought, but with a fatal flaw. He is more than a 5 percent owner of his consulting business, and the rule about deferring the MRD after 70½ if you are still working does not apply to individuals with a 5 percent or greater ownership in the company.

Special Rule for 403(b) Participants

Both employee and employer contributions to a 403(b) plan made before January 1, 1987, are not subject to minimum required distributions until age 75. As a result, the balance in your 403(b) as of December 31, 1986, is not subject to MRDs until you reach age 75, not age 70½, even if you have retired. If you fall into this special category of 403(b) account holders, you should consult with your organization's benefits office to determine the balance of the account as of December 31, 1986. Surprisingly, many institutions, including TIAA-CREF, do a good job of tracking that balance.

On the other hand, when you actually calculate the tax advantage of keeping the funds in the 403(b) to defer a portion of the minimum distribution, it is relatively small. If you think you could get even a slight investment advantage by doing a trustee-to-trustee transfer from your 403(b) to an IRA to gain additional investment options, it would still be worthwhile.

Schedule your IRA distribution
for Thanksgiving

Would you like more cutting-edge information on distribution planning for TIAA-CREF participants? Go to www.retiresecure.com for a free report or fill out the order form at the back of this book. Please sign up now while it's fresh on your mind!

When Should You Schedule Taking Your MRD?

Theoretically, you should take your MRD on December 31 to delay as long as possible withdrawing money from the tax-favored environment. Another little trick is by taking the MRD in December and having federal income tax withheld. The tax withheld is treated as if it had been withheld throughout the year as opposed to being treated like a late year estimated tax payment. In the real world, however, it is difficult to get any work done with financial firms in December, and trying to comply with a deadline between Christmas and the last day of the year is a total nightmare. Remember, if you miss taking a withdrawal by year-end you face the 50 percent penalty for failing to take your required minimum distribution—an expensive penalty. If you don't need the cash, I recommend scheduling your distribution for Thanksgiving or early December. If you need the MRD for your spending needs, it may be best to schedule 12 equal monthly distributions throughout the year.

> **If you don't need the cash, I recommend scheduling your distribution for Thanksgiving or early December.**

A Key Lesson from This Chapter

Keep your MRD to the minimum required. Do not take out more money than you need so that you keep the balance in your tax-deferred accounts as large as possible.

6

|||||||||||||||||||||||||

Should You Transfer Your 401(k) Account to an IRA at Retirement?

Rollovers Versus Trustee-to-Trustee Transfers and Other Strategies

They say it is better to be poor and happy than rich and miserable, but how about a compromise like moderately rich and just moody?
—Diana, Princess of Wales

Main Topics

- Assessing the flexibility of your retirement plan
- Advantages of IRA investment options
- Advantages of trustee-to-trustee transfers
- Disadvantages of trustee-to-trustee transfers
- The mechanics of initiating the transfer or rollover

KEY IDEA

In most cases retirees should consider a trustee-to-trustee transfer of the majority of their company 401(k) plan to an IRA or, alternatively, a one-person 401(k) plan. There are circumstances, however, where a retiree will be well served by retaining at least a portion of his or her retirement plan in the original company 401(k).

When someone retires or is "service terminated," the big question is, "What should I do now?"

Without getting into specific investment ideas, let's consider whether it makes sense for you to keep your money in your existing retirement plan, transfer it to an IRA, take a lump-sum distribution or, my newest idea, make a trustee-to-trustee transfer into your new one-person 401(k) plan.

Contingent on the specifics of any given retirement plan, the basic options are as follows:

1. Transfer the money into a separate IRA.

2. Leave the money in the current plan.

3. Annuitize the balance. (For more information on annuitizing, see Chapter 8.)

4. Use some combination of options 1, 2, and 3 (often my favorite choice).

5. Take a lump-sum distribution.

6. Transfer money to your new one-person 401(k) plan.

Rolling Over to an IRA

Retirees often talk about rolling over to an IRA or rolling money out of a retirement plan and into an IRA. Technically we should use the term *transfer,* simply because the IRS makes a significant distinction between the mechanics and regulations of a rollover versus a trustee-to-trustee transfer. The trustee-to-trustee transfer is simpler, and what I usually recommend. I'll explain about the distinctions between rollovers and transfers later in this chapter. (In keeping with common usage, when referring to a transfer, I will use the terms *rollover* and *transfer* interchangeably throughout this book, but please understand that what I am referring to is a trustee-to-trustee transfer and not a rollover.) (See the section in this chapter called "The Mechanics of IRA Rollovers and Trustee-to-Trustee Transfers.")

Though there are a few downsides, transferring retirement plan accumulations into an IRA or into your own one-person 401(k) via a trustee-to-trustee transfer is usually the best option. As with most decisions, there are advantages and disadvantages.

> **Retirees often talk about rolling over to an IRA or rolling money out of a retirement plan and into an IRA. Technically we should use the term *transfer,* simply because the IRS makes a significant distinction between the mechanics and regulations of a rollover versus a trustee-to-trustee transfer.**

Tax Advantages of Transferring a Company 401(k) (or Other Retirement Plan) into an IRA

The biggest tax advantage of transferring a company 401(k) to an IRA revolves around what happens to the inherited 401(k) versus the inherited IRA at death. To really understand this section, it is best to have a working knowledge of what happens when the IRA owner dies and eventually the IRA is inherited by a nonspouse beneficiary. A detailed discussion of this topic is presented in the section "Laying the Foundation for Estate Planning: Using the MRD Rules After Death."

> The law governing the discussion in this entire section of the book is currently in flux. At press time, what is stated in this section is accurate. However, if the Pension Protection Technical Corrections Act of 2008 is passed, this section and the following case study will become obsolete. I have heard top experts disagree on what will eventually happen to the law on this subject. We will present the law as it is today at press time. Nonetheless, some of the concepts discussed in this section will have enormous value to the reader, even if the future law makes the particulars of this section obsolete. To get an update on this law, please visit www.retiresecure.com.

The stretch IRA concept—limiting distributions from an inherited IRA to the minimum to maintain money in the tax-deferred environment for as long as possible after the death of the IRA owner—is sound. I discuss the stretch IRA in detail in Chapter 13.

Proper planning requires the appropriate steps while you are alive and after you and your spouse have died. If done correctly, your heirs could stretch taxable distributions from an inherited IRA and certain retirement plans for decades, sometimes as long as 80 years after the original owner dies. If, however, your employer's retirement plan document stipulates the wrong provisions, the stretch may be replaced by a screaming income tax disaster. Dad's heirs could be in for a tax nightmare if dad never transferred his retirement plan into an IRA.

Many investors fail to realize that the specific plan rules that govern their individual 401(k) or other retirement plan take precedence over the IRS distribution rules for inherited IRAs or retirement plans. The distribution rules that come into play at the death of the retirement plan participant are usually found in a plan document that few employees or advisors ever read. Some plan documents read that in the event of death, a nonspouse beneficiary must receive (and pay tax on) the entire balance of the retirement plan the year after the death of the retirement plan owner. These retirement plans don't allow a nonspouse beneficiary to stretch distributions. (The new law, if passed, will dictate that employers must give nonspouse beneficiaries the right to stretch the inherited IRA over the course of their life.)

Upon retiring, some employees prefer to keep their retirement plan balances where they currently are rather than transferring it to an IRA because their 401(k) plans may offer favorable fixed-income investments and/or the possibility of lower transaction fees. However, if the 401(k) plan does not offer the stretch IRA feature for a nonspouse beneficiary, and the employee dies with a balance in his or her 401(k) plan and has named someone other than a spouse as a beneficiary, the entire balance must be withdrawn by the beneficiary in the year following the 401(k) plan owner's death. This distribution can result in a huge acceleration of fully taxable income. If there is a $1 million balance, the nonspouse heir or heirs will have to pay income taxes on $1 million. Then, the remaining balance, roughly $650,000 ($1 million minus the $350,000 immediate income tax hit) would be outside of the tax-deferred protection of an inherited IRA.

If the 401(k) participant had taken that money and transferred it into an IRA before he died, the nonspouse beneficiary would have been able to stretch the distributions based on his or her life expectancy. Failing to make the IRA transfer could result in an unnecessary massive income tax burden for the nonspouse beneficiary. I know of many real-life examples where the acceleration of taxes on an inherited 401(k) resulted in an income tax nightmare for the beneficiaries. Please don't compound the tragedy of your death by creating a tax nightmare for your heirs. Even if the new law is implemented and the company allows your nonspouse beneficiary to stretch the inherited IRA, Figure 6.1 is still informative. The $1 million loss shown in this graph will become a reality if there is a mechanical mistake in the way the 401(k) or IRA beneficiary form is filled out or if the actions of the beneficiaries themselves after the death of one or both parents are not appropriate. This graph essentially proves that failing to stretch an inherited IRA or 401(k) could easily cost the heirs $1 million.

Rolling the 401(k) into an IRA

Figure 6.1 compares the results of inheriting a retirement plan that makes no allowances for nonspouse beneficiary stretch distributions versus an inherited IRA where the beneficiary can stretch the distributions (and defer taxes).

The following assumptions are reflected in Figure 6.1.

1. The inheritances begin with a beneficiary IRA of $1 million versus $650,000 of after-tax funds, assuming 35 percent tax would be paid on a $1 million taxable withdrawal in one year.

2. Annual spending needs of $40,000 after taxes are deducted annually from each inheritance, indexed for 3 percent inflation.

Figure 6.1

**Stretched IRA or Retirement Plan Balance vs.
Accelerated Lump-Sum Distribution**

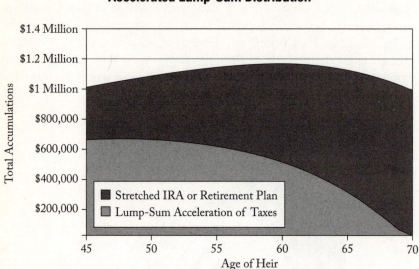

3. Assumptions for the $650,000 of after-tax funds are as follows:

   • Investment returns are 7 percent annually, 70 percent is capital appreciation and 30 percent is ordinary interest income.

   • Capital gains are realized on 15 percent of the prior year's cumulative unrealized capital appreciation (a 15 percent portfolio turnover rate).

   • Capital gains are also realized on withdrawals for payment of expenses and income taxes.

   • A small capital gains tax rate of 9 percent is used for the realized capital gains on after-tax funds.

   • Ordinary interest income is taxed at a rate of 15 percent, a lower rate than the rate on the retirement plan distributions.

4. Annual withdrawals from the inherited IRA are taxed at a higher rate of 25 percent and are equal to the spending amount plus taxes.

The dramatic difference noted in the two inheritances shows the value of continuing tax deferral on a large amount of money. The accelerated lump-sum distribution scenario shows that all the funds are depleted by the time the beneficiary reaches age 70, when the IRA or retirement account's value of the inherited IRA is nearly $1 million.

If your nonspouse beneficiary must withdraw the money all at once—thus ending the deferral—the large amount of ordinary income will likely move him or her into a higher tax bracket. This accounts for the significantly lower starting amount for the accelerated 401(k) fund, that must be converted into after-tax funds.

Are you considering navigating these potentially rocky waters without a professional who is qualified and experienced in distribution and estate planning for IRAs and retirement plans?

If so, please read this next tragic story. This happens all the time. You can avoid it with the right professional and proper planning.

MINI CASE STUDY 6.1

True Story of the Disastrous Consequences of Not Making a 401(k) Rollover to an IRA (details adapted)

Even before the divorce papers were final, the mother of a young son had her divorce attorney draft a new will and retirement plan beneficiary designation. In her will and in her retirement plan, she cut out her ex-husband and left everything to her son via a trust that provided for his education, among other things. Making provisions for her son was particularly important because she was in poor health and was no longer able to work.

She saw a financial planner about the possibility of rolling her retirement plan into an IRA. She hated to pay fees and found it particularly distasteful because she liked the fixed-income account of her employer's 401(k) plan. She was not aware that the rules of her retirement plan, as stated in the plan document, stipulated that the entire plan balance must be withdrawn within a year of her death. Her retirement plan would not permit her son to use his own life expectancy for minimum required distribution purposes.

The financial planner, using only investment-related advice, could not convince her to roll over her 401(k) into an IRA. The attorney preparing the will and the beneficiary designation of the 401(k) never recommended an IRA rollover.

The mother died with over $250,000 in her former employer's retirement plan. Because of the mandatory withdrawal, the trust for her son had to pay massive income taxes on the balance of the entire 401(k) in the year after she died. Also, the trust for her son had an even higher income-tax rate than he would have had individually, that meant the retirement monies were taxed at the highest rate of 35 percent.

Had the mother taken her retirement plan and rolled it into an IRA the day before she died, and used the appropriate beneficiary designation, the money would have remained as an inherited IRA in a tax-deferred environment. Distributions and thus taxation could have been spread over the son's life expectancy. For at least a portion of that money, income tax could have been deferred for more than 80 years.

If either the client, the attorney, or the financial advisor had read *Retire Secure!,* they would have foreseen the problem of the accelerated income tax rules in the employer's plan. The advisor could have pointed to compelling reasons to transfer the money into an IRA that went beyond investment issues. They might have considered rolling everything but the fixed-income fund into an IRA, but they didn't. The result of the lack of planning and the lack of a knowledgeable advisor left the son financially handicapped, in addition to suffering the loss of his mother.

> **Retirees who still have their money in a retirement plan that doesn't allow the stretch should strongly consider rolling their retirement plan, or at least a major part of their retirement plan, into an IRA.**

The Moral of the Story: Retirees who still have their money in a retirement plan that doesn't allow the stretch should strongly consider rolling their retirement plan, or at least a major part of their retirement plan, into an IRA to protect the next generation from an unnecessary massive acceleration of income tax. If you are unaware of your plan's death distribution rules, please learn them right away. It could save your family a bundle in the long run.

Investment Reasons to Transfer to an IRA or to a One-Person 401(k)

One of the most compelling reasons to transfer the money out of the retirement plan and into an IRA is the opportunity to take advantage of the universe of investment choices offered by IRAs. A big challenge facing most IRA owners is choosing among the thousands of investments such as mutual funds, stocks, bonds, etc. Leaving the money in the company plan will generally limit your options. The argument for greater investment choices becomes even more critical if your plan does not offer good investment choices. Though the trend is to give employees more choices and more advice than in the past, transferring the money into an IRA or a one-person 401(k) will always give the retiree more and often better choices.

Advantages of Leaving the Money Where It Is

Let's assume for a moment that you are retired and have the option of transferring your retirement plan into an IRA or a one-person 401(k). Are there good reasons to leave the money where it is and not make the trustee-to-trustee transfer? There sure are. Don't skip this part.

The best reason for leaving the money in the plan is that your current retirement plan may have an excellent fixed-income fund, often guaranteed in the form of a guaranteed income contract (GIC). Many of the fixed funds that purchased long-term bonds, mortgages, and commercial paper a number of years ago when interest rates were higher than today are still holding those investments. As a result, many of these fixed-income accounts are paying out higher returns than those available for comparable current investments with the same degree of safety.

But, in general, if you hold stocks or alternate investments—other than a much-better-than-average type of fund that you could not replicate outside your retirement plan—I would like to see you make a trustee-to-trustee transfer out of the retirement plan and into an IRA or a one-person 401(k) (subject to other exceptions coming up). Even with that good investment, in general, I still prefer the trustee-to-trustee transfer.

On the other hand, some commentators feel that naive retirement plan owners are likely to be the victims of unscrupulous financial advisors. The argument goes that if you stay in your 401(k) plan, you will avoid some of these unscrupulous advisors. Though I hate to admit it, the concern has merit. However, if you find a good advisor, transferring the money into an IRA or a one-person 401(k) is certainly the indicated course.

Music to the Ears of a CD Investor

I bet all you CD investors are tired of hearing everyone talk about the benefits of a well-balanced portfolio, aren't you? You don't want to hear that inflation will eat at the purchasing power of your CD investments. You just want some good advice on how to manage your CDs. Okay. Fair enough. This is for you.

Maybe you just don't want to be in the market no matter what all the financial advisors say. Many people feel this way in light of the recent market volatility. If you feel this way, you will be happy to know that the FDIC insurance for CDs has been increased from $100,000 per person to $250,000 per person. Those seeking additional security can add a transfer on death designation to the CDs adding $250,000 of FDIC insurance protection per beneficiary named on the transfer on death designation.

Conservative retirees are also attracted by the offers made by some banks to allow seniors to upgrade their CDs annually to a higher interest rate and for a longer term. When the maximum term, typically 10 years, is reached, the annual upgrade in rates is still permissible, but you have to ask for it. Choosing CDs with a term of 5 to 10 years should alleviate some of the worry about market ups and downs. Also many retirees are unaware that many banks permit annual minimum required distributions to be taken from CDs without breaking the CD or incurring any penalty or loss of earnings. Virtually all institutions follow this rule when taking minimum required distributions from IRA CDs. But, don't just arbitrarily roll over a sizeable portion of your 401(k) into CDs that you buy from your current bank. It would be better to get quotes from at least three or four banks. Share the quotes with the bank manager you really want to do business with, and ask her for their best and final rates.

Weighing the Investment Advantages versus the Threat of Income Tax Acceleration

My clients who have good guaranteed investment contracts in their 401(k) plans often tell me they understand about the stretch IRA and the acceleration of income taxes for their heirs, but they don't want to give up the security of their fixed-income account that is paying higher-than-current interest rates on comparable investments. At least to some extent, they are right. What should you do if you are in that situation? For one thing, just because a GIC is paying a higher rate now, please don't assume that will be an indefinite arrangement. As the old bonds and paper mature, the GIC will be forced to lower its return in keeping with the lower current rates. Therefore, the investment advantage, while real, will likely only be temporary. Beyond the investment issue, I would like to revisit the distinction between spouse and nonspouse beneficiaries.

As with the previous section on the tax advantages of transferring a 401(k) (or other retirement plan) into an IRA, the information in this section may also be dated if there is a change to the rule regarding income tax acceleration of the inherited 401(k).

To get an update on this law, please visit www.retiresecure.com.

Let's assume you have named your surviving spouse as the primary beneficiary of your 401(k). Your strategy is that after your death, your spouse will choose to retain the retirement plan as his or her own rather than disclaiming to the children. In that case, under the rules of most retirement plans, the surviving spouse will be allowed to inherit the retirement plan with no obligation to withdraw it all and pay the income taxes. By naming your spouse as beneficiary, he or she will get the lifetime stretch even if the money remains in the 401(k) and income tax acceleration will be avoided at the first death.

The problem arises upon the death of the second spouse when the money is left to the children or any nonspouse beneficiary. The income tax could be accelerated at the death of the second spouse. Over time, as shown in Figure 6.1, this income tax acceleration could cost the children $1 million. The only rational justification for risking the $1 million is that you prefer the fixed-income account and the projected time frame for the income tax acceleration problem seems very far removed. Both you and your spouse have to die before the income tax is accelerated.

In trying to prepare for the death of the second spouse, the general strategy might include having the surviving spouse transfer the 401(k) into an IRA when the first spouse dies. The reason for thinking ahead is that you never want to be in a situation where there is only one life separating the family from accelerated income taxation. The strategy might even include the idea that if the 401(k) owner gets sick, he or she would abandon taking advantage of the fixed contract, guaranteed investment advantage. The plan is to transfer the money into an IRA to avoid the massive income tax hit in the event of the employee's death and the subsequent death of the employee's spouse.

If we use this straddle plan, that is, leave the money in the 401(k) but be prepared to roll it over into an IRA on short notice, you could argue that you are getting the best of both worlds. You and your spouse get the higher fixed-income-fund interest during your life and the stretch afterwards for your children. This solution is comfortable.

Is it a reasonable strategy? Not really. Too many things could go wrong. Failing health and advanced age seriously complicate the picture. In addition, my experience has been that people don't like to acknowledge how sick they are, and putting decisions off until you reach that state is not wise. A sick person often pushes financial matters aside. I have often seen sick clients who just were not up for dealing with money. Justifiably, they want to devote all their remaining time and energy on their health and family.

The strategy above would fail if upon the first death (it could be either spouse), the surviving spouse fails to make the transfer from the retirement plan to the IRA. After a death, I have seen surviving spouses freeze, that is to say, become afraid to do anything. If this happens and the surviving spouse dies before the transfer to an IRA is made, then we have the income tax acceleration disaster. If there is a sudden or unexpected death, the trauma can be even more paralyzing.

If you are currently a plan participant that accelerates income at your death for nonspouse beneficiaries, you must transfer this money to an IRA before the nonspouse beneficiary inherits the funds to avoid the acceleration. If you do not, the nonspouse beneficiary will face massive taxation. I recommend moving the money out of the 401(k) while everyone is healthy and choosing the appropriate investments, perhaps with the help of a qualified and reputable investment advisor or money manager to compensate for the loss of the fixed income fund.

One compromise might be to leave the fixed asset portion of your portfolio that is currently invested at higher-than-current market rates in your 401(k) and transfer the rest into an IRA. I would consider this approach the minimum that you should do to avoid the income tax acceleration.

My New Recommendation: The One-Person 401(k) Plan

Throughout this chapter and in other parts of this book, I have mentioned the possibility of creating a one-person 401(k) plan and using that as your primary retirement plan vehicle as many people now use IRAs. The difficult part to using this strategy is that an individual requires self-employment income to open his or her own one-person 401(k) plan. Many retirees, by definition, don't have self-employment income. If that is your case, the best solution might be to roll the money into an IRA or if your retirement funds are in an IRA now, to leave them there. If possible, it would be better if you could get some self-employment income. Do some consulting, work on a project, do something where you earn some income and based on that self-employment income set up a one-person 401(k) plan. You will have control of the plan, and you can do a trustee-to-trustee transfer of all your retirement plans to this one-person 401(k) plan.

If you are retired and still have money in your former employer's 401(k) plan, subject to exceptions mentioned in this chapter, I would consider rolling at least a portion, if not all, of your existing 401(k) plan from your former job into your new one-person 401(k) plan. I would even suggest that you consider rolling your IRA to your new one-person 401(k) plan. This offers the following benefits:

* Extremely flexible investment choices are possible.

* In the event of your death, your beneficiaries would still be able to make a Roth IRA conversion of the inherited 401(k).

* There are expanded Roth IRA conversion possibilities (new).

* You will have better protection from creditors than traditional IRAs.

It is not that having a lot of money in a company 401(k) or even a traditional IRA is bad, but having it in a one-person 401(k) plan that is completely under your control is, for many retirees, a better strategy. If you don't have any self-employment income and have no realistic way of getting self-employment income, the classic trustee-to-trustee transfer to an IRA will usually be best with at least the majority of your retirement assets.

However, to be fair, there are some advantages to leaving your company 401(k) plan where it is and not rolling the money into an IRA or one-person 401(k).

Additional Advantages of Retaining a 401(k) Rather Than Rolling into an IRA

1. *Superior credit protection:* Many ERISA (Employee Retirement Income Security Act of 1974) type plans enjoy the federal protection against creditors and bankruptcy that IRAs do not enjoy. It should be noted, however, that the Bankruptcy Abuse Prevention Act of 2005, signed in April 2005 by President Bush includes a $1 million exemption for contributory IRAs and Roth IRAs. It further exempts all rollovers from retirement plans to IRAs. Because there are two different types of creditor protection, owners of large IRAs are advised to keep their rollover IRA in a separate account from their contributory IRA. IRAs usually have state law protections, but over time, even these state law protections have diminished. For the vast majority of participants, a good umbrella

insurance policy providing coverage of at least $1 million or possibly $2 million or more (to protect against unexpected liabilities) is the best solution. For participants with serious liability issues, such as emergency room doctors or surgeons, the superior credit protection may be more important than the investment and estate planning advantages of the IRA. For example, I recently worked with a physician who decided not to terminate his qualified retirement plan for these reasons when it would have been easier to terminate the plan and roll the plan balance into an IRA. For the physician, the additional asset protection feature of keeping his 401(k) plan from work intact was more important than the simplicity and reduced fees of an IRA. Now, under my new strategy, if the physician can develop some self-employment income, he could have his own one-person 401(k). This is one of the reasons I like having the one-person 401(k) plan. It has all the benefits of an IRA but also the superior creditor protection of the ERISA retirement plan.

2. *Deferment taking MRDs:* Special rules allow employees of companies whose ownership interest is 5 percent or less, to defer taking their minimum required distributions until they retire, even after they turn age 70½. For example, let's assume you are such an employee, aged 72, and still working. Half of your retirement assets are in a 401(k) where you currently work. The other half is in an IRA, which came from a rollover from a previous employer. Regarding the 401(k) where you are still working, there is no required minimum distribution as long as you continue to work. You must take your annual minimum distribution from your traditional IRA. Even if the company allows you to transfer a portion of the 401(k) into an IRA, there is at least an argument for leaving it in the 401(k) to continue deferring taxes until the time arrives for minimum required distributions.

3. *Borrowing privileges:* The 401(k) plan may have provisions that allow you to borrow against the plan. There are situations when it may be handy to borrow money from a 401(k) plan. Borrowing from an IRA is not permitted.

4. *Net unrealized appreciation:* Before you initiate a trustee-to-trustee transfer out of a 401(k) into an IRA you might be giving up an enormous opportunity if you do not check to see if there is any net unrealized appreciation (NUA) stock and any after-tax money in the 401(k) or other qualified plan. If there is any NUA stock or after-tax money in the retirement plan, then special treatment is

highly recommended. (Please see Chapter 9 for more on NUA.) Checking for NUA is even more important since recent tax law changes have temporarily reduced capital gains tax rates.

5. *Roth IRA conversion possibility for nonspouse beneficiary:* Notice 2008–30 provides a unique opportunity for a nonspouse beneficiary to do a Roth IRA conversion. Nonspouse beneficiaries of inherited IRAs do not have the same opportunity to do Roth IRA conversions, so this conversion possibility for nonspouse beneficiaries of qualified plans is an additional reason to retain assets in a qualified plan.

6. *Direct Roth IRA conversion from 401(k) and 403(b) plans:* It used to be that you had to transfer your 401(k) balance into a traditional IRA before you could convert that traditional IRA to a Roth IRA. The new law makes it possible to transfer your 401(k) account directly to a Roth IRA. But the good news doesn't stop there. There is an additional—and likely unanticipated by Congress—tax benefit with respect to a direct Roth IRA conversion from a 401(k) account. This development relates to the potential opportunity to transfer after-tax contributions (basis) from your qualified plan account into a Roth IRA without having to pay the tax.

Bear with me here, while we review some of the technicalities that you need to understand to appreciate this new opportunity. Under Section 408(d)(2) IRA aggregation rules, a retirement plan participant who wants to transfer the balance of his plan, including the basis from after-tax contributions, to a traditional IRA cannot isolate the after-tax contributions and convert that money to a Roth IRA, and transfer the balance of the account to a self-employed retirement plan or a qualified retirement plan with another employer without considering the balances of his other existing IRAs. Let's look at an example.

Assume you have a $1,000,000 IRA with no basis and have a $300,000 401(k) with basis from after-tax contributions of $50,000. You want to convert the $300,000 to a Roth IRA. Under the IRA aggregation rules, if you wanted to convert all the $50,000 of after-tax contributions in an IRA to a Roth IRA, you would have had to previously convert the entire balance of the remaining other traditional IRAs as well as the $300,000 401(k). This would cause a whopping income tax bill in the neighborhood of $437,500 ($1,250,000 taxes at 35 percent) to get the $50,000 of after-tax contributions into a Roth IRA.

But now, with the ability to transfer directly from a 401(k) account to a Roth IRA, you avoid the aggregation rules that apply only to IRAs. Now, you will not have to consider any preexisting IRAs when you transfer a 401(k) account that includes after-tax contributions directly into a Roth IRA.

Here is an example of Roth conversions of the inherited funds under the old and new laws:

	Old Rules	New Rules
Starting with		
Inherited 401(k) (Includes basis of $50,000 from nondeductible contributions)	$300,000	$300,000
Other IRAs—no basis	1,000,000	1,000,000
Convert inherited 401(k) to a Roth:	1,300,000	1,300,000
Conversion via an IRA only	300,000	
Conversion directly to Roth IRA		300,000
Basis allocated	(11,538)	(50,000)
Taxable amount	$288,462	$250,000
Tax—assume 35% federal and state	$100,962	$87,500
Tax savings under new rules		$13,462

As a bonus, if the retirement plan allows you to separate the after-tax contributions from the pretax contributions, you may have a situation where you can convert the after-tax contributions directly from a 401(k) plan into a Roth IRA and move the balance of the 401(k) account into a rollover IRA without paying any taxes on the Roth IRA conversion. If you have any basis from after-tax contributions in your qualified plan account, you should consult with a qualified advisor who can review your situation prior to completing a rollover to an IRA. To download a free report that examines this new strategy, or more accurately applies one of my old secret strategies to the new law, visit www.retiresecure.com.

Combining Distribution Options

Frequently, my clients who have been associated with TIAA-CREF decide to leave the fixed-income component of their retirement plan (TIAA) in their 403(b) plans because of the favorable rate of return. Some of them will choose to transfer their CREF balances to an IRA because of the diversity of investment options. Finally, some participants will annuitize part of their TIAA-CREF balance to guarantee a set amount of income regardless of how long they live. (Please see Chapter 8.) Although not all plans offer the annuitization option, it is still beneficial for retirees to consider splitting their retirement accumulations between their 401(k) plans and their IRAs in situations where there are investment and/or tax reasons to maintain a separate IRA and 401(k) plan account.

Many of my Westinghouse retiree clients follow a similar strategy. They opt to keep the fixed-income portion of their 401(k) plan in the Westinghouse plan and transfer the remaining funds into an IRA. Although not all plans offer the annuitization option, it is still beneficial for retirees to consider splitting their retirement accumulations between their 401(k) plans and their IRAs in situations where there are investment and/or tax reasons to maintain a separate IRA and 401(k) plan account.

Lump-Sum Distribution

First, let's get the terminology straight. When I refer to the *lump-sum distribution,* I am referring to the special tax treatment afforded retirees when they withdraw their entire account and pay income tax on the entire amount. Ouch!

Many retirees say they "took the lump sum," but what they really mean is that they chose *not* to annuitize their retirement plan accumulations—that is, not to accept regular monthly payments for the rest of their lives. (For more information on annuitizing, see Chapter 8.) What actually happened was that they rolled or transferred the money into an IRA or left the money in the existing retirement plan. Few retirees actually elect the special tax treatment per Internal Revenue Code (IRC) Section 402(d), which is the proper meaning of *taking a lump-sum distribution.*

The advantage of a lump-sum distribution is the special tax calculation applied to the entire lump sum. The tax calculation is called *10-year averaging,* and it is available only to individuals born before 1936. The essence of 10-year averaging is that you may take your entire retirement plan and pay income taxes on it immediately but at a reduced income tax rate. In addition, a 20 percent capital gains tax rate is available for the amount attributable to pre-1974 contributions to the plan. This amount will often be less than the ordinary income tax that would otherwise be due.

Only participants in Section 401(a) qualified retirement plans (i.e., a Section 401[k], pension, or other benefit sharing plans but not a Section 403[b], IRA, or SEP-IRA plan) can qualify for lump-sum distribution treatment. A lump-sum distribution is only permitted when the participant reaches 59½, or if the participant is separated from service, or if the participant dies. Finally, a lump-sum distribution must be made within a 12-month period from the triggering event for the distribution (i.e., death, attainment of age 59½, separation from service), subject to certain exceptions, to qualify as a lump-sum distribution.

Ten-Year Averaging Is a Hellish Calculation

Do you qualify? Should you do it?

The answer in both cases is usually no. I will spare you the details. Even assuming you are willing to jump through enough hoops to qualify, for most employees it will result in a needless acceleration of income taxes, though admittedly at a lower-than-normal rate.

In practice, I have never recommended a 10-year averaging plan but have preferred to take advantage of the net unrealized appreciation (NUA) provisions when available (described in more detail in Chapter 9) and roll the rest into an IRA. My reason for not getting too excited about the 10-year averaging is not the restrictions, but the fact that you must come up with taxes now. Remember: *Pay taxes later.* Nonetheless, running the numbers is a prudent approach.

The general idea behind the lump-sum distribution is that if you successfully jump through a series of hoops, the IRS will discount your taxes. That said, even at a reduced tax rate, it would require some very compelling arguments to persuade me that accelerating taxes is a good idea—especially if large sums of money are involved, which is often the case.

In theory, I can picture the lump-sum distribution (LSD) being useful in two situations.

1. You have a phenomenal use for the money. Some physicians, who have pensions in addition to a 401(k), have taken a LSD and used the money to speculate in real estate. They paid the reduced tax on the LSD and used the remaining proceeds as a down payment on commercial real estate. If the rent covered the mortgage, the idea was that the building appreciation would be on the entire purchase price of the real estate and not the amount invested (the down payment). With the boom real estate market of the past decade that strategy worked for a number of taxpayers, leading invariably to unrealistic expectations for the next generation of would-be landlords. During the best of times, that strategy was too aggressive for me, and in today's environment I would not even think about it.

2. I could picture considering the LSD if the retirement-plan owner was rich and either terminally ill or extremely old and if the value of the total estate was worth well more than the exemption equivalent amount ($3.5 million in 2009). In that case, he or she might want to consider the LSD to avoid the combined income and estate taxes on the IRA after death.

Other professionals certainly disagree with me. My natural bias is toward keeping retirement assets in IRAs or retirement plans rather than withdrawing the money and paying the tax earlier than necessary. If there were a good reason to make early IRA or retirement plan withdrawals, then the LSD becomes attractive. I just hate paying taxes up-front.

You may find a situation where the LSD may be a good choice, but approach it with a predisposition against the LSD and make a qualified financial professional prove to you, with hard numbers, that it would be a good thing. If you take that approach, you will likely be safe from making a bad decision.

Of much greater benefit is the discussion about NUA (please see Chapter 9), which often is found with the discussion of LSDs.

Deciding on a good strategy for handling your retirement assets is an area where the appropriate financial advisor can be worth his or her weight in gold, particularly if they are number runners. Getting good advice at this point can have a significant impact on your future.

Deciding on a good strategy for handling your retirement assets is an area where the appropriate financial advisor can be worth his or her weight in gold.

The Mechanics of IRA Rollovers and Trustee-to-Trustee Transfers

Let's assume the goal is to move your retirement plan funds from one retirement plan to either another retirement plan or an IRA or your new one-person 401(k) plan (what I generally recommend). The lay public usually calls this kind of transfer a *rollover*. But you need to be aware that according to the proper terminology, there are, in fact, rollovers *and* trustee-to-trustee transfers.

Individuals planning to move money from a 401(k) retirement plan (or similar plan) to an IRA generally will want to conduct a trustee-to-trustee transfer.

A rollover from a 401(k) or other type of qualified retirement plan into an IRA is tax-free, provided you comply with the rules. IRC Section 402 states that retirement plan distributions are not taxed if rolled over to a retirement plan or an IRA. Technically, a rollover is a distribution from one retirement plan or an IRA to the owner and then taken by the owner to the new retirement plan. If you affect a transfer of funds through a rollover, you have to worry about the following rules:

- The 60-day rule

- The 20 percent withholding-tax rule

- The one-rollover-every-12-months rule

The best way to avoid the problems of the 60-day rule, the 20 percent withholding-tax rule, and the one-rollover-per-12-months rule is via a trustee-to-trustee transfer of a retirement plan to an IRA. In a trustee-to-trustee transfer, no participant or IRA owner ever touches the actual money. It is an electronic blip; a few pieces of paper (not green) pass from one financial institution to another. Alternatively, some institutions make the check payable to the new trustee but send it to the participant who is then responsible for forwarding the check to the new trustee. Although this is a permissible method of completing a trustee-to-trustee transfer, please speak to a qualified advisor and the plan administrator before completing a trustee-to-trustee transfer under these circumstances.

The following three sections provide a short description of the problems you may encounter if you do not do a trustee-to-trustee transfer. If the merit of doing the trustee-to-trustee transfer rather than a rollover is established in your mind, you may safely skip the next three sections and jump to "What You May Roll Over and What You May Not."

Avoiding the 20 Percent Withholding-Tax Rule

When someone elects to roll over a 401(k) or other retirement plan to an IRA without using a trustee-to-trustee transfer, the transferring company must withhold 20 percent of the amount rolled over. This can be a nightmare if the objective is to roll over the entire amount. Obviously, we want to keep this transaction income tax-free. By not doing a trustee-to-trustee transfer, however, you create an unnecessary 20 percent withholding of income taxes. This withholding trap has caught many unwary 401(k) owners off guard. If your former employer must withhold 20 percent, the only way you will not have to pay any income taxes on the rollover is for you to come up with the 20 percent amount yourself, from other sources. If you don't have the 20 percent amount to restore to your retirement plan, you have even more headaches because you will have to pay income taxes on the rollover to the extent that the 20 percent withholding is insufficient to cover the taxes. The best way to avoid the 20 percent withholding-tax rule is by simply doing a trustee-to-trustee transfer.

Note that the 20 percent withholding-tax rule does not apply when transferring one IRA to another.

The 60-Day Rule

Let's assume you can get around the 20 percent withholding problem. Another problem remains. You must comply with the 60-day rule. You must restore the funds to another retirement plan or an IRA within 60 days of receiving the distribution. Otherwise, income taxes must be paid on the entire amount; furthermore, if you are 59½ or younger, you have the added 10 percent premature distribution penalty—a nightmare.

Are there exceptions? A few—but basically, you don't want to go there. If you are planning to do a rollover as opposed to a trustee-to-trustee transfer, get the money back in a retirement plan or IRA within 60 days. Most of the reasons the IRS will accept as excuses are so terrible that you would never want to plan for any of them to happen. If you do miss the 60-day rule accidentally, then you can start looking at the reasons the IRS will waive the rule, but don't expect to obtain relief.

In practice, people who want to do a rollover versus a trustee-to-trustee transfer may be looking for a short-term loan, and the only source of money is the IRA or a qualified plan. If the money was in an IRA that didn't allow a loan or the loan allowed by the qualified plan wasn't enough or had some undesirable restriction, some people who think they are clever might choose to withdraw their IRA or retirement plan and attempt to restore the account within the 60 days. That might work, but it is risky at best.

The classic reason for trying to finesse the system is to use the money for some type of real estate transaction. However, that is what bridge loans at the bank are for. If avoiding those fees is so critical, and you are certain that there will be no hang-ups with either the sale or purchase of whatever the money is needed for, good luck. But if the deal goes sour because of some unforeseeable event, don't expect the IRS to have any sympathy.

Perhaps the Horse's Ass Award goes to the guy who wants to take advantage of some type of financial tip on an investment that isn't listed on one of the popular exchanges. He is told he can double his money in a month. The Horse's Ass has no other funds to invest except his IRA or retirement plan. He goes to his retirement plan, withdraws funds as a loan, invests in his sure winner, and plans to restore the retirement plan before 60 days pass. The sure winner implodes, and the Horse's Ass not only lost money on his investment, but he will have to pay income taxes on money he doesn't have anymore. The $3,000-per-year loss limitation on deducting the capital loss will virtually make the tax benefits of the loss meaningless, and the income tax he must pay on the retirement plan withdrawal will be draconian.

If the hot tip were a stock or mutual fund that is traded over any of the recognized stock exchanges, he would have been better off rolling the money into an IRA and purchasing the security in his IRA. That way, when the account gets clobbered, at least he will not face the tax liability in addition to the loss.

The One-Rollover-Per-12-Months Rule

An individual is allowed only one rollover per any 12 month period, but the number of trustee-to-trustee transfers anyone can make is unlimited. If you have different IRAs or different retirement plans, you may have one rollover per separate IRA or separate retirement plan.

Also, the one-rollover-every-12-months rule applies only to IRAs. For example, a reader who initiates a direct rollover from a 401(k) to an IRA on January 2, 2009, can roll over to another IRA on January 15, 2009, if he or she so desires. This move is permissible because the first distribution was not from an IRA.

Again, life is complicated enough. Do a trustee-to-trustee transfer, and don't worry about this rule, the 60-day rule, or the 20 percent withholding-tax rule.

What You May Roll Over and What You May Not

The general rule of thumb under the new expanded portability rules is that an individual can roll anything into anything. Of course, that is a slight exaggeration, but the general idea now is that funds can go from one qualified plan to another without taxation, though some restrictions may apply.

> ... the general idea now is that funds can go from one qualified plan to another without taxation, though some restrictions may apply.

Most of the recommended rollovers—or to be more technically correct, trustee-to-trustee transfers—will be from taxable retirement plans to IRAs. For example, a retired or service-terminated employee owning a fully taxable account, such as a 401(k), a 403(b), a 457 plan, a SEP, a Keogh, and so on, will usually be well served to institute a trustee-to-trustee transfer to an IRA. The employee is allowed to transfer from account to account if he or she likes. For example, if you leave your university job and go into the private sector, you might think it's a good idea to consolidate your old 403(b) with your new company's 401(k). You can, but I don't think it would be in your best interests. I would prefer you transfer the old 403(b) into a separate IRA or your own one-person 401(k) and then start new contributions in the 401(k), which will eventually leave you with balances in an IRA, or your own 401(k) and a 401(k) from work.

Now, there will be times when it might be advisable to go backwards. For instance, if a working or self-employed IRA owner wanted to use retirement funds to purchase life insurance, he or she might take his or her IRA (through which he or she is not allowed to purchase life insurance), transfer it into a different qualified plan, and then purchase his or her insurance inside the qualified plan. Caution is advised, however, for retirement plan owners who want to purchase life insurance inside a retirement plan. We do not cover that risky strategy.

You cannot do the following:

- Transfer or roll over the minimum required distributions from a retirement plan or an IRA into another retirement plan. You must pay tax on that money.
- Make a Roth IRA conversion from your MRD.
- Open a Roth IRA with your MRDs.
- Transfer or roll over inherited IRA distributions.

- Transfer or roll over Section 72(t) payments (a series of substantially equal payments distributed from a qualified plan for the life of the employee or the joint lives of the employee and his designated beneficiary that qualifies for an exception from the 10 percent penalty otherwise imposed on 72[t] payments).

Special Exception for 403(b) Owners with Pre-1987 Balances

Even if retired, a 403(b) owner's pre-1987 balance is not subject to minimum distribution until he or she is age 75, not age 70½. If he takes the 403(b) money and rolls it into an IRA, he will be required to take his MRD on the entire balance in the account (including his pre-1987 dollars).

If the terms of the 403(b) retirement plan allow the stretch for the nonspouse beneficiary, then there is no tax motivation to do the rollover (assuming the retiree is happy with the investment accounts offered). In fact, there is a tax disincentive because of the acceleration of the minimum required distribution. The tax disincentive ends up being so minor, however, that if you think you can do even a tiny bit better by investing outside of the 403(b) with an IRA, then don't worry about the minor acceleration of income you will make by losing the option to defer the pre-1987 MRD until you would have reached age 75.

Would you like more cutting-edge information on distribution planning for TIAA-CREF participants? Please go to www.retiresecure.com for a free report, or go to the back of the book and fill out the order form. Please sign up now while it's fresh on your mind!

Inexact Language on a Beneficiary Form Can Spell Disaster

Sloppy titling could ruin the entire stretch IRA concept for nonspouse beneficiaries of an IRA. It is imperative that the deceased IRA owner's name remain on the account.

MINI CASE STUDY 6.2

The Difference between Proper and Sloppy Language on a Beneficiary Form

Grandpa and Grandma both name a well-drafted trust for their grandchild, Junior, in the beneficiary designations of their respective IRAs.

They both die during the same year. Due to a quirk in estate administration, Detailed Danny becomes the administrator for Grandpa's IRA, and Sloppy Susan becomes the administrator for Grandma's IRA. Detailed Danny, when transferring the inherited IRA to the trust for Junior, follows the advice of Grandpa's financial planner and titles the account "Grandpa's IRA (deceased, December 2008) Trust for Benefit of Junior." Junior, being only 10 years old at Grandpa's death, ends up stretching Grandpa's IRA for his entire lifetime. Even when Junior is 70 years old, the account continues to have Grandpa's name. Because the inherited IRA makes a tremendous difference in Junior's life and since his financial security is assured, he often thinks of Grandpa's thoughtfulness and also appreciates Detailed Danny's care in handling the inherited IRA.

> Sloppy titling could ruin the entire stretch IRA concept for nonspouse beneficiaries of an IRA. It is imperative that the deceased IRA owner's name remain on the account

Sloppy Susan, when doing similar work for Grandma's IRA, titles the account "Trust for Junior." The trust is audited, and the IRS requires the trust to pay income tax on the entire balance. If the titling of the account does not make it clear that the IRA is inherited from the deceased IRA owner, the income tax on the inherited IRA is accelerated. The trust is then required to pay income tax on the entire balance and, to make it worse, at the higher trust income tax rates. When Junior turned 21, he finds out what happened and his attorney suggested he sue Sloppy Susan for negligence in the handling of his IRA.

Junior decides not to sue Sloppy Susan because it isn't nice to sue your mother. His mother, Sloppy Susan, did, however, deprive Junior of the stretch for Grandma's IRA, which will end up costing him over $1 million. His only consolation is that he will still receive inherited IRA benefits from Grandpa's IRA for the next 60 years. When Junior is age 70, he shakes his head while thinking of his grandmother. Grandma's legacy, of course, has long since vanished—ravaged by taxes due to sloppy titling.

Do you have a trusted advisor to help you with your retirement plan? Do you feel confident he or she is qualified and experienced in distribution and estate planning for IRAs and retirement plans? If you do, great. Please—finish reading this book; make a list of questions, comments, and concerns; and set up an appointment as soon as possible.

If, however, you don't have a trusted advisor and can't find anyone who you feel has the appropriate expertise in retirement plans and IRAs, there is another option for some readers. I and some of the CPAs and attorneys in my office are offering a number of free IRA assessments, and taking on a limited number of private clients who will work with us directly. If you are interested in working with one of us one on one and you are a resident of Pennsylvania, California, Florida, Ohio, New York, or Virginia, please visit www.retiresecure .com or refer to the end of the book for more information.

Make sure that your executor or administrator knows how to title the inherited IRA correctly. If you are a financial planner, I hope I have made a compelling case for the correct titling of an inherited IRA. If you are in charge of internal office procedures at a financial institution, create a policy that ensures that all inherited IRAs retain the name of the deceased IRA owner; you will do a lot of beneficiaries much good.

Also, please don't assume that your financial professional, whether a CPA, financial planner, or (with all due respect) an attorney, will know about proper titling and act accordingly. Recently I received a call from a planner in California. This is a true story. He said, "Jim, my client died, with more than a million dollars in an IRA. The IRA owner left the IRA to his son. When my secretary saw that the son was the beneficiary, she took the money and transferred it to his son's account. Is that okay?" Oh no! She just accelerated the income tax on $1 million. He said to me, "Oh, Jim, I'm sure the IRS will understand that it was just my secretary and she didn't mean to do it." No. The IRS won't. The client's son had to pay tax on $1 million instead of stretching that million out over the course of his life. Boom! Income tax on the whole thing. So instead of having $1 million, the son now has only $600,000. I hope his malpractice premiums were paid up. Whether he actually gets sued or not, the planner has to live the rest of his life knowing that that mistake cost his client a bundle.

Other Titling Notes

If there are multiple beneficiaries (as is typical with accounts left to "children equally"), the accounts should be split after death and the inherited IRAs should then be kept separate. Please note that under the new rules, each child will be able to take minimum required distributions from the inherited IRA based on his or her own life expectancy. In addition, although the deceased IRA owner's name will remain on the account, the Social Security number of the beneficiary should be used.

Choosing an Investment Institution after the Death of the IRA Owner

Let's assume that Detailed Danny knows all about the titling and takes equal care in looking at Grandpa's portfolio. As a result of his analysis, he determines that he wants to replace the financial institution where the money currently resides—the High Fee, Low Service Bank—to the firm where he invests his own money with his own trusted financial advisor who was actually the person who told him about the titling problem.

He requests the appropriate paperwork for transferring the account from the High Fee, Low Service Bank where Grandpa invested to his firm. He is informed that Grandpa's bank will not allow a trustee-to-trustee transfer of the inherited IRA. He objects but soon realizes that it is well within the power of the bank not to accommodate him on a trustee-to-trustee tax-free transfer. Sure, he can demand the bank be forced to distribute the money, but the bank cannot be forced to do a trustee-to-trustee transfer. Also, *the 60-day rule does not apply to inherited IRAs!* The High Fee, Low Service Bank could make Detailed Danny choose between leaving the money with them or suffer the income tax acceleration if the bank makes the transfer.

My approach to these problems is to try to be nice at first. That failing, I would apply relentless pressure and use whatever leverage I have to make the bank accommodate my wishes. The best way to approach the problem is for the IRA owner to know in advance the financial institution's policy with respect to this type of transfer. Don't work with one that imposes these types of limitations.

A Key Lesson from This Chapter

For most individuals approaching or at retirement, initiating a trustee-to-trustee transfer of a qualified retirement plan to an IRA or a one-person 401(k) is a good decision. With proper titling, you can preserve the stretch, and you can offer your heirs the continued advantage of tax-deferred growth and take advantage of a wider variety of investment choices during your lifetime. That said, you still have to weigh the decision carefully and look at the particular circumstances of your situation. Deciding how to manage your retirement assets at the time you retire is important and deserves your full attention.....

7

||||||||||||||||||||||

Roth IRA Conversions

Did you ever notice that when you put "THE" and "IRS" together it spells "THEIRS"?

—Author Unknown

Main Topics

- Roth IRA conversions
- Qualifications—Modified adjusted gross income limits
- 2010: The first year for Roth IRA conversions for the wealthy
- Factors to consider before a Roth conversion
- Mini Case Study 7.1: Benefits of a Roth IRA conversion

Roth IRA Conversions: A Proactive Strategy to Benefit You and Your Heirs

First, let me start by saying that it really riles me to see my clients and readers paying taxes now if they can pay taxes later. So, if I advocate for Roth IRA conversions, there have to be some very compelling reasons.

A Roth IRA conversion requires paying taxes *now*—which flies in the face of my long-cherished mantra, *Pay taxes later!* What's the story here?

First, let me start by saying that it really riles me to see my clients and readers paying taxes now if they can pay taxes later. So, if I advocate for Roth IRA conversions, there have to be some very compelling reasons.

The advantages of a Roth IRA conversion for many, if not most, IRA owners are so powerful that I firmly believe every IRA owner should consider a Roth IRA conversion, and most should adopt a long-term Roth IRA conversion strategy. We've run the numbers, and they have persuaded me of the Roth's advantage. When you do the analysis as we have done, you learn that a Roth IRA conversion can create thousands, sometime millions, more dollars of purchasing power for your family than maintaining the status quo. If I were to summarize my tax strategies into one slogan it would be *Pay Taxes Later—Except the Roth*. I thought about making that the subtitle for this book.

Of course Roth IRA conversions aren't for everyone. But I have seen more people make the mistake of failing to convert an optimal amount than I have of people who made a conversion when they shouldn't have, or who have converted too much at one time.

A Roth IRA conversion has the potential to provide thousands, sometimes millions, of dollars of income tax-free growth for your family. The conversion strategy is usually advantageous for older people for their own use (a fact that many people are unaware of), but its greatest advantage will likely be conferred on the heirs who will inherit the Roth and enjoy the long-term benefits of the tax-free growth after the Roth IRA owner dies. I think Roth IRAs, Roth 401(k)/Roth 403(b)s, and Roth IRA conversions are so important that I recently established The Roth IRA Institute; an organization designed to provide information to taxpayers and their advisors regarding Roth IRAs and Roth IRA conversions. Interested readers can learn more by going to www.therothirainstitute.com

A Roth IRA conversion has the potential to provide thousands, sometimes millions, of dollars of income tax-free growth for your family.

The key to understanding the essence of the Roth IRA conversion is perhaps best expressed philosophically as "You pay income tax on the *seed* and you (or possibly your heirs) *reap the harvest* income tax-free." When you convert your traditional IRA to a Roth IRA, you must add the amount you converted to your income and pay the income tax on that increased amount. That is like paying tax on the seed. Then, after you or your heirs enjoy growth on that account and eventually take distributions from that account, all the proceeds, including the dividends, growth, and interest are income tax-free. In other words, you and/or your heirs reap the harvest tax-free. The key to understanding the advantage of the Roth conversion is that the taxes on the growth of after-tax funds are reduced once a conversion is done. After-tax funds are burdened with annual income taxes on the growth. Once those after-tax funds are used to pay the taxes on the Roth conversion, they are no longer fodder for further taxes. Furthermore, Roth IRAs have no minimum required distributions for the original owner, so the money can grow for a long time in the tax-free environment. And, if and when you do make a withdrawal, no taxes are due on that money that you take out.

Later in this chapter I will give examples of my number-running assessments that will provide compelling proof that paying tax on the seed and reaping the harvest income tax-free is a wonderful long-term strategy that most IRA owners should consider. The importance of your current and projected tax bracket cannot be over emphasized in this analysis. In Chapter 3, I examined the impact of different tax rates during the year an individual makes a contribution in concert with an assessment of future tax rates. Though it was done in the framework of Roth 401(k) versus traditional 401(k), the analysis is equally if not more important for readers interested in Roth IRA conversions. After reading this chapter, if you are motivated to consider a Roth IRA conversion, I would urge you to read or reread Chapter 3.

Our examples, which will quantify the Roth's advantage over the status quo of not making a conversion, will span three generations of Roth IRA owners: the original IRA owner (most likely you!), the child of the original owner, and the grandchild of the original owner. The bottom line is that the future tax savings on the tax-free growth of the Roth IRA ultimately outweigh the benefits of a tax-deferred traditional IRA combined with the after-tax investments that would be used to pay the income tax on the conversion.

A Roth IRA conversion converts money that is growing income *tax-deferred* (e.g., your traditional IRA) and *taxable money* (e.g., ordinary after-tax investments) into money that grows income *tax-free* (i.e., your Roth IRA). You are required to add to your adjusted gross income (AGI) the amount that you are converting to a Roth IRA. For example if your AGI is $40,000 and you make a $100,000 Roth IRA conversion, your AGI will be $140,000. Because you are required to pay income taxes on the amount converted, and because I recommend paying those taxes from funds you have outside of your IRA, you deplete your after-tax investments by the amount required to pay the taxes on the conversion.

Readers have questioned our math. They say that if all our assumptions are steady (interest rate, tax rate, growth, etc.), then the Roth IRA conversion ends up being a breakeven for the IRA owner. We concede that would be true, up until minimum required distributions begin, if we paid the tax on the conversion from the IRA itself. However, if you pay the tax on the conversion with after-tax dollars, the math favors the conversion, and the benefit measured in purchasing power is compelling. Once MRDs begin at age 70½, the advantage grows and it even grows in cases where the tax is paid from the IRA itself. The longer the time horizon for tax-free growth, the greater the benefit it can provide.

However, if you are like many of our clients, your wealth is primarily in your retirement plans and traditional IRAs. If you do not have the money to pay the income tax on the conversion from funds outside the IRA, then my advice would change—don't do a conversion or do a much more conservative conversion. Another instance where I would not recommend making a Roth IRA conversion would be if you plan to leave all your money to charity. The charity will not benefit from the tax-free growth of the Roth IRA.

> **If you do not have the money to pay the income tax on the conversion from funds outside the IRA, then my advice would change— don't do a conversion.**

A Series of Small Conversions Rather than One Big Conversion

Depending on the circumstances of the individual contemplating the Roth IRA conversion, I often recommend a series of partial conversions of their traditional IRA to a Roth IRA—one every year over a period of years. How much to convert is a significant decision because if you convert a large amount, it could result in a high tax rate on the conversion. Your best strategy might be to convert just enough to bring your taxable income to the top of your present tax bracket. Then repeat that process in subsequent years. This keeps the conversion-related taxes to a reasonable amount, and it prevents you from paying income taxes on the conversion at a high rate.

Although a Roth IRA conversion may not be right for everyone, it can eventually mean hundreds of thousands of dollars of additional purchasing power (in today's dollars) for families in the right situation. Even a modest Roth IRA conversion of a portion of your IRA could mean tens of thousands of dollars (in today's dollars) in additional purchasing power for your family.

Who Qualifies for a Roth IRA Conversion?

For 2009, the Roth IRA conversion strategy has a significant limitation. A regular IRA can be converted to a Roth IRA only if the owner's modified adjusted gross income (MAGI) does not exceed $100,000 (whether you are married or single). The reason it is called your *modified* adjusted gross income is because your MAGI is a modification of your adjusted gross income from your tax return, computed after the conversion. Your AGI has amounts subtracted from it, such as the conversion amount, and amounts added to it, such as deductions for certain tuition expenses and deductions for IRA contributions to finally become your MAGI. There are strategies for lowering your AGI, which in turn might get your MAGI below $100,000. Common methods include contributing more to your retirement plan at work to reduce taxable wages, selling investments at a loss to reduce net capital gains, deferring bonuses and salary where possible, and taking business deductions if self-employed.

I am currently working on a book devoted to the entire spectrum of opportunities within the Roth environment. In that book I will delve much deeper into the discussion of when and how to effectively capitalize on Roth IRA conversions. If you would like a report that has more details about the Roth IRA conversion, visit www.retiresecure.com.

The really big news is the opportunity opening up in 2010 for Roth IRA conversions for individuals with incomes greater than $100,000. If your income is greater than $100,000, you should love the change in the tax law and the next section of the book.

> **The really big news is the opportunity opening up in 2010 for Roth IRA conversions for individuals with incomes greater than $100,000.**

2010 Will Provide a Great Opportunity for Higher Income Taxpayers to Move into the Roth Environment

In 2010 higher income taxpayers will, for the first time, qualify for Roth IRA conversions. Your income level will not matter for the purpose of whether you are allowed to make a Roth IRA conversion. In Chapter 3 we pointed out that high income taxpayers can now participate in the tax-free investment world through the use of Roth 401(k)/403(b) plans, and why it was advantageous to do so. Beginning in 2010, however, they can do even better—they can make a Roth IRA conversion.

As a special bonus, if you make a conversion in 2010 you may elect to recognize half the income in 2011 and half in 2012. For example, you make a $100,000 Roth IRA conversion in 2010 and elect to recognize $50,000 for tax year 2011 and $50,000 in tax year 2012. (There is one caveat, however; we are not sure what the tax rates will be in future years. We are running a large deficit in this country, and tax rates may change.) The deferral, however, is just a bonus. The true benefit of the conversion is the many years of tax-free growth.

This is an especially good opportunity for very high income taxpayers, that is to say, those individuals who are in the top tax bracket and who will likely remain in the top tax bracket because their incomes are so high. Whereas other taxpayers can push themselves into a higher tax bracket if they make a significant conversion, a top tax bracket taxpayer cannot pay taxes at a higher rate. Some low- or middle-income tax bracket readers could actually make an inappropriately large Roth IRA conversion that would not only increase their taxes but also increase their tax rate on the conversion. This is not likely for high income taxpayers who opt to make a conversion in 2010 as long as they have the money to pay the taxes on the conversion from outside the IRA. And the wealthy are the most likely to be able to take advantage of a long time horizon of tax-free growth, because there is less chance that they will need to spend that money.

For the very high income, top tax bracket family, the benefit of a Roth IRA conversion is potentially phenomenal. But even a moderate income family can eventually realize significant financial benefits from conversions. Our estimate is that over a generation—passing the Roth from parent to child—a taxpayer's family could benefit by as much as twice the amount converted. That is an estimate of the potential long-term benefit of making a Roth IRA conversion as we will demonstrate in Case Study 7.1.

Factors to Consider before Converting to a Roth IRA

The potential for tax-free growth is so compelling that *all* taxpayers who have substantial IRA balances and who qualify for conversions should consider converting at least a portion of their IRA. As I mentioned at the outset of this chapter, a Roth IRA conversion is one of the rare actions that contradicts the advice "Don't pay taxes now, pay taxes later." This is because, by paying the associated taxes *now* you *avoid* additional taxes later.

However, many factors must be considered pertaining to both you, as the IRA owner, and the beneficiaries of your IRA. Let's look at each.

If you are the IRA owner, you need to consider the following:

- Your current and future income tax rates

- The rate of return on your investments

- Your age and life expectancy

- Your anticipated spending needs during retirement

- Your other sources of income (including any pensions, Social Security, wages, and other)

- The balances in your IRAs from which you can convert

- The balances of other investments including after-tax money and investments

- Other assets and liability balances you may have, such as real estate and loans

Regarding your IRA's probable beneficiaries, you need to consider these factors:

- Their age and life expectancy

- Their planned use of the IRA or Roth IRA funds after inheritance

- Their future income tax rates

That is quite a list of things to consider, which is why we strongly recommend that you consult with a qualified financial advisor prior to making any decisions about how to proceed. But now let's look at the numbers that will persuade you that considering a Roth IRA conversion should be on your to-do list.

MINI CASE STUDY 7.1
Benefits of a Roth IRA Conversion

In Chapter 2 we introduced the advantages tax-free Roth IRAs can have over traditional tax-deferred IRAs. There were two salient points to remember:

1. The growth in the Roth IRA is tax-free.

2. The Roth eliminates the problem of the taxable growth on the tax savings from a deductible contribution.

These advantages also apply to Roth conversions. A conversion results in more *purchasing power value* in a *tax-free* account than there would be in a *tax-deferred* IRA account combined with other nontax-sheltered after-tax investments. Additionally, there are no minimum required distributions from the Roth IRA (for either you or your spouse) as there are with a traditional IRA. If you don't need the money, the Roth account keeps growing tax-free compared to a traditional IRA which gets distributed to after-tax investments over time.

Suppose you have an identical financial twin and you are both 65. Because you read *Retire Secure!* and after consulting with your financial advisor, you make a $100,000 Roth IRA conversion at the end of 2007. Your twin, however, never even learns about the possibility of a Roth IRA conversion.

Your $100,000 Roth IRA conversion adds $100,000 to your income, and you pay the $28,000 in federal income tax from money outside your IRA. Your financial twin, on the other hand, doesn't make the conversion. He keeps his $28,000, invests it in a diversified portfolio, and enjoys income and appreciation on money that you sent to the IRS.

You and your twin invest identically, and you each receive an 8 percent return on your investments. The graph in Figure 7.1 shows the balances of purchasing power over time for both of you.

Figure 7.1

The Roth Conversion Advantage

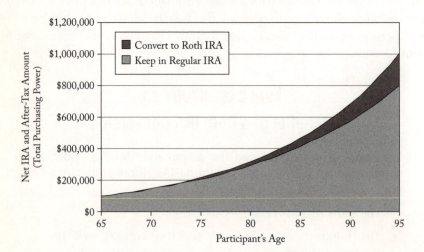

The graph in Figure 7.1 reveals that 20 years after your conversion to a Roth—i.e., when you are age 85—*you will have $51,227 more purchasing power* than your twin! And after 30 years, the difference is *$206,386*! If we assume 3 percent inflation every year, the purchasing power advantage of the conversion to the Roth IRA in today's dollars is $28,363 at age 85 and $85,028 at age 95.

The assumptions for this figure include the following:

1. Each investor starts on 12–31–07 with $100,000 in an IRA and $28,000 in after-tax investments.

2. Investments earn an 8 percent rate of return.

3. After-tax funds are considered diversified such that, of the total investment income, 50 percent is realized as long-term capital gains subject to 15 percent federal tax through 2010 and 19 percent thereafter; 25 percent is dividends taxed at the same long-term capital gains rates through 2010; and 25 percent is taxed as ordinary income (interest and short-term gains).

4. Ordinary federal income tax rates are 25 percent for regular IRA minimum distributions and ordinary investment income.

5. State income taxes of 3 percent are levied against after-tax investment income, but not on the conversion amount or IRA withdrawals (similar to tax laws in Pennsylvania).

6. Tax on the conversion and in measurement of the purchasing power of remaining traditional IRA balances is in the higher 28 percent tax bracket.

7. Required minimum distributions from the regular IRA are reinvested with the after-tax investments.

8. No withdrawals are made from the Roth IRA after conversion.

These results indicate that the Roth IRA offers enormous advantages over the course of a lifetime for the smart twin who made the conversion. Furthermore, a long-term analysis of this situation reveals that the results shown in Figure 7.1 understate the advantages of a Roth IRA, because they do not consider *your beneficiary's time frame* for taking distributions from the inherited Roth IRA. The analysis does not consider the potential benefits your beneficiary may receive from tax-free growth of the inherited Roth IRA when compared to the tax-deferred growth of the traditional IRA and taxable growth of after-tax-savings.

So, what will the situation look like if we extend the time frame to include a child as a beneficiary?

Roth IRA Advantage to the Beneficiary

Let's return to our example of you and your financial twin. Suppose you make a $100,000 conversion at 65, your twin does nothing, and you both die at age 85, which is 20 years after your Roth IRA conversion. Both you and your financial twin have 55-year-old sons, and you both leave your money to your sons. At this time, the balances of your assets' purchasing power are shown below.

	No Roth Conversion	Roth Conversion
After-tax investments	$251,325	$0
Traditional IRA investments	227,144	0
Roth IRA investments	0	466,096
Liquidation tax allowance at 28%	(63,600)	0
Total purchasing power	$414,869	$466,096

Figure 7.2 assumes that the child will withdraw only the required minimum distributions from both the inherited IRA and the inherited Roth

Figure 7.2

Roth IRA Advantage to the Child Beneficiary

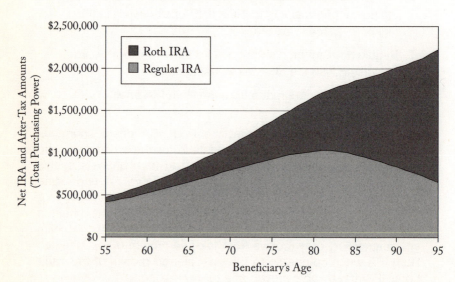

IRA. Both examples assume that the amount of the required minimum distributions from the inherited regular IRA is actually spent each year from the after-tax funds, so spending is the same in each example. This spending is continued at the same rate even after all funds are completely removed from the IRA and the Roth IRA accounts. After-tax balances are invested with similar returns and tax rates as in the parent's example above.

Figure 7.2 shows that the child who inherited the Roth IRA will eventually be left with over twice what the child received who inherited the traditional IRA will have. The numbers are compelling. By age 85, 30 years after the death of the original IRA owner and 50 years after the conversion, the child of the twin who did not make the conversion has $980,800 whereas the child with the Roth IRA has $1,853,426. The conversion created an advantage of $872,626 (which is $199,052 in today's dollars adjusted for 3 percent annual inflation). This is an advantage amount approximately equal to twice the original conversion amount, with the total value about three times the original conversion amount.

These results are quite favorable using a child as your beneficiary. However, the results for a *grandchild* beneficiary are even better because of the lower required minimum distributions of an inherited IRA or inherited Roth IRA for a younger person. Figure 7.3 shows the results if we assume

Figure 7.3

Roth IRA Advantage to the Grandchild Beneficiary

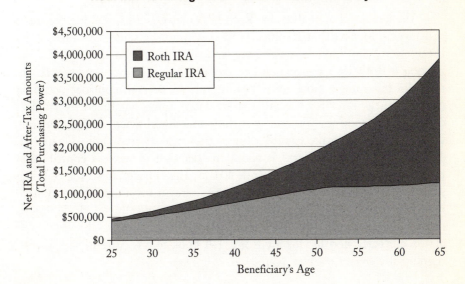

there is a 25-year-old grandchild beneficiary instead of the 55-year-old child, with the same after-tax spending amounts as in the example of the 55-year-old child.

Figure 7.3 shows that the converter's grandchild is much better off pursuant to the Roth conversion than without it. Considering both graphs in Figures 7.2 and 7.3, after 30 years from inheritance, the relative purchasing power advantages from the Roth conversion are as follows:

	Advantage in Future Dollars	Advantage in Today's Dollars
Child as beneficiary	872,626	199,052
Grandchild as beneficiary	1,239,762	282,799

After 40 years from inheritance, the graphs show the relative purchasing power advantages from the Roth conversion are as follows:

	Advantage in Future Dollars	Advantage in Today's Dollars
Child as beneficiary	1,562,742	265,249
Grandchild as beneficiary	2,681,974	455,220

The advantages shown in the tables, even in today's dollars, are well in excess of the original $100,000 conversion amount. The conclusion here is that, from the beneficiaries' standpoint, there is much to be gained from Roth IRA conversions when they are able to continue the tax-free growth in the inherited Roth IRA.

The next level of analysis for Roth IRA conversions is making the more realistic assumption that income tax rates will not be static over time. Even if they were, your income tax bracket is likely to change at retirement. Also, making a Roth IRA conversion can put you into a higher tax bracket. So, to make this information more meaningful, we need to consider potential changes in tax rates for the purpose of determining whether a Roth IRA conversion is good for you and, if so, how much and when should you convert. We actually covered quite a bit of this type of analysis in Chapter 3. The discussion in Chapter 3 is about the decision to make a contribution to a traditional 401(k) versus a Roth 401(k). The concept, however, of being sensitive to tax brackets at different times, and using that information to influence your Roth IRA conversion decision, is practically identical. Serious readers interested in Roth IRA conversions should review Chapter 3 and get on our early alert list for my Roth IRA book that is currently in process. Sign up at www.retiresecure.com.

The Downside of a Roth IRA Conversion

The analysis thus far has assumed that your investments will grow over time. Even if the rate of growth is slower than I assume, you would still be better off, just not by as much. But what if your converted investment drops significantly after you make the conversion? Then, you would not be a happy camper and the advice to make a Roth IRA conversion would hurt you, not help you. The fear of losing money on investments is on everyone's mind as we experience such volatility in the market.

The traditional response is that if you wait long enough, then the investment will recover. But, what if it doesn't? What if you just decide it was a mistake. Are there steps you can take if the investment goes down soon after you make the Roth IRA conversion?

Yes. In short, you can recharacterize your Roth IRA conversion. *Recharacterize* is the formal jargon to describe undoing your conversion. You can recharactize a Roth IRA conversion by October 15 of the year following the year of the conversion. Of course recharacterizing doesn't help you recover the loss in your investment, but you can recover the taxes you paid on the conversion, which will put you in a position similar to where you would have been if you had not completed the Roth IRA conversion.

After the recharacterization, you could then do another Roth conversion of the reduced amount and end up with a Roth IRA of the same value as if you had not recharacterized it. This strategy has the significant advantage of your greatly reduced tax liability to the IRS.

There are waiting rules regarding these "reconversions" of IRAs. You must wait until the calendar year after the first conversion or, if longer, 30 days from the first conversion, to do another conversion of the same money. However, if you only did a partial conversion, you avoid this restriction. You could immediately convert a different amount of money to a different Roth IRA account.

MINI CASE STUDY 7.2
Recharacterizing the Roth IRA Conversion

Carrie Convert converts $100,000 of her traditional IRA in July, 2009. She files her tax return in April, 2010, reports an additional $100,000 in income, and pays the tax in a timely manner. In October 2010, her Roth IRA has decreased in value to $50,000. Carrie is disgusted and wants to strangle me for telling her how great it would be to make a Roth IRA conversion. Of course, she could stay the course and hope the investment will recover. Carrie does, however, have a better course of action.

She should recharacterize or undo the Roth IRA conversion. She would fill out the appropriate paper work with the IRA custodian to recharacterize the Roth IRA returning it to a traditional IRA. After filling out the appropriate paperwork, she will have a $50,000 regular IRA instead of a $50,000 Roth IRA. Then, since she filed her tax return and paid the tax on the conversion, she should file an amended tax return, Form 1040-X showing the necessary election is made under IRS regulations, and request a return of her taxes on the conversion. If, rather than filing her tax return on time she filed an extension on April 15, then she would not have to file an amended return—she would simply file her return.

Granted, her investment is still $50,000 instead of $100,000, but had she not made the conversion her investments would still be down; she is no better nor any worse off. If she then decides to convert another $50,000, she would have the same value in a Roth IRA as she had before the recharacterization, but would only owe the IRS taxes on $50,000 of income instead of on $100,000 of income.

In our office, October 2008 was a big year for recharacterizations of Roth IRA conversions that were made in both 2007 and 2008. The reason is that in October 2007 the market was considerably higher than October 2008 and many clients that made conversions, often on my advice, were then advised to recharacterize or undo the conversion after the investment lost money.

The fact that the tax laws allow you to recharacterize a Roth IRA offers some protection against making a Roth IRA conversion and experiencing a significant downturn in the investment in the short term. The ability to recharacterize might give additional confidence to IRA owners considering a conversion.

I do concede however, that if you make a Roth IRA conversion and the investment loses money over the long term, then the conversion will have been a mistake. That is one of the risks of the Roth IRA conversion.

Other risks are congressional changes to the tax laws. I confess to having some concerns about this, but not significant concerns. It is written into the Internal Revenue Code that Roth IRA conversions will stay income tax-free. True, they said the same thing about Social Security and we are now paying tax on Social Security. The difference is that the Social Security provision was never part of the Internal Revenue Code.

If Steve Forbes got his way and the United States switched to a value-added tax or national sales tax and eliminated income tax, then the tax you paid on the conversion would presumably be wasted. However, since there is over $7 trillion dollars in the IRA and retirement plan system and since most taxpayers are expecting to pay taxes on that amount and since the government really needs the revenue, I can't see the taxes on IRAs and retirement plans being forgiven.

What is more likely is a tax increase and in that case making a Roth IRA conversion while taxes are lower will yield even more benefits than my analysis shows.

Furthermore, at least while I am writing this, the market is depressed. If you make a Roth IRA conversion and the market improves, you will be a happy camper. If it goes down further, you can recharacterize. Further analysis on recharacterization is available for interested readers. Please see www.retiresecure.com for more information.

After the first edition of *Retire Secure!* was published, I was invited to make presentations and train financial planners all over the country. One night one of the financial planner attendees offered me a ride from my speaking engagement to my hotel. He told me that he read my book and talked to his parents about changing their wills and IRA beneficiary designations consistent with my recommendations. Even though both of his parents were in good health at the time, they listened to their son and changed their estate plan to the cascading beneficiary plan and made a series of large Roth IRA conversions. Unexpectedly, not long after making the recommended changes, his father died. In terms of benefits for the next generation, the planner conservatively valued the difference between the old plan and the new plan in millions of dollars. His "aha" moment was realizing that this advice works. But more important he did something about it! If you think this advice is right for you, take action, preferably with the help of a qualified expert.

A Key Lesson from This Chapter

A Roth IRA conversion can provide the Roth IRA owner and his or her family with an exceptional vechicle for increasing purchasing power.

8

||||||||||||||||||||||

Annuitizing Your Financial Accumulations

Does It Make Sense for You?

I advise you to go on living solely to enrage those who are
paying your annuities.

—Voltaire

Main Topics

- Defining annuitizing
- Types of annuities
- Picking among survivorship options
- Drawbacks of annuitizing

KEY IDEA

Annuitizing your retirement plan or after-tax accumulations can
be a method of making sure you don't outlive your money.
For some individuals, annuitizing part of their financial assets is
a totally reasonable choice.

What Is Annuitizing?

An *annuity* refers to receiving a specified income payable at stated intervals for a fixed or contingent period. The counterpoint to an annuity is a lump sum.

Annuitizing your retirement plan accumulations or after-tax money involves surrendering all or a portion of your money to purchase an immediate annuity in exchange for receiving regular, recurring payments for a defined time period, most commonly the rest of your life or if married the rest of your and your spouse's life.

There are other annuities, such as nonqualified tax-deferred annuities, which allow you to accumulate after-tax funds in an annuity vehicle prior to the time it is annuitized. That is often referred to as a commercial annuity. Commercial annuities usually are sold by life insurance companies. In exchange for higher fees, there are usually guarantees associated with commercial annuities that many advisors and clients find attractive. Commercial annuities are not discussed in this book.

> Choosing to annuitize your retirement plan is essentially the same as what a retirement plan participant is forced to do in a defined-benefit plan. That is, you get regular payments for the rest of your life as opposed to having access to a large chunk of money.

Choosing to annuitize your retirement plan is essentially the same as what a retirement plan participant is forced to do in a defined-benefit plan. That is, you get regular payments for the rest of your life as opposed to having access to a large chunk of money. The total of the monthly annuity payments is usually going to be more than the lump-sum amount, provided the owner does not die prematurely.

We combine the discussion of annuitizing your retirement plan and purchasing an immediate annuity because they are conceptually quite similar.

The basic concepts of annuitizing apply to both retirement funds and after-tax funds. The major difference is the income tax treatment of the annuity payments.

- Payments from an after-tax or commercial annuity are partially taxable in the early part of the payment stream; they are *partially taxable* because one portion of the payment is considered a return of the original capital and is not taxable until the entire original cost is recovered. The other portion of the payment is considered ordinary taxable income, such as interest income. After the initial period of cost recovery, which can last for many years, the payments become fully taxable.

- Distributions from annuities purchased with retirement funds, on the other hand, are fully taxable like pension income.

In light of the recent volatility of the stock market, readers who can't stand the roller coaster ride may derive some comfort from purchasing an immediate annuity.

Payment Schedules

The terms and the duration of the annuity payments depend on what is offered and the choices made. Usually, the choices include receiving payments for:

- The remainder of your life

- The remainder of your and your spouse's life

- A fixed number of years

- One of the above plans with an extra provision to extend benefits to your heirs

There are many variations in payment schedules, including various guaranteed periods such as payments for life with 10 years of payments guaranteed. If the owner dies within 10 years of annuitizing, the remaining payments within the 10-year period are paid to his or her heirs. Sometimes you can choose a higher payment while both the owner and his or her spouse are alive and a lower payment after the death of the owner, such as a 100 percent benefit initially and a 50 or 66 percent benefit for the surviving spouse. Remember, unless you pick one of the survivorship or guarantee options, there will be no money left to pass on to your heirs.

> **Remember, unless you pick one of the survivorship or guarantee options, there will be no money left to pass on to your heirs.**

Which is the better deal? It depends. An ideal candidate for an annuity is a healthy single person with a long life expectancy who doesn't care about leaving any money behind. If the person is married, then a joint life annuity to last through both lifetimes is often the best choice. Annuitizing a portion of a retirement plan is also a reasonable choice in many situations.

Most insurance companies and retirement plans will calculate your annuity payment according to your actuarial life expectancy based on age and sex. Your actual physical condition does not enter into the calculation unless you ask the insurance company to rate you. This is the opposite of life insurance. When purchasing life insurance, you want to show the life insurance company how healthy you are. The sooner you die, the better the decision to buy life insurance. With an immediate annuity you want to show the life insurance company that you have a much reduced life expectancy. The longer you live after purchasing the annuity, the better it will work out for you and your family. Please note: Annuitizing at least a portion of your assets is a method that ensures your money lasts at least as long as you do.

Annuitizing would not be a good choice if you have a reduced life expectancy. Usually the annuity company or retirement plan does not give sufficient weight to the health of the applicant for me to recommend an annuity for someone with a dramatically reduced life expectancy. Occasionally, a company considers these factors, but not always. For example, I had a client with multiple sclerosis who was denied a favorable annuity rate in spite of her health condition.

Annuitizing: A Conservative Strategy?

One view holds that annuitizing over a lifetime or joint lifetimes is a conservative strategy because it practically ensures that you will not outlive your money. Although you lose access to the large lump sum of money immediately after purchasing the annuity and the lifetime-based payments stop after your death, the payments will not run out in your lifetime, no matter how long you live.

Annuitizing a large amount of money is sometimes an emotionally hard choice to make. It feels like you are giving it all away despite the fact that you are actually ensuring a secure income source. One solution to the fear of annuitizing is to annuitize only a portion of the available funds. Annuitizing a portion, but not all, of your assets is probably sound for many situations. Jonathan Clements, a great financial writer and defender of the consumer, wrote the following in his column for the *Wall Street Journal.*

> I often suggest that income-hungry retirees take maybe a quarter of their nest egg and use it to purchase an immediate-fixed annuity, thus buying a lifetime stream of income. But if you really want to generate a lot of income and you think you will live to a ripe old age, here is an even better strategy. Buy that immediate annuity—but wait until age 75, so you get a generous income stream based on your shorter life expectancy.

There are also some products that offer guarantees that provide some return of the capital invested if you die early. For example, one option would be to choose payments for life with a guaranteed 10-year payout to your heirs if you die prematurely. Sometimes, a policy will specify that a large portion of the original cost will be returned to the family if the owner dies early. Alternatively, you might want to consider forgoing the extra expense of an annuity guarantee feature, and instead buy a life insurance contract with money not spent on any guarantee feature. My personal preference is to keep it simple: If you choose to purchase an immediate annuity, make it for your life or the lives of both you and your spouse. The common advice among financial planners and attorneys is "Don't sell a client an immediate annuity without a guarantee feature, because if the client dies early, the heirs might sue you or at least give you plenty of grief." From a financial planner or insurance agent's viewpoint, that is probably good advice. For the client, however, it might not be the best advice.

> If you haven't done it yet, please get out a pad of paper, a pen or pencil and/or your computer spreadsheet. A great start is making a list of all your assets (preferably on one sheet of paper) and all your income.
>
> Just the process of assembling this information could be eye opening. Ideally, you would then take that sheet of paper with you to your appointment with a financial professional who is qualified and experienced in distribution and estate planning for IRAs and retirement plans and who inspires your confidence.
>
> I know I sound like a broken record, but I hate to think you'll make a mistake and then really regret doing this completely on your own!

MINI CASE STUDY 8.1
When Annuitizing the Majority of Your Assets Is a Good Choice

Ida is a retired 65-year-old woman in excellent health with no children and no heirs. After her daily yoga and meditation routine, she enjoys her steamed organic tofu and broccoli sprinkled with ground flax seeds. After her breakfast, she swallows a host of vitamins and supplements with wheatgrass juice. Then she walks three miles to visit her 95-year-old parents who are both in excellent health.

She has a $400,000 CD and no other considerable assets. She receives $16,000 a year in Social Security. She hates thinking about money, but fears that she will become destitute or at least miserable if she invests unwisely and another downturn in the market takes place. She spends $36,000 per year before taxes. Though she would prefer to spend a little more, she never wants to be in a position where she has to spend less. Her five-year CD, however, is about to mature, and she discovers from her bank that she would only get 4.25 percent interest if she renews it.

If she continues the investments in 60-month CDs, based on a 4.25 percent interest rate, she would earn and receive only $17,000 of interest income plus her Social Security of $16,000 for a total income of $33,000 per year. Because her Social Security is nontaxable, she pays only a small amount of taxes ($1,220 federal and Pennsylvania state income taxes, based on 2007 rates), and she is left with only $31,780 of net income. So she must eat into the principal amount every year if she wants to spend $36,000. With principal deterioration and inflation to worry about, particularly in today's volatile stock market, she legitimately fears she will out-live her money. Though she has been advised about the advantages of diversification, she is not comfortable owning stocks and doesn't want to be an investor. Even with a diversified portfolio, there are no guarantees that she would meet her financial goals, and her fear of being forced to reduce her spending could become a reality.

Alternatively, she could also purchase a $400,000 lifetime annuity. She will discover that there are an overwhelming number of varieties and choices. She could take an annuity over her lifetime only, or over both her and a beneficiary's lifetime if she chooses to name a beneficiary. She could have fixed payments or increasing payments at a flat interest rate of increase, or payouts that could increase by various amounts based on stock market returns to some degree. Based on recent rate quotations, she could choose one of the following guaranteed fixed annuities that would pay her the following amounts no matter how long she lived:

	Monthly Payment	Annual Total
Fixed payments, no increases	$2,637.91	$ 31,654.92
Payments increasing 4% per year	1,807.70	21,692.40

Joint lives, fixed payments, no increases	2,387.76	28,653.12
Joint lives, payments increasing 4% per year	1,581.69	$ 18,980.28

Taking inflation into account, Ida feels that increasing the payments by 4 percent per year should provide her with adequate safety. She is not interested in lowering her payment to provide for an heir. She decides to purchase the increasing single life annuity providing $21,692.40 initially, which, combined with her Social Security, gives her an income of $37,692; it also generates a better cash flow and less tax than the CD option because with the annuity, only about 38.1 percent of the annuity payment will be taxable to her. A comparison of the CD option and the annuity option is shown below:

	CD Option	Increasing Single Life Annuity Option
Social security income	$16,000	$16,000
Interest income	17,000	0
Guaranteed annuity income	0	21,692
Income before taxes	33,000	37,692
Less income taxes	(1,220)	(0)
Less spending needs	(36,000)	(36,000)
Amount available for savings (or required savings withdrawal)	($4,220)	$1,692

The annuity meets her needs. She will have a guaranteed income stream that, with the 4 percent inflation adjustment protection, should be sufficient to meet her needs for the rest of her life. She realizes an initial return of 5.42 percent on her $400,000, and it will increase annually by 4 percent, which is probably better than she could do with any safe investment. If she had to continue with CD investments, future interest income would be reduced since the principal is deteriorating at $4,220 per year, and the deterioration will increase. On the other hand, with the annuity option, she is able to put $1,692 in savings.

Comparing the annuity option with the CD option, her annuity payments are always increasing 4 percent annually while the CD interest income decreases. This causes the CD balance to become fully depleted when Ida is about 87 years of age, at a time when there is a surplus balance of about $83,000 under the annuity option. Figure 8.1 shows the principal balance remaining under these two options.

Figure 8.1

Balance of Funds Available
CD Investments vs. Lifetime Annuities

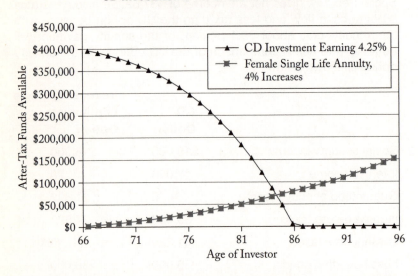

Figure 8.1 assumes that Ida's spending increases at a rate of 4 percent per year. You may not be able to see it in the figure, but the annuity option levels off very slightly when Ida is about 86 years old. This is due to a slight increase in the income taxes associated with the annuity. Only 38.1 percent of the annuity is taxable income initially, but when the nontaxable amounts received exceed the annuity cost of $400,000, the entire annuity payment becomes taxable. Most of Ida's Social Security income, however, is still not taxable even when this happens, and her taxes never exceed 10 percent of her income.

Though the annuity will end when she dies, she doesn't care because her needs are met and she has no heirs. This plan not only meets her psychological need for security, but it also is probably the best course of action for her. Perhaps your investment goals are somewhat more aggressive than Ida's. In other words, you feel that to make the example more meaningful, we should compare the annuity with after-tax investments earning a rate of return of 5 or 6 percent instead of just a 4.25 percent CD. Using the same assumptions except for the interest rate, the after-tax investment pool would be fully depleted by the time Ida was 89 or 92 years old (for 5 or 6 percent rates of return, respectively), when there would still be either $95,000 or $116,000 remaining with the annuity option.

Annuitizing Retirement Accumulations

Many people are faced with taking required minimum distributions from their retirement plans once they reach age 70½, the required beginning date. Instead of taking these payments based on the annual value and life expectancy factors, they can choose to annuitize the balance. This way, they no longer have to worry about managing the money and what happens if the balance dwindles or becomes depleted. In many situations, annuitizing at least a portion of the retirement assets is a good choice. In the late 1990s, when the market was up and you could smell confidence in the air, annuitizing was frowned upon. "Why annuitize when you can make 25 percent in the market? Even if the market levels out at 10 percent, you could still do better than annuitizing."

After three years in a row of significant losses in the stock market in 2000 to 2002, and enormous losses from October 2007 to press time, heightened fears of economic downturns, the price of energy, the foreclosure crisis, banking crisis, energy shortages, terrorism, federal deficits, and stock market downturns, there is a new attitude. Many people just want to make sure they have financial security for themselves and their spouse. I rarely recommend that someone with large accumulations annuitize everything. Even with Ida, I would probably advise that she only annuitize a portion of her assets and keep a portion of her assets outside of the annuity. In many real-life situations, annuitizing a portion of your retirement holdings is consistent with a desire for

In many real-life situations, annuitizing a portion of your retirement holdings is consistent with a desire for security. It provides a stable income that, combined with Social Security, will provide a minimum base of income and a sense of financial security not available with other strategies.

security. It provides a stable income that, combined with Social Security, will provide a minimum base of income and a sense of financial security not available with other strategies.

MINI CASE STUDY 8.2

When Annuitizing a Portion of the Retirement Plan Is Appropriate

George and his wife, Susan, both 65, retired in 2007 with $1.1 million in their combined retirement plans. George didn't do a good job of diversifying their holdings and to make matters worse, against Susan's wishes, he invested too much of their money in S&P large-cap growth stocks. After the market declines, they now have $800,000. No longer do George and Susan talk of a worry-free retirement. At the moment, they are more concerned about themselves than the stretch IRA for their grandchildren.

They have seen financial planners who have recommended a diversified portfolio striking a balance between income-bearing and growth investments. Still, Susan worries. The planners explain that if George and Susan invest too conservatively in an all-income portfolio, inflation and taxes will reduce the value of the principal and their estate will decline in purchasing power, something that makes Susan uneasy. George isn't as worried as Susan, but he would also like a long-term solution that would provide the possibility of an upside but with the assurance they will always have a roof over their heads, food on the table, and gas in the car.

They may choose a one-life annuity, a two-life annuity with full benefits to the survivor, or three-quarters or half benefits to the survivor, an annuity with a guaranteed payment for 5 or 10 years, and so on. My purpose here is not to analyze all the annuity choices but to let you know that annuitizing a portion of a retirement plan is often a reasonable option that can be customized for your needs and goals.

My preference for George and Susan is to combine the concepts of annuitizing and maintaining a retirement plan. If George and Susan annuitize one-fourth of their $800,000 in retirement funds, they would then be free to invest the remaining $600,000 of funds in a well-diversified portfolio and still look to enjoy the benefits of any future gains in the market. A $200,000 annuity would provide them with a retirement annuity income of $14,327 per year for as long as either of them lived. Even replacing the fixed income portion of their portfolio with an immediate annuity and investing the remainder of the portfolio is a safe strategy.

Changes in interest rates and inflation may affect the economic outcome of annuitizing. If interest rates are low, the quoted annuity payout amount may be lower in anticipation of lower investment returns by the annuity-issuing company. If interest rates are low and going higher, and you like the idea of annuitizing, you may want to consider waiting for the interest rates to rebound somewhat so the payout gets better before annuitizing a portion of your retirement plan.

Would you like to determine if you are a good candidate for an immediate annuity for a portion of your portfolio? Please visit www.retiresecure.com for more advice, or fill out the request form in the back of the book to see if either I or someone in my office would be able to advise you or refer you to someone who could help you determine whether an immediate annuity would be appropriate for your situation.

Annuitizing Has Worked Out Well for Many Investors

Annuitizing has worked out well for many of my older clients who were forced to annuitize. For example, most TIAA-CREF participants who retired in the 1980s or before were forced to annuitize most of their significant TIAA (bond) and CREF (stock) holdings. (They may also have been able to take some taxable withdrawals.) They currently enjoy both a fixed payment stream from the TIAA annuity and a variable payment stream from the CREF annuity. The retirees, in addition to whatever they saved, have their TIAA-CREF annuities and Social Security. They may not be rich, but they are usually comfortable. Usually they don't worry about money and, barring any unforeseen events, don't have to. There is no need for any trusts, no money management, and no messing around. When the market is up, they get larger distributions from CREF but still enjoy a steady income from the TIAA fixed annuity that has outperformed the guarantee. Although the CREF annuities were subject to large declines in the 2001–2003 time frame, the payment amounts greatly exceed the TIAA payments based on growth over the last 20 years. This income, combined with their Social Security, will be something on which they can rely. I am particularly familiar with this type of person because one of them is my mom. When she retired from her job as a professor of journalism (back then they had mandatory retirement at 70), she had to annuitize her retirement plan accumulations. My dad predeceased her, so I recommended she take out a one life annuity without a guaranteed number of years. Since I preferred she get more income, I told her to forget the survivorship feature and just get the most for herself. Against my advice, she chose an annuity with a survivorship feature. If she died within 10 years of retirement, my brothers and I would have received some income. She has had a steady dependable income for the last 22 years and will for the rest of her life. However, if she had listened to me, she would have had more income. I guess she paid me back for all the times I didn't listen to her, but her decision actually hurt her.

This example, however, is not limited to TIAA-CREF participants. This example will apply to many taxpayers who either had to or have chosen to receive a regular payment for life in the form of a pension.

Annuitizing: A Risky Strategy?

Another view of annuitizing is that it is not conservative but rather a gamble. Since most annuities are based on an actuarial life expectancy, you are gambling that you will outlive your actuarial life expectancy, and the company holding the annuity is gambling that you won't.

Evaluate the potential for you according to these criteria:

• If you have reason to believe that you will not survive your actuarial life expectancy, then annuitizing is probably a mistake.

• If you think, however, that you and your spouse are going to substantially outlive your actuarial life expectancy, then annuitizing will provide an assured income stream for a long life.

• If you have terminal cancer and your wife has a long life expectancy, consider having your wife purchase an immediate annuity on her life only.

Although annuitizing will provide fixed monthly amounts for a lifetime, there are other risks involved that make even this conservative strategy a gamble. One risk is that the issuing insurance company will go bankrupt and be unable to meet its obligations to pay the annuity. Although the state governments provide some guarantees to protect against their insolvency, you can minimize the risk by choosing insurance and annuity companies with Standard & Poor's quality ratings of at least AA or preferably AAA.

Another way to reduce your risk exposure is to buy immediate annuities from more than one company. For example, if you want to purchase an immediate annuity of $300,000, which represents 25 percent of your portfolio, consider three separate annuities of $100,000 each from three different companies.

Another risk involves the effect of inflation and the fixed nature of the *fixed* annuity payments. If the payout results in the same payment amount every month, the long-term effects of inflation can lead to the annuity income becoming inadequate to meet growing expenses. Some options are available to offset inflation risks when purchasing an annuity. One is choosing a payment stream that increases every year by a fixed rate of interest, although this option is not available for most retirement plan annuities, just after-tax annuities. This fixed rate of increase, however, is not directly tied to inflation, and could become insufficient in times of high inflation.

CREF annuities, for those in a TIAA-CREF plan, or any similar plan may help to protect your annuity payment stream from inflation by providing a payment that changes based on market investment returns. This can be both good and bad. If the stock market (or other investment index) does well, then you will be better off, but if the market returns are negative, you face the risk of the payments decreasing. Either can happen in times of high inflation. Pick your poison—do you risk the effects of inflation or of a market decline? Although there is no single correct answer, diversification may be the key to help in such decision making.

> **Another problem with annuitizing a retirement fund is that money is paid out on a regular schedule, and this may not be in tune with your needs.**

- If you do not need the money, then annuitizing retirement plan assets needlessly accelerates the payment of income taxes on your retirement accumulations. In theory, at least in the early years, the annuity payment will be somewhat higher than minimum required distributions since it reflects a return of principal. This is unlike the favorable tax situation we saw earlier in Case Study 8.1 where Ida annuitized after-tax assets.

- If you need more than the annuity payment amount and you have annuitized everything, then you are just plain out of luck unless you can borrow from a bank or other lending institution. If you are taking minimum required distributions from a retirement plan, you can always eat into the principal for a large distribution when and if you need it. This is, of course, the fundamental risk of annuities.

A Variation on the Annuity Theme: The Longevity Annuity

If your most consuming, most sleep-depriving worry is running out of money before you die—despite all your best planning, perhaps a longevity annuity is something you should consider. In effect, a *longevity annuity* is a type of annuity that requires immediate payment for a deferred benefit. You buy the annuity now, but you receive nothing immediately other than the guarantee that a number of years from your purchase date you will begin receiving annual or monthly benefits. An example might be helpful.

Assume you are age 65, healthy, and think you have a long life expectancy. You don't need any additional income now and you think you have more than enough money to last you for the next 20 years. Your fear is that you might very well live beyond those secure 20 years and then you would outlive your money. You don't want to buy an immediate annuity because you really don't need the income now. So, you purchase a longevity annuity that will provide you with an income 20 years from now. In its purest form, if you die before 20 years, too bad, you get nothing, your heirs get nothing from the insurance company, and buying the annuity would have been a mistake. If, however, you live until 95, the decision to buy this type of annuity will have proven to be of tremendous benefit. Obviously, if you live longer, the annuity would be even more valuable. It is like many forms of insurance: If you need it, you will be very glad that you have it. Not needing it is the risk you take. But being the number runners that we are, let's look at specific examples to help quantify the benefits and drawbacks. As you would expect, you can purchase longevity annuities, also known as deferred immediate annuities, with various survivorship features.

MINI CASE STUDY 8.3
Buying a Longevity Annuity

Phil is age 65 and he is confident that he will have sufficient income for the next 20 years to maintain his standard of living. He also has $100,000 of discretionary after-tax dollars to immediately fund a longevity annuity. He is unmarried, but he does have a son to whom he would like to leave something. Phil is intrigued by the idea of the immediate deferred annuity, and Phil wants to look at the cost and benefits of the immediate deferred annuity and also compare and contrast the numbers for purchasing the longevity annuity on a life only basis versus an installment refund basis. If he opts for the life only option, then in the event that he dies before turning 85 there would be no benefit paid to his son. If he opts for the installment refund option, then if he dies before turning 85 his son or other heirs will be guaranteed the monthly income for 15 months—basically a return of the original investment.

Based on current rates (May 2008) once Phil reaches age 85, the longevity annuity with the life only option will provide him with a fixed lifetime monthly income of $8,502.65 ($102,031.80 per year). If he chooses to go with the installment refund option, his monthly income will be $6,852.22 ($82,226.64 per year).

If we assume an inflation rate of 3.1 percent per year, these amounts provide an annual income in today's dollars of about $52,666 for the life only option or $42,443 for the installment refund option at age 85. Each year thereafter, the real income in today's dollars drops due to the continued effects of inflation.

These two amounts mean that if we don't take into account interest or the time value of money or if Phil lived 12 or 15 months beyond his 85th birthday, this would be a winner. However, that isn't a fair analysis. A fair analysis must take into account the time value of money and taxes on the annuity income. If we make certain assumptions and run the numbers, we have a much less favorable breakeven point.

Let us run the numbers assuming investment income on an alternative investment of either 4, 6, or 8 percent. The annuity income received at age 85 is taxable to the extent that the income exceeds the $100,000 investment. For example, let us also assume the income at age 85 is considered 70 percent withdrawal of cost basis and the rest ordinary income until the total cost of

$100,000 is returned. Also assume taxes of 25 percent on ordinary income but net of only 20 percent on after-tax investment income due to the favorable capital gains rates and deferral of taxes due to appreciation. The following table shows the various breakeven points:

Rate of Return on After-Tax Investments	4 Percent	6 Percent	8 Percent
Approximate Breakeven Point in Years of Age for:			
Life only option	87y 4m	88y 5m	90y 1m
Return of premium guarantee option	87y 11m	89y 3m	91y 7m

Now that Phil has the numbers, his options are much better defined, but he still has to decide if his fear of running out of money outweighs the risk of not realizing a return on the investment

That is a dilemma that people have to assess for themselves. But I offer this observation from Larry J. Kotlikoff, a Boston University economics professor and developer of important software that does a dynamic analysis of multiple variables affecting retirement spending. His model is superior to other models that use constant and static spending targets. Larry says if the whole point is to never run out of money, we should be willing to pay a premium over the actuarial breakeven number—in effect, for peace of mind. The reason it has so much appeal to me and other advisers is that it helps alleviate the #1 fear facing most retirees—outliving their money.

By the way, I would not recommend it in its simplest form if you are married. In that case, unless there are extenuating circumstances (such as one of you has life insurance or a pension or other resources), you should purchase the immediate deferred annuity for both lives. The above example does not analyze these numbers. For now, suffice it to say that the annuity payment would be reduced because the insurance company must continue paying until both the husband and wife die.

What Are the Disadvantages of a Longevity Annuity?

What are the biggest arguments against it? Well, right off the bat, you are writing a check for $100,000 (actually it could be for any amount), and you are not getting any immediate benefit. You could die before 85, and your decision would not have worked out well for your family. For many people with heirs to consider, that will be the end of the discussion. For you hearty souls who are worried about running out of money and are willing to take some extra risks to address your fear, please read on for even more reasons not to do it.

The insurance company could fail and you end up with nothing. However, insurance companies are highly regulated by the states. During the bailout of AIG and other companies, stockholders suffered, but owners of annuities and beneficiaries of life insurance policies were completely protected. Of course, I can't deny there is some amount of risk, even with well rated companies.

Another reason not to buy it now is that today, interest rates are low and as a result, the future annuity payments will be less than they would be if interest rates were higher. Perhaps the best solution to this issue is keep your options open and when interest rates go back up and the benefit per dollar of the premium goes up, buy one then.

In addition, we could face hyperinflation and even if you survive, you would get paid in devalued currency.

On the other hand, if you think that the economy is not going to do well over the next 20 years and you want a guarantee of not running out of money, and you can live with the downsides that I pointed out, this is a great idea. But perhaps the best use for a longevity annuity comes not from purchasing one outright, but rather trading up.

The "Aha!" Moment with Respect to Longevity Annuities

I often rely on Tom Hall, an insurance broker with Pittsburgh Brokerage Services, LLC, to find my clients the best deals on life insurance. Tom often has astute recommendations. This "aha" moment came from Tom.

Before introducing Tom's idea, I have to give you some background information on one problem I often encounter as an estate planner. Many of my clients, at some point in their lives, have purchased a tax-deferred annuity. A discussion of that type of annuity is beyond the scope of this chapter. In any event, sometimes they work out well, but sometimes retirees who have purchased a tax-deferred annuity don't have a good plan for their eventual disposition.

Tom Hall says, "That's fine. Do a tax-free exchange of your tax-deferred annuity for this longevity annuity." What a great idea! The reason this is such a good idea is a taxpayer can do a tax-free exchange disposing of an asset he or she did not want to keep in exchange for guaranteed payments in the future as long as the client lives. This could be a much better choice than electing the annuitizing option that is usually part of a tax-deferred annuity contract. The reason is, if you annuitize a tax-deferred annuity contract now, the payments will be much lower than if you elect to defer payments for a number of years in the future.

At the moment, the longevity or immediate deferred annuity is not a well-known option for many taxpayers. I predict it will become more important in the future as people will be willing to pay money up front to avoid the risk of outliving their money.

Special Idea: Using Annuities for Spendthrift Children

Over the years, our legal practice has drafted many spendthrift trusts for adult children as beneficiaries of wills and trusts and retirement plans (see Chapter 17 for more details regarding spendthrift trusts). We usually draft these trusts when a parent feels that an adult child is not capable of handling money responsibly. Sometimes it is drafted to make sure the no-good son-in-law doesn't get one red cent of mom and dad's hard-earned money. The trust is set up for the benefit of the irresponsible child (or the daughter who is married to the no-good son-in-law). A trustee is named to invest the funds and make distributions according to the terms of the trust.

Many times naming a spendthrift trust as a beneficiary is a good solution. Sometimes it isn't. There are multiple problems with spendthrift trusts, including aggravation; an additional tax return; and legal, accounting, and trustee expenses. Perhaps the biggest problem with the spendthrift trust is choosing a trustee. Usually, the parents of the adult child decide who should be the trustee of the spendthrift trust. Many of my clients do not want a bank or trust company as a trustee or, even if they did, the value of the trust isn't enough to get a bank interested. I personally will not act as a trustee and neither will a lot of attorneys. (We don't want to have to deal with whiney beneficiaries wanting more money than our prudent natures would allow.) One logical choice of trustee is one of the spendthrift's siblings because the sibling is likely to have a greater understanding of the situation than a bank or other corporate trustee. Do you, however, really want to set the stage for family strife? What happens when the trustee doesn't give the spendthrift what he wants? What would Christmas dinner be like after Brother Trustee just said, "No, Sister Spendthrift, you can't use the money from your trust fund for a new sports car." Or "No, Sister Spendthrift, paying for tuition and room and board at the University of the Sun Devil Worshiper doesn't qualify as funds for education, and I won't pay tuition for that institution out of your trust!"

Naming a bank as trustee is often a problem, too. Often there isn't enough money in the trust for a bank to be willing to serve as trustee. Even if there is a sufficient balance, there are fee issues, and ultimately many clients just don't want a bank involved.

The Solution to Providing for the Spendthrift Adult Child

Let's assume the goal is to provide an income stream for the adult spendthrift child for the rest of the child's life. Mom and dad want the assurance that the child will be properly provided for. They may not see the need for the child to accumulate money. They also may not care about what happens to the money after the child dies.

One potential solution to the problem is to eliminate the trust entirely. Assume the parents have three children, and they want to treat all three equally. The parents could give a direction in their will or other document that the spendthrift's share would be used to purchase a lifetime annuity for the benefit of the spendthrift. The annuity would be purchased from the estate after mom and dad die. An annuity will assure a future income stream and provide protection against the spendthrift's creditors.

MINI CASE STUDY 8.4

Using an Annuity in Lieu of a Spendthrift Trust (a True Story)

Concerned Parent is trying to figure out how to provide for his son, one of three children. He trusts his daughters completely and is planning to leave both of them their one-third of the inheritance directly. The issue is how to leave money to his son, who he doesn't trust with money. If he leaves it to his son outright, he is afraid his son will deplete the principal through excessive spending or be vulnerable to potential creditors of both his son and his daughter-in-law. He also fears his daughter-in-law will put pressure on his son to spend more than he might be comfortable spending, or what may be prudent to spend, but he doesn't want to be too controlling from the grave or jeopardize his son's marriage.

If he leaves the money in some type of spendthrift trust, the money is tied up and perhaps overprotected. He would also have to choose a trustee. If the bank is a trustee (a corporate fiduciary), there will be fees and extra layers of administration. If he names one of his daughters as trustee, there is a good chance that he will harm the relationship between the son and the daughter. Then he would have to decide among the different possibilities for terms of the trust. Should the trust have a mandatory distribution? How much judgment license should the trustee be authorized to use? Should it be a total-return trust? (Another subject, another day, but a total-return trust is a new type of trust that makes sense in some situations.)

Does Concerned Parent really want to control from the grave? *No!* The Concerned Parent doesn't want to control his son's life. He just wants to provide him with the highest degree of financial security.

At the Concerned Parent's death, the executor is directed to take all or a portion of what would have gone to the son directly to purchase an annuity with monthly annuity proceeds going to the son. Son gets an annuity for the rest of his life and most likely ends up with a larger monthly or annual distribution than he would have received had the inherited money been left in a trust.

Disadvantages include reduced flexibility for the son and the same disadvantages of annuitizing as were listed previously.

This idea of directing the executor to purchase an annuity has been used in practice to the total delight of the Concerned Parent setting it up and to even greater delight of the responsible sibling who doesn't have to be trustee for the spendthrift sibling. If you make this provision in your will or revocable trust, I recommend giving the executor the right to shop for the best deal on an annuity at the time of your death.

Protection from Creditors

Another advantage of the immediate annuity is that it provides some protection from creditors. Once the annuity is purchased, the principal itself will be protected from creditors because it is gone—that is, outside the control of the annuitant. In some situations, a creditor may be able to reach the proceeds (a payment) of the annuity, but that is unlikely. For example, a creditor can't get an order directing an annuity company to pay the son's annuity directly to the creditor. It could, however, strategically levy a checking account where the proceeds of the annuity check would be deposited, in which case the son should learn to be an effective sleazebag or pay up.

This idea of buying an annuity is also a good idea for the father of a child who has substantial debts or who practices in a profession where there is significant personal liability, such as medicine. Of course, one of the downsides of annuitizing for the benefit of a child is that there will be nothing to pass on to the grandchildren.

To address that flaw, I offer several responses.

1. So what? With the exception of providing for education, most grandparents are much more interested in providing for their children than their grandchildren. Of course this isn't always the case, but it is in my experience.

2. You don't have to have the executor annuitize all the proceeds. You can have the executor annuitize just a portion.

3. Something could be set up for the grandchildren directly. If you purchase an annuity for your child, you could leave some portion of the inherited IRA to a trust for the grandchildren to allow the greatest stretch.

A Key Lesson from This Chapter

Annuitizing a portion of your retirement plan or purchasing an immediate annuity for roughly 25 percent of your retirement assets is often a good strategy to help ensure that you never run out of money. A new strategy of purchasing an immediate deferred annuity will be very attractive to some individuals.

9

||||||||||||||||||||||

Withdrawing Retirement Plans Funded with Company Stocks and Net Unrealized Appreciation

If you do not know how to ask the right question, you discover nothing.
—W. Edwards Deming

Main Topics

- What is Net Unrealized Appreciation?
- Limits on funding qualified plans with employer stock
- Case studies (that save a bundle)

KEY IDEA

The difference between the market value of your company stock still invested in your retirement plan at the time of the distribution and its value at the time your employer made the contribution to your plan is called *net unrealized appreciation*, or NUA. At retirement, it is critical to check for NUA before rolling money into an IRA. NUA qualifies for favorable tax treatment.

The underlying premise of this book is that the key to significantly greater overall wealth accumulation for you and your family is delaying, for as long as possible, taxes on distributions, of any amounts, from the tax-deferred environment—in other words, pay taxes later. There may be situations in the pension area, however, where we should make an exception to the rule. Paying tax on NUA now is one of the exceptions to the "Don't pay taxes now—pay taxes later" rule. This is particularly true if the capital gains tax and qualified dividends are taxed at 15 percent.

What Is NUA, and Why Should I Care?

When an employee retires and takes a lump-sum distribution from a qualified plan, such as a 401(k), the distribution may include employer stock that is worth more than its fair market value at the time it was contributed to the plan. The difference between the market value of your company stock invested in your retirement plan at the time of the distribution and its value at the time your employer made the contribution is called *net unrealized appreciation* (NUA). You should care because NUA receives favorable tax treatment.

The difference between the market value of your company stock invested in your retirement plan at the time of the distribution and its value at the time your employer made the contribution is called *net unrealized appreciation* (NUA).

Employers have been and are still allowed to fund qualified plans with their own stock, using the fair market value of the stock to value the contribution. Though this practice has been frowned upon since the Enron fiasco, it is still common and exists in many of the older plans. A pension plan may not have more than 10 percent of its assets invested in employer stock. For certain plans, such as stock bonus plans, all contributions are in employer stock. Profit-sharing plans may have 100 percent of their assets invested in employer stock.

If the stock was contributed by the employer, the employee gets to treat the NUA portion as a special entity as long as the distribution initially qualifies as a lump-sum distribution as described in Chapter 6. If the proposed distribution qualifies as a lump-sum distribution, then the NUA is not taxed at the time of the distribution. The employee pays tax only on the original value of the stock from the time his employer contributed it to the plan. That amount becomes the basis of the stock in the hands of the employee. Employees do not pay tax on the NUA portion until they sell or otherwise dispose of the stock in a taxable transaction. Also, the employee then pays taxes at capital gains rates instead of ordinary income rates. No matter how long the employee has held the stock, the NUA portion is taxed as a long-term capital gain. The essence of the advantage of the NUA is that distributions will be taxed at capital gains rates rather than ordinary rates as with traditional IRAs. If the employee dies, there is no step-up in basis for NUA, which means that tax is still due on the total amount of the long-term capital gain.

Would you like to continue your IRA and retirement plan education? You can listen to my MP3 and read my special reports from the comfort of your home. Please go to the last several pages of this book for ordering information. In addition, this information can be accessed at www.retiresecure.com.

MINI CASE STUDY 9.1
When Checking for NUA Saves a Bundle

Joe Employee retires and takes a lump-sum distribution from his company's stock bonus plan, consisting totally of his company's stock, which had been contributed by his employer. The total value of the stock at the time of the distribution is $500,000. The company's cost basis in the stock is $100,000.

Joe gets a Form 1099-R from his employer showing a total distribution of $500,000 and a taxable distribution of $100,000. The amount of NUA is $400,000. Joe pays tax on $100,000 of ordinary income at the time of the distribution. If Joe sells the stock immediately for $500,000, he will also report a $400,000 long-term capital gain.

Already Joe is better off than if he cashed in a $500,000 traditional plan or even an IRA. If he cashed in a $500,000 IRA, he would have to pay income taxes on the entire amount at ordinary income tax rates. At the top marginal rate, the tax is $500,000 × 35% = $175,000 of income tax on an immediate cash-out. This leaves Joe with $325,000 after taxes.

If, instead, the transaction qualifies for NUA, he sells $400,000 at capital gains rates of 15 percent and $100,000 at ordinary income tax rates: ($400,000 × 15% = $60,000, plus $100,000 × 35% = $35,000), or a combined tax of $95,000. This leaves Joe with $405,000 after taxes. Better yet, Joe can take his NUA, keep track of the NUA status, and not pay immediate income taxes.

- If Joe holds the stock for three months and then sells it for $550,000, he will report a $400,000 long-term capital gain (the NUA portion) and a $50,000 short-term capital gain on the stock.

- If Joe holds the stock for a year after the distribution, and then sells it for $600,000, the entire $500,000 of gain on the stock, not only the NUA, qualifies as long-term capital gain.

- If he just sits on the NUA, the account will continue to accumulate, but some day he will be subject to capital gains taxes. Even at death you can't escape the capital gain, and there is no step-up in basis.

In most cases, it is beneficial to roll over a distribution from a qualified plan into an IRA to get the benefits of tax-deferred growth. But Joe has done even better! While he holds the stock, all the appreciation is accumulating in a tax-deferred manner, since gain on the stock is not taxed until he sells it. And he will pay tax on the gain at capital gains rates when he sells the stock, rather than ordinary income rates like distributions from an IRA. Joe also has the option of keeping part of the stock and rolling over the balance of the shares into an IRA. In this situation, Joe would pay income taxes only on the basis of the shares he keeps and would maintain NUA status on those shares. If Joe rolls the stock over to an IRA, and later takes a distribution in stock from the IRA, the taxable amount of the distribution is the fair market value of the stock, and Joe is taxed at ordinary income rates. Rolling shares into the IRA is a bad idea for Joe, because he loses the tremendous benefit of the capital gains rates for the NUA portion.

This is why it is critical when you retire and are considering an IRA rollover that you check to see if there is any NUA in your retirement plan. If you do not have company stock in your plan, and there was no type of stock swap, you will not have NUA. If you do own employer stock in your retirement plan, then you will have to find out from the payroll department whether you have NUA. If some of the NUA on employer stock is relatively small due to the difference in the stock basis and fair market value at the time of the contribution, a rollover of those shares into an IRA may be a better approach. Preserving the tax-deferred status of those shares may outweigh the minimal long-term capital gains benefits derived from taking the distribution.

Getting a handle on NUA could present a tremendous savings opportunity. When you calculate how much money you can save in taxes, you will find you may be in a much better situation using the NUA rules to your advantage.

MINI CASE STUDY 9.2
A Typical NUA Opportunity

It is rare for an employee to have a retirement plan funded 100 percent with employer stock. More typical is the case of Bob, who retires from his company and receives a lump-sum distribution from the company's pension plan consisting of $450,000 in cash and other securities and employer stock worth $50,000, of which $40,000 is NUA. That is to say, the stock value at the time the company contributed it to Bob's retirement plan was $10,000. This is a reasonable range that you might find for an employee who has worked at the same company for many years.

- Bob should roll over the noncompany stock portion (the $450,000) to an IRA and keep the stock while still excluding the NUA portion from income—the best of both worlds.

- Bob will end up with a $450,000 IRA and $50,000 in company stock and will have current taxable income of $10,000. The $40,000 in NUA won't be taxed until Bob sells the stock.

If the employer contributed the distributed stock to the plan, then the deferral and capital gains treatment apply only if the distribution meets all the qualifications for a lump-sum distribution, other than the subsequent rollover of a portion of the plan to an IRA. Such a partial rollover would prohibit the 10-year averaging treatment as discussed in Chapter 6, but would not prohibit the special tax treatment for NUA. If the distribution does not qualify as a lump-sum distribution, then only the NUA of stock that the employee himself contributed to his plan would qualify for this special treatment of income deferral and capital gains.

If you have substantial NUA in your retirement plan, I highly recommend that you get someone to run the numbers for you and help determine a long-term NUA plan. If the people you work with don't have this special expertise in NUA (frankly, I don't), I know of no one better than one of the top IRA and retirement planning experts in the country, Robert Keebler, CPA.

A Key Lesson from This Chapter

The difference between the market value of a stock when it was contributed to your IRA and its value upon distribution is called the *net unrealized appreciation*, or NUA, and NUA receives favorable tax treatment. The most important piece of information to carry with you from this chapter is always check for NUA before rolling money into an IRA. If you have NUA, please, either get professional advice or dig further into the matter.

Part Three

ESTATE PLANNING

It Is NeverToo Early To Start

OVERVIEW

I find it hard to draw clear lines between retirement planning and estate planning because I view both as a continuum. Optimal estate planning for IRA and retirement plan owners usually involves the same principle I have been consistently preaching throughout: Don't pay taxes now—pay taxes later.

In this part of the book, I expand on that concept and present what many experts and I feel is the ideal beneficiary designation of an IRA and/or retirement plan, known as Lange's Cascading Beneficiary Plan™. I mentioned this plan in a peer-reviewed article back in 1998 and published the first full dedicated article on this plan in *Financial Planning* magazine in March 2001, right after the change in the tax law made this plan so favorable. I have given talks on the subject at some of the top estate planning seminars in the country. Since then, Lange's Cascading Beneficiary Plan has been widely quoted with attribution to me in such sources as *Kiplinger's Retirement Reports* and the *Wall Street Journal*, and by Jane Bryant Quinn in *Newsweek*. The *Wall Street Journal* acknowledges the explosive growth of the use of the key concept of the plan—disclaimers.

Well, you made it over the hump; you've accumulated well and planned your retirement. What happens next? You need an estate plan for your heirs. Please picture yourself after the necessary changes have been made, knowing that you have set things up in the most beneficial manner for your family. Your spouse may not be immersed in the details now, but he or she will be thrilled with the gift of security you are providing. Imagine how good you'll feel knowing that you have protected your estate from both the IRS and that no-good son-in-law who you never trusted!

If all your documents are in great shape (and after reading this book you will be in a better position to know), you should be congratulated! If, however, things aren't in great shape or if you have questions, please read on and take action so that your legacy won't be decimated by taxes.

As much as I like the plan, it isn't for everyone, so I also present a more traditional estate plan. A certain core of information is important to truly understand the benefits of Lange's Cascading Beneficiary Plan and the traditional plan. After learning the core information, you will be in a better position to know how to approach estate planning for you and your family.

Finally, a trend has emerged. With the continuing escalation of exemption equivalent amounts, many clients who would have been subject to or at least worried about estate taxes when the exemption amount was $600,000 today do not have that fear. Even if you don't anticipate estate taxes and the federal estate and gift tax structures aren't important to you, the concepts of disclaimers and the stretch IRA are still critical.

The three critical concepts of this plan are:

1. The federal estate and gift tax structure

2. The concept of using disclaimers in the planning stages

3. The concept of the stretch IRA

Chapters 10 to 13 address those topics in some detail. Chapter 10 presents an extended case study of a sophisticated retirement and estate plan to optimize wealth for a professional married couple when the bulk of the money (roughly $2 million) is in the husband's IRA and 401(k).

10

Eddie and Emily: A Retirement and Estate Planning Case Study

You can always amend a big plan, but you can never expand a little one.
I don't believe in little plans. I believe in plans big enough to meet a situation
which we can't possibly foresee now.

—Harry S Truman

Edward J. Engineer ("Eddie"), age 68, is a retired engineer. Eddie is married to Emily, age 65. They have two married children and four grandchildren. Their son, Bill, is doing quite well financially and is in a solid marriage. Their daughter, Sarah, unfortunately, has significant marital problems and, to make life even more difficult, her finances are a mess and this is a major concern to Eddie and Emily. To make matters even worse, Eddie doesn't trust his son-in-law. Period.

Though Eddie made a reasonable salary as an engineer, it was difficult to save money. Taking care of the mortgage and maintenance on the house, buying groceries, braces, and raising their children took most of his paycheck. They also paid for their children's college education. Eddie did make regular contributions to his retirement plan, and when it was deductible, to a voluntary IRA. Emily has a small IRA.

Just 10 years ago, Eddie had $1,000,000 in total retirement assets. He was just hoping that the accumulations would provide for his and Emily's comfortable retirement. With time and compounding, however, Eddie's retirement assets then grew to $2,200,000 in his 401(k) and $280,000 in his IRA. The year 2008 was rough for Eddie, and his accounts shrunk to roughly $1,800,000 in his 401(k) plan and $200,000 in his IRA. The Engineers do not think of themselves as wealthy, and they have not changed their spending habits. Eddie continues to drive his 10-year-old car. He would consider it absolutely foolish to spend money on a new car. His current one is reliable and certainly serviceable.

Eddie and Emily remain in their modest house where they raised their children. They haven't remodeled the kitchen or bathrooms. Emily still clips coupons. Now Eddie and Emily are facing enormous taxes on their retirement assets both during their lifetimes and at their deaths.

Eddie and Emily have wills that are several years old. They were drafted when there was a greater risk of federal estate taxes when Eddie and Emily died. Eddie's will reflects traditional planning decisions that were quite common when there was a concern about paying estate taxes. It includes a trust that basically says that in the event Eddie predeceases Emily, a significant portion of his money will go into a trust from which Emily will receive income, and she will have the option to invade the principal for health maintenance and support.

Eddie was never really comfortable with the planning for his retirement plan or IRA. For instance, he wasn't sure how the beneficiary form of the IRA and 401(k) plan should be filled out.

The Engineers have an approximate net worth of $2.5 million, including life insurance. A detailed list of the Engineers' assets is as follows:

Eddie's 401(k) plan	$1,800,000
Eddie's IRA	200,000
Emily's IRA	30,000
After-tax investments and savings	130,000
House	185,000
Cars and personal property	45,000
Whole life insurance	50,000
Term life insurance	60,000
Total estate	$2,500,000

Eddie and Emily were never confident of the advice they received regarding their IRA and retirement plans until they met me. What follows is a summary of some of Eddie and Emily's concerns and how I addressed the concerns.

Eddie and Emily's Retirement and Estate Planning Issues

- Eddie and Emily's first concern is providing for a comfortable retirement as long as they both live. Their second concern is providing for the survivor upon the first death.

- Though Eddie and Emily would prefer leaving money to their children rather than paying taxes, avoiding taxes is secondary to providing for each other.

- Eddie and Emily's Social Security and other income do not cover their expenses, and they must make withdrawals from their portfolio. They wonder if they should spend their IRA or 401(k) funds first, or whether they should spend after-tax money first—money on which they have already paid taxes.

- Eddie and Emily trust each other completely, although Eddie is a little tighter about money than Emily.

- Eddie and Emily wondered if life insurance should play a role in their planning, and, if so, what kind and how much.

Eddie is pretty sharp and he realizes that the years between entering retirement and being required to take minimum distributions will give him more control over his income than he has ever had. After he reaches 70½, his minimum required distribution will be taxed for federal income tax purposes and his tax rate will increase. From now until then, his taxable income is relatively low. If he chooses not to make any IRA or 401(k) withdrawals and live off his after-tax funds (money not in his 401[k] or IRA), his income and his taxes will be extremely low. He wonders if these "low tax years" create an opportunity for him and his family.

- One of the issues the low tax years bring up is whether Eddie and Emily should convert a portion of their IRA or 401(k) into a Roth IRA. If they choose to convert a portion of their 401(k) and/or IRA into Roth IRAs, what is the optimal amount to convert? When should the conversion take place? Which assets should they use to pay the taxes on the conversion?

- The reason Eddie never rolled the money out of his 401(k) into an IRA: One-third of the money in the 401(k) is invested in a guaranteed income fund that is paying

6 percent, which makes Eddie happy. Was it really smart to leave the money in the 401(k)?

- Despite the fact that their children have widely disparate needs, Eddie and Emily want to treat the children equally, but he doesn't want his no-good son-in-law to get one red cent of his money. He is also worried about his daughter's bleak long-term financial situation.

- Eddie and Emily want to know more about optimal beneficiary designations for their retirement plans to pass that money on to their children and possibly their grandchildren.

- Eddie knew that with the higher exemption amounts (the amount you are allowed to die with, without having to pay federal estate taxes), the traditional trusts that were part of his wills and retirement plan and IRA beneficiaries might not only be unnecessary, but possibly financially disastrous. Even though Eddie has known about this problem for several years, he is still a stubborn engineer and to get him to do anything outside his routine often takes a Herculean effort. Emily gave up trying to get Eddie to do anything he didn't want to do years ago but I stilled wanted to optimize the plan for the family, even if Eddie is a little reluctant to make changes.

- Eddie, even more so than Emily, doesn't want to see his no-good son-in-law get one red cent of his money. The thought of that no-goodnik living off his inheritance makes Eddie sick. This problem, in addition to his daughter's bleak financial prospects, though not his primary concern, weighs heavily on Eddie's mind.

Retirement Planning

Eddie knew the maxim Don't pay taxes now—pay taxes later. He recognized the benefits of spending his after-tax dollars before his IRA dollars. He wondered if there were exceptions to that rule. He also knows minimum distributions are around the corner, and he wants to know what impact that will have on his planning. Specifically, he knows his income tax bracket is lower now than it will likely ever be again. With my help, Eddie decided to make Roth

IRA conversions up to the top of the 15 percent bracket as per the advice in Case Study 4.4.

Calculating the Minimum Required Distribution (MRD)

Fortunately for Eddie and Emily, the massive changes passed by Congress in 2001 actually simplified projecting Eddie's minimum required distribution. Though we are oversimplifying for this case study, using the minimum distribution calculator and Table III of the IRS tables (found at www.retiresecure.com and in the appendix of this book), Eddie realized that when he turned 70½ his minimum required distribution would be roughly 4 percent of the balance of his account. As he and Emily age, they will be required to take out more and more money from their IRA and 401(k) and pay income taxes on those withdrawals, whether they like it or not.

Estate Planning*

Eddie's new estate planning/attorney team was quick to stress that the beneficiary designation of his IRA and his 401(k)—not his will or living trust—determine the disposition of the retirement plan funds upon his death. Most of Eddie's assets were in retirement accounts. Thus, focusing on the design of Eddie's retirement plan beneficiary designations was the single most important portion of Eddie and Emily's estate plan.

Eddie and Emily also wondered whether the trusts they had drafted when the exemption amount was $600,000 were still appropriate today with the higher exemption amounts. In addition, their previous attorney wasn't able to satisfy Eddie's concerns about the beneficiary designation of his 401(k) and his IRA. Eddie now realizes his planning is not appropriate for his family's current needs.

Eddie and Emily found out that their will and retirement plan and IRA beneficiary designation severely limited the options available to survivors and/or heirs upon either Eddie's or Emily's death. In fact,

---

*A discussion of taxation at the state level is beyond the limited scope of this case study; thus, all references to taxes refer to taxes at the federal level.

given the increases in the exemption amount, Eddie's and Emily's current documents are a disaster waiting to happen. They have the old A/B system whereupon if Eddie dies first, his IRA and other assets in his name go into a trust for Emily's benefit. True, Emily can draw income and invade principal for health maintenance and support, but as it turns out the trust as drafted for them would be a monumental mistake. Please read the section in Chapter 11 called "The Nastiest Trap of All."

Eddie's attorney looked at Eddie and asked him point-blank, "Do you trust your wife?" After a little kidding, he answered, "Yes." The attorney asked Emily if she trusted her husband, and Emily also answered affirmatively. The attorney then took the opportunity to explain to Eddie and Emily the keystone of an estate planning technique that seemed tailor-made for their situation: "Lange's Cascading Beneficiaries Plan." (See Chapter 15 for more details.) In addition to the main features of Lange's Cascading Beneficiaries Plan, Eddie also wanted some type of protection for Sarah's benefit to protect Eddie and Emily's assets from their no-good son-in-law.

Eddie also sensed that it might not be a smart thing to keep the majority of his retirement plan in his 401(k). I asked Ed something none of the other advisors had asked. I asked to see the plan document, which has the rules that govern Eddie's 401(k) plan at work. I told Eddie that his children and grandchildren had a potentially big problem if he and Emily died before the money was rolled into an IRA. Eddie found out that when he and Emily died, depending on whether certain new laws were implemented, his heirs might have to pay income taxes on $1,800,000 the year after he and Emily died. (For the purposes of this case study, we have assumed that employers are still not required to provide nonspouse beneficiaries with the option to transfer their plan balances to inherited IRAs. There is currently a proposal in Congress which may become law by the time this book is published that would make it mandatory for employers to permit nonspouse beneficiaries to transfer their plan balances to inherited IRAs which would prevent the immediate income taxation described above.) The attorney also explained that even though you can never get out of paying income taxes on those retirement plans and IRAs, it was usually advantageous to pay the taxes later via a stretch IRA. The stretch IRA can defer income taxes for 40 or even 80 years after Eddie and Emily's death. The 401(k) retirement plan may not accommodate stretching Eddie's 401(k) distributions over the lives of his children—a critical component of Lange's Cascading Beneficiaries Plan. Eddie learned that this difficulty with his employer's 401(k) was typical of many corporate retirement plans—that is, the required distribution of the entire plan balance to a nonspouse beneficiary after the plan owner's death causes an enormous and otherwise unnecessary acceleration of income taxes. (Please see the section in Chapter 6 called "Tax Advantages of Transferring a Company 401[k] [or Other Retirement Plan] into an IRA.")

Though Eddie was reluctant to let go, with the exception of the fixed income account, he decided to roll his retirement plan account into his one-person 401(k) plan that he started after earning $10,000 consulting for his old company. With his one-person 401(k) he can direct his investments, take advantage of a great technique to make a Roth IRA conversion of his after-tax dollars inside his 401(k) without having to pay the tax (see www.retiresecure.com for a report on this technique), and his children will be able to stretch his 401(k) when he and Emily die. The children will also be able to do a Roth IRA conversion of the inherited 401(k). As a bonus, Eddie will enjoy added creditor protection because his one-person 401(k) plan falls under the ERISA act and affords better creditor protection than IRAs. He can also take full advantage of Lange's Cascading Beneficiary Plan.

As I was saying good night to my daughter one evening, we talked about the most important thing about *Retire Secure!* She asked, "Dad, what about all of the people who will be able to live better lives because of your book? Isn't that the most important thing?" My daughter made me stop and think. I often get so lost in the material that I forget about the impact *Retire Secure!* is having on people's lives.

So, please don't just read this book as an intellectual exercise. After reading the material, please implement the appropriate strategies either on your own or with the help of an advisor and put yourself and your family in a better position for the future.

Now that they were comfortable with the way their retirement assets will be left to Bill and Sarah, Eddie and Emily considered that those assets would be taxable to the children when withdrawn and used. Even with all this planning, the kids will face some big income tax bills as well as potential estate and inheritance tax issues. Taking a lot of money out of the retirement plan all at once after Eddie and Emily die would not only cut short the stretch but also create a higher tax rate. What if Eddie and Emily died prematurely? They only had $50,000 in whole life insurance and the $60,000 of term life insurance was going to become increasingly expensive to maintain. They decided to review the costs and benefits of survivorship life insurance to address these concerns.

They investigated a survivorship life insurance policy with a death benefit of $1,000,000, which amounted to 40 percent of their total estate. This amount would provide the estate and the children with sufficient liquidity to fund taxes and other expenses. This solution also allows the stretch IRA and Roth IRA to continue as long as possible, even to the grandchildren. Using a broker to search for what the top-rated companies could offer, and following a process similar to the one cited in Chapter 12, they found their premium was going to be about $14,500 per year. They had hoped for a lower premium of about $12,400 per year—which would have been possible if they had received a preferred rating on their health assessment from the insurance company. However, Eddie's cholesterol situation and extra weight would not allow that.

Even so, the $14,500 was within their budget. They could still afford to give money to the children annually or on an as-needed basis during their lifetimes. To think the children would then be guaranteed such a large amount of $500,000 each, gave comfort to Eddie and Emily that their children would be well provided for even if their spending began to reduce the savings accumulations in later years. They also realized that should they die earlier than expected, Eddie and Emily's family would be very well provided for compared to not getting the survivorship policy. They also decided that they would stop the term policy as part of the funding for the survivorship policy.

They used a life insurance comparison calculator to compare the survivorship policy to gifting money to the children directly rather than using the money to buy survivorship life insurance. They assumed a 7 percent rate of return and a 28 percent federal and state income tax rate that the children would have had to pay on the growth of the gifted money. Assuming Emily lives longer than

Eddie and that she reaches age 87 (her life expectancy), the gift fund would contain $589,249, but the insurance policy will guarantee the children $1,000,000. This is an additional $410,000 for the children! In addition it is income and inheritance tax-free upon receipt. They decided to commit to the $1,000,000 survivorship life insurance policy since it was not only a great deal for the family but they also felt much more secure in using their own savings and retirement money as they needed. (See chapter 12 for a more detailed discussion of survivorship life insurance.)

Conclusions

With expert guidance, Eddie and Emily designed a retirement and estate plan that optimized their assets for themselves and eventually their children. The Engineers were relieved. Finally they had made the decisions they had been delaying for years.

The information contained in this case study is not intended as legal advice. Due to the personal nature of retirement and estate planning, the fictional estate plan discussed in this case may not be appropriate for another situation.

We get more excellent suggestions on our case studies from our readers than any other topics discussed in this book. If you have suggestions on how we could improve planning for Eddie and Emily, please give us your suggestions. The best suggestions will be published and acknowledged in our next edition. Please go to www.retiresecure.com for an opportunity to make suggestions and thank you in advance for your efforts.

A Key Lesson from This Chapter

There is a reason that the words *retirement* and *estate planning* seem to just roll off the tongue—they belong together. It is important to understand that the consequences of your decisions may have immediate, short-term, and long-term tax ramifications. Plan with the big picture in mind, and keep things flexible when you can. Integrated planning always beats out something that is cobbled together.

11

How to Reduce Your Federal Estate Tax Burden

Collecting more taxes than is absolutely necessary is legalized robbery.
—Calvin Coolidge

Main Topics

- Defining estate and gift taxes
- Avoiding estate and gift taxes
- The importance of annual giving
- Different types of gifts
- Tax traps on the death of the second spouse
- The problem with B trusts intended for the benefit of the spouse
- The nastiest trap of all
- Funding trusts with retirement assets

KEY IDEA

For married couples whose assets exceed the Applicable Exclusion Amount ($3.5 million beginning in 2009), the concern is not with the estate tax at the first death, but rather the estate tax at the second death. For single or married taxpayers, simple gifts of $13,000 per year per beneficiary may save your heirs a bundle.

Defining Estate and Gift Taxes

In its simplest form, the federal gift and estate tax system is a transfer tax levied when individuals transfer assets during their lifetime or at their death. It is rare that individuals pay gift taxes during their lifetime. Therefore, it is much more common for the transfer tax to be imposed on the transfer of assets at their death.

With respect to transfers to spouses, the unlimited marital deduction allows you to transfer an unlimited amount of property to your U.S. citizen spouse, during his or her lifetime or at death, free of transfer taxes. If your spouse is not a U.S. citizen, the situation is more complicated and is beyond the scope of this book.

With respect to transfers to nonspouse beneficiaries, the IRS sets the upper lifetime limit on how much money individuals are allowed to transfer out of their estate before they incur a transfer tax. The amounts allowed are now different for lifetime transfers than for transfers at death. There is a $1 million Lifetime Gifting Exclusion amount that an individual is allowed to transfer to non-spouse beneficiaries during lifetime without incurring a federal gift tax. There is also an annual exclusion amount of $13,000 (in 2009), which can be transferred to each non-spouse beneficiary without using the Lifetime Gifting Exclusion. Please see additional discussion under Gift Taxes later in this chapter. The amount an individual is allowed to transfer at death without incurring a federal estate tax to nonspouse beneficiaries is referred to as the *Applicable Exclusion Amount*. The Applicable Credit Amount (formerly, and now often incorrectly, referred to as the Unified Credit Amount) is the amount of federal estate tax that would be due on the Applicable Exclusion Amount but for the existence of the credit. In 2009, the Applicable Exclusion Amount equals $3.5 million. The Applicable Credit Amount (the amount of federal estate tax that would be due on $3.5 million but for the credit) equals $1,455,800. Married individuals may each transfer an amount equal to the Applicable Exclusion Amount to nonspouse beneficiaries. Any reduction of the Lifetime Gifting Allowance also has the effect of reducing Applicable Exclusion Amount for estate tax purposes.

The amounts vary by year as follows:

Applicable Exclusion Amounts

2009	$3.5 million
2010	Estate tax is repealed*
2011	$1 million*

*Unless Congress takes action which we think is quite likely

This schedule is a mess, and chances are that this is only the tip of the iceberg. Right now a lot of taxpayers and their advisors are trying to guess what changes will be made in the next two years. Some are waiting to draft will and trusts till more information is available, and others are drafting based on their best guess as to what the exemption amount might be.

Personally, I don't think it is terribly pertinent for the purposes of drafting wills and trusts. The plan that I draft for my clients would survive intact in the face of most changes to the exemption amount. It is likely there will be many major changes of the exemption amount during our lifetime. I firmly believe that no one can accurately predict what will happen with the estate tax exemptions. Even if Congress repeals the estate tax entirely, they could easily bring it back, as they have on three separate occasions during times of war when Congress needed more money. My objective is to show you how to build a flexible estate plan that accommodates all the scheduled changes and adapts for those changes about which we can only speculate. At press time, the conjecture is that the exemption will be frozen at $3.5 million per year for the next several years.

This book does not address the potential impact of decoupling, the decision by some states to freeze the federal estate tax exemption at prior levels so the states can assess transfer tax on smaller estates. Individuals who live in those states should not assume that their estates are exempt from death taxes if their estate is below the $3.5 million federal estate tax exemption because the estates may be subject to a state estate tax known as the *pick-up tax*. Please consult with a qualified advisor to determine the impact, if any, of state death taxes on your estate plan.

> *Prediction is very difficult, especially if it's about the future.*
>
> —Niels Bohr

> *The groundhog is like most other prophets; it delivers its prediction and then disappears.*
>
> —Bill Vaughan

Given that the Applicable Exclusion Amount is a moving target, I think the safest way to plan is to recognize that your family may or may not be subject to the federal estate tax in the future. Whether your estate will be subject to federal tax will be determined by the combination of what your estate happens to be worth, what the Applicable Exclusion Amount equals in the year of your death, and how well you plan.

Avoiding Estate and Gift Taxes

In the United States there are several common ways to avoid federal gift and estate taxes. The first is simply to die with less than the Applicable Exclusion Amount (subject to exceptions) in your estate. That sounds obvious, but with the shifting Applicable Exclusion Amount, it becomes problematic, and planning for individuals with total estates over $3.5 million, or estates that have the potential to grow greater than $3.5 million, becomes more challenging. Also, though currently remote, we could see lower exemption amounts in the future. I will discuss additional ways to minimize and perhaps avoid federal gift and estate taxes later in this chapter.

> *Unlimited marital deduction:* The unlimited marital deduction leads to a deferral of federal gift and estate taxes and perhaps avoidance of the taxes entirely depending on the surviving spouse's spending and the federal estate tax exemption at the time of the surviving spouse's death. U.S. citizens (it is the citizenship of the beneficiary spouse, not the deceased spouse that is important) are entitled to inherit an unlimited amount of money from their deceased spouses, without paying any federal estate taxes. This applies to retirement plans, IRAs, and every other type of asset.

How You Can Save Millions without Spending a Nickel on Attorney Fees: The Importance of Annual Gifting

> *A lawyer is a learned gentleman who rescues your estate*
> *from your enemies and keeps it himself.*
> —Henry Peter Brougham

I had an uncle who planned to take his money with him. Why else wouldn't he make annual gifts to his deserving children and grandchildren? Why would he allow that money to be taxed at 50 percent and make his family wait until after he died to enjoy what was left?

I have a client who I have nagged for years to make annual gifts to his children and grandchildren. The last time I saw him I said now was a great time for a gift. He agreed and then said he was ready to receive any gifts his children wanted to give him.

Control is nice, staving off the fear of running out of money is important, but saving what could be millions of dollars in estate taxes for your children is also important. Of course you have to consider your own individual circumstances. If you are in a position where gifting is advisable, I offer a short description of the most basic types of gifts.

Different Types of Gifts

I like to focus on three important forms of gifts:

1. The classic $13,000 per year per beneficiary, usually children

2. Gifts of education

3. Gifts of second-to-die insurance

The most important estate planning tool for many people is simple gifting. Before you even look at all the more sophisticated gifting models, seriously consider plain old, nonsexy gifts of $13,000 per year per beneficiary.

James Narron, an excellent estate attorney I met at the Heckerling Institute, likes to say with a strong southern accent, "Keep your eye on the pine." He tells the story of when he was a little boy and his father was teaching him to drive a tractor. His father would tell him to "keep your eye on the pine." When he did, James would travel in a straight line toward the pine. When he looked around, he veered off course and lost his straight line. When he returned to keeping his eyes glued to that pine off in the distance, he would get back on course.

The most important estate planning tool for many people is simple gifting.

Most of my wealthy clients need to be told and then later reminded to "keep your eye on the pine." What is "keeping *your* eye on the pine"? It is making annual tax-free gifts of $13,000 per year per beneficiary. If you are married, that means both you and your spouse can give each of your children or grandchildren (or anyone you choose) a gift of $26,000 per year without incurring a gift tax or a reduction of your Lifetime Gifting Exclusion. It is simplest for the money to come from a joint account showing the gift came from both spouses.

Of course, one of the reasons this example is questionable is because we really have no way of predicting what estate taxes are going to be. This lack of predictability is a terrible problem for estate planners, and they have different methods of handling the problem.

MINI CASE STUDY 11.1
The Measurable Benefits of Simple Gifting

Tom and Judy, both 60 years old, have two children and four grandchildren. Even though they have grown their estate to $4 million, they are relatively frugal. They live comfortably on their pension and Social Security. They don't want Uncle Sam to get any of their hard-earned money at their deaths. At the very least, they want to drastically reduce the taxes their children will owe upon their death. Let's assume they reject all of the more sophisticated gifting techniques. They opt for simple gifts of $13,000 per year per beneficiary (with adjustments for inflation). They have six beneficiaries and each parent may give $13,000 per year per beneficiary. Thus they give away $156,000 (6 × $26,000 per donee) per year. Their plan is to continue making these gifts as long as they are comfortable with their own finances. They know that if they do nothing, they run the risk of growing too old and too rich to effectively use simple or even more complex gifting techniques.

The gifts continue for 25 years, in annual amounts increasing with 3 percent annual inflation. Over time the amount gifted comes to $5,532,000. Assuming a 45 percent estate tax rate, the savings to the family, not including appreciation, would be $2,489,400. That is really significantly less than the savings if we assume that the cash gifted will appreciate at an after-tax rate of 4 percent. If the cash appreciated at 4 percent, then the projected value of the gifts at life expectancy would be $8,671,416 for a total savings to the family of $3,902,137. If we assume a 6 percent after-tax rate, the savings are approximately $4,996,087. If we use an 8 percent after-tax rate, the savings are approximately $6,482,535.

Whether you will have a taxable estate for federal estate tax purposes will depend on the year of your death and the taxable balance of your estate. I do not like to assume there will be a tax, nor do I want to ignore the possibility that estates over $1 million may be taxed. I like to make wise choices that work out well for the family, whether there is an estate tax or not. On to another important type of gift.

The Gift of Education: A Favorite for Grandparents

Economists report that a college education adds many thousands of dollars to a man's lifetime income—which he then spends sending his son to college.

—Bill Vaughan

Most grandparents who can afford it (convincing them they can afford it is a different matter) like the idea of at least partially funding their grandchildren's college education.

Grandparents as well as parents can pay tuition (as well as medical expenses) directly for their children or grandchildren, and these payments do not count against the $13,000 per year exclusion. These direct payments for tuition as well as direct payment of medical expenses could almost be considered a fourth type of major gift.

Section 529 College Savings Plans are really a variation of a gift. Section 529 plan contributions, which presumably will be used by the beneficiary for college expenses, are unique in that when you die, the proceeds of the gift and the appreciation of the gift are outside your estate. But while you are alive you retain the power to take the money back if you like. Though I have never seen anyone take back a Section 529 plan contribution, the assurance that the donor has that option appeals to practically every grandparent.

Section 529 plans accomplish the following:

- Provide income tax-free growth

- Give you the freedom to change beneficiaries within the family, including first cousins

- Allow you to divert the fund from the beneficiary back to the contributor and use the proceeds for nonqualifying purposes (subject to a 10 percent penalty)

- Are excluded from the estate of the contributor

These four factors make the decision to invest in a Section 529 plan compelling, particularly for wealthy grandparents who want to provide for their grandchildren's education. Joe Hurly's web site, www.savingforcollege .com, is one of the best web sites, if not the best, for Section 529 plans.

Gifts of Life Insurance Premiums

Many planners recommend second-to-die life insurance to pay the estate tax at the second death. I agree that this is a great way to use second-to-die life insurance. What if the second death comes in a year when there is a high exemption amount or in a year when there is no federal estate tax? Second-to-die insurance is still usually a good deal and is an effective method of transferring assets to the next generation (or two generations). Therefore, if you can afford the premiums and are looking to pass money to the next generation, second-to-die insurance is worthwhile whether there is an estate tax or not. Of course, there are many types of insurance besides second-to-die that are worthwhile variations of a gift. I emphasize second-to-die insurance because it is the well-deserved classic. Please note, however, I would only recommend second-to-die life insurance if the underlying investment in the insurance policy seemed like a reasonable investment even if it is not used to pay estate taxes. Usually it is. Please refer to Chapter 12 for a more detailed discussion regarding second-to-die or survivorship life insurance.

Variations on Gifts

There are a number of sophisticated estate planning techniques that are really variations of making a gift. They include:

- Gifts beyond Annual Exclusion Gifts that consume the $1 million Lifetime Gifting Exclusion
- Family-limited partnerships
- Grantor-retained annuity trusts
- Grantor-retained unitrusts
- Intentionally defective grantor trusts
- Private annuities
- Qualified personal residence trusts
- Irrevocable trusts, including life insurance trusts
- Life insurance without trusts but owned by the heir, not the client
- Generation-skipping trusts

I leave discussions of most of these and other legitimate estate planning techniques for another day—or another book.

Gift Taxes

If your gifts exceed the $13,000 annual exclusion amount, the excess is subject to a graduated gift tax with rates ranging from 18 to 45 percent in 2009. To avoid owing gift tax, you may elect to deduct the excess of the gift over and above the $13,000 from your $1 million Lifetime Gifting Exclusion. For example, Daddy Donor chooses to give his son a gift of $63,000. Of that money $13,000 takes advantage of the annual exclusion. The $50,000 is subject to the gift tax. Daddy elects to have the $50,000 deducted from his $1 million Lifetime Gifting Exclusion rather than pay the gift tax. This leaves him with $950,000 that can be used for additional taxable gifts.

It is important to make this election by filing a gift tax return, Form 709. That tells the IRS that the gift consumed part of the $1 million Lifetime Gifting Exclusion. Please also note that filing the gift tax return starts the statute of limitations on the gift. This is particularly important in the event that the value of the gift could be open to interpretation, such as a gift of an interest in a family-limited partnership, a piece of land, a business, or any other asset that by its nature is difficult to value. It is conceivable and common among proactive wealthy clients and readers to use up part or all of their Lifetime Gifting Exclusion during their lifetime, depending on the nature of their lifetime gifts to nonspouse beneficiaries.

The best strategy for wealthy clients who could end up in a taxable estate situation is to take advantage of the annual $13,000 per year per beneficiary exclusion, assuming they can comfortably afford to make the gifts. If the annual gifts of $13,000 per year are not sufficient because there is still too much money in the estate, further gifts that consume a portion of the entire Lifetime Gifting Exclusion can still be a good idea. Though annual gifts above $13,000 will eat into the Lifetime Gifting Exclusion and reduce what may be inherited at death without tax, it also transfers out of the estate all the appreciation that would have been in the estate had the gift not been made.

MINI CASE STUDY 11.2
Gifts That Use the Total Applicable Exclusion Amount

Jill, a widow with a pension and Social Security that covers her needs, has $4 million and only one beneficiary, her daughter Lucky. Giving away $13,000 per year to the beneficiary is fine, but it hardly makes a dent in the potential estate tax at Jill's death. The $13,000 per year gifts will not be part of this example. Let's compare Jill giving Lucky $1 million in year one vs. making no gift. Also, assume Jill gets 7 percent on her investments and she lives 10 years.

To simplify the math, use the rule of 72s, which roughly holds that Jill's money will double in 10 years. Let's also assume a flat 50 percent estate tax. If Jill makes the $1 million gift and is left with $3 million, her estate will double to $6 million at her death. If the applicable exclusion is $3.5 million at that time, Lucky will have to pay estate tax on $3.5 million (total estate of $6 million plus $1 million [the amount of the Lifetime Gifting Exclusion used] minus $3.5 million [the Applicable Exclusion Amount at Jill's death]). Using the flat 50 percent estate tax rate, Lucky pays $1,750,000 in taxes. In the meantime, Lucky also earned 7 percent on her $1 million, which is worth $2 million at Jill's death.

Lucky will have $6 million less $1,750,000 estate taxes plus her $2 million = $6.25 million.

If Jill did not make the gift, her estate would have grown to $8 million. She would have a $3.5 million exclusion, so she would have to pay tax on $4.5 million, which would be $2.25 million in estate tax. Lucky would be left with $5.75 million. By using the applicable $1 million Lifetime Gifting Exclusion in the prior example, Jill managed to reduce Lucky's taxes by $500,000.

In the real world, Jill would probably be well advised to make a leveraged gift such as a grantor retained annuity trust (GRAT), a family limited partnership (FLP), a gift of life insurance, or one of the other gifting techniques. Lawrence Katzenstein, an excellent estate attorney with a head for figures and a heart for charity, presented a wonderful original analysis at the Heckerling Institute. He showed that in many cases under the previous law it was prudent to make a gift so large that it triggered gift taxes while the donor was still alive. The result of the gift and the gift tax paid was a reduction of the overall tax burden at death. The problem with the analysis today hinges on the uncertainty of future investments and, perhaps more importantly, future changes in the amount of the federal exemption. I would hate to see you pay gift tax now and then later, through changes in the law and/or in your portfolio, find out that you would not have been subject to estate taxes anyway.

Freezing the Lifetime Gifting Exclusion at $1 Million

Be aware that in 2004, the Lifetime Gifting Exclusion was frozen at $1 million, while the Applicable Exclusion Amount for estates rises to $3.5 million in 2009. The Lifetime Gifting Exclusion will remain at $1 million, as the Applicable Exclusion Amount for estates increases. This is different from previous years where the gift and estate tax exclusion amounts were the same. We now have lost the unified system where the gift and estate tax exclusions were the same; thus we can no longer properly refer to the unified credit shelter amount.

This is important for gifting strategies. Don't get caught thinking that because the Applicable Exclusion Amount will be $3.5 million that you can give away more than $1 million without paying a gift tax. In the prior example, had Jill given Lucky $2 million, that would have triggered an immediate gift tax on $1,000,000 ($2 million gift minus $1 million Lifetime Gifting Exclusion).

Be aware that in 2004, the Lifetime Gifting Exclusion was frozen at $1 million, while the Applicable Exclusion Amount for estates rises to $3.5 million in 2009.

Once your excess lifetime gifts are greater than $1 million, the amount over $1 million cannot be applied to the Applicable Exclusion Amount, but rather you must pay the gift tax. Thus, you can die with more than $1 million and not be subject to estate tax; but if you give away more than $1 million you will be subject to gift tax.

If taxable lifetime gifts exceed $1 million, the following gift tax rates apply:

	Rate	Years
Taxable gifts between $1 million and $1.25 million	41%	All except 2010
Taxable gifts between $1.25 million and $1.5 million	43%	All except 2010
Taxable gifts between $1.5 million and $2 million	45%	All except 2010
Taxable gifts over $2 million	45%	2008–2009, 2011, and on
For all taxable gifts over $1 million	35%*	2010

*Rate is based on highest individual income tax rate.

The Importance of Having After-Tax Dollars to Pay Taxes and Expenses

Inheritance taxes are so high that the happiest mourner at a rich man's funeral is usually Uncle Sam.

—Olin Miller

There is an entire world of literature just on gifting, both simple and sophisticated techniques. I include this brief summary because it is such an important area. It is also particularly important for large estates that are IRA heavy. If clients follow my advice and spend (or give away) their after-tax dollars before their IRA dollars, they will be left with IRA dollars at the end of their lives. Many readers have substantial IRAs and not much else. If you die with nothing but IRA dollars, and your heirs need money after you die for expenses, taxes, or even their own personal needs, they will have to go into the inherited IRA for the needed funds. When they go into the inherited IRA, the distribution triggers income tax. In addition to the immediate income tax on the withdrawal from the inherited IRA, beneficiaries lose the opportunity to stretch (defer taxes) on the inherited IRA over their life expectancy.

In the case where a beneficiary must make withdrawals from the inherited IRA to pay estate taxes, you end up in the horrendous situation where the withdrawal from the IRA to pay the estate taxes triggers an income tax, and the only source of paying the income tax that you have to pay because you withdraw money to pay the estate tax is further withdrawals of the IRA—withdrawals and taxes ad nauseam. This is a circular calculation that makes you want to weep. For clients who will be subject to estate taxes, it is particularly important that there be some after-tax dollars available to pay the estate taxes. Preferably, the money available to pay the estate taxes would be in the hands of the heir no later than when the estate taxes are due. That is, during the life of the IRA owner, he makes gifts (either simple, sophisticated, or through life insurance) so the beneficiary will have a stack of money to pay any estate tax. In the event the IRA owner dies in a situation where, because of the increased exemption equivalent amount, there is no tax, there is nothing lost; in the case of second-to-die life insurance, it can be an excellent investment for the family with or without the estate tax.

> For clients who will be subject to estate taxes, it is particularly important that there be some after-tax dollars available to pay the estate taxes.

MINI CASE STUDY 11.3
Using Life Insurance to Pay Estate Taxes

Joe and Carol, both 70 and in good health, have an estate of $2 million consisting mainly of Joe's IRA. In addition to their portfolio, they have a pension and Social Security income. Depending on a number of factors, there is a reasonable chance that their family will never pay estate taxes when Joe and Carol die. On the other hand, they might.

They are interested in passing on a significant amount of money to their heirs. They examine the benefits of a second-to-die life insurance policy. They decide they can safely afford the premiums for $500,000 worth of coverage. They know that one of the benefits of the coverage is that upon the second death, their beneficiaries will receive $500,000 free of income and estate taxes. If they have a taxable estate, that $500,000 could go to pay the taxes and expenses, and the beneficiaries would be able to preserve the stretch IRA. This is a classic and effective planning strategy.

Suppose that at the second death, the amount of the survivor's estate is less than the Applicable Exclusion Amount so that the only costs will be the expenses of administering the estate and the state inheritance tax. The $500,000 purchase of the second-to-die policy will still have been a good decision because, assuming a good and appropriate choice of policy, it is a good way of passing on wealth even in the absence of the estate tax.

Gifting, particularly with large estates that are "IRA heavy," is particularly important, and individuals who are extremely interested in passing on wealth to the next one or two generations are encouraged to examine the numbers in the second-to-die analysis before rejecting the idea out of hand.

Why Should I Care about the Applicable Exclusion Amount if I Have Less Than $7 Million in My Estate?

You may be asking yourself why you need to be concerned about the Applicable Exclusion Amount if your and your spouse's assets are worth more than $3.5 million but less than $7 million in 2009. "Didn't you just tell me that each spouse could shelter $3.5 million in 2009 from the federal gift and estate tax?" Yes, each spouse can shelter $3.5 million in 2009 from the federal gift and estate tax. However, planning must be done to ensure the proper ownership of assets, and the proper wills and trusts must be in place to maximize the use of the Applicable Exclusion Amount for each spouse.

For example, suppose that husband and wife jointly own assets worth $4 million. If the husband dies in 2008, there will be no taxes due at his death because all of the joint assets passing to the surviving spouse will qualify for the unlimited marital deduction, provided that she is a U.S. citizen.

If the surviving spouse accepts all of the assets, she will have $4 million in her name, which is more than the current applicable exemption amount of $3.5 million. (For this example, I am assuming that she only spends the growth and earnings on her assets and that the amount of her assets remains level during her lifetime.) If the surviving spouse dies later in 2009 when the Applicable Exclusion Amount is $3.5 million, her estate will be subject to federal estate tax.

In situations where there is a possibility of an estate tax and the husband and wife have roughly equal life expectancies, I recommend, to the extent possible, that the husband and wife divide their assets equally or as close to equally as possible by transferring some of the joint assets to the spouse who has less money in his or her name. You might also consider simply splitting joint assets so that each spouse gets a portion. That way, each spouse can pass on the maximum amount possible, free of federal estate tax, by properly using their Applicable Exclusion Amount. Of course, the advice might change if there is a significant difference in life expectancy or amount of assets in one spouse's retirement plan.

I have seen far too many situations where assets were not equalized and the family was unable to capitalize on both spouses taking advantage of his and her own Applicable Exclusion Amount. Proper titling of assets prior to the first spouse's death enables the surviving spouse to have the maximum amount of possible options to reduce the total amount of transfer taxes ultimately due from both estates.

The Dreaded Double Tax on IRA Assets at Death

Although we attempt to provide you with the tools to avoid this problem, heirs of IRA owners with significant estates often face the dreaded combination of estate taxes and income taxes at the IRA owner's death. The combination of income taxes and estate taxes can be more than 50 percent of the estate. If you leave more than $3.5 million to a grandchild (a "skip" person), the grandchild may face a triple tax of income taxes, estate taxes, and generation-skipping taxes. The combined taxes could be as high as 70 percent or more of the estate.

If the IRA owner provides funds other than the IRA to pay the estate tax, the income tax on the inherited IRA, if everything else is done right, may be deferred over the life of the beneficiaries, which are usually children and/or grandchildren. If the only money available to pay the estate tax is the IRA itself, withdrawals from the IRA to pay the estate tax will trigger income taxes. Then the income taxes must be paid from distributions from the IRA, and this cycle continues, depleting the IRA very rapidly.

Some financial advisors have "pension rescue" programs. Under the right circumstances, these programs are a good idea. They are variants of

what is recommended in the gifting section. The pension rescue involves taking a portion of your IRA, paying tax on the IRA distribution while you are still alive, and giving the proceeds to your beneficiaries. This serves to reduce your estate and to provide your beneficiaries with after-tax dollars to pay any estate taxes. This strategy is often combined with the purchase of life insurance (often a second-to-die policy) where the proceeds from the IRA distributions are given as gifts to children (usually through a trust) to purchase life insurance on the parents. When the policy matures (or, in other words, when both parents die), the insurance proceeds are distributed to the children who can then use the proceeds to pay any estate taxes or other expenses.

Conceptually, pension rescue is similar to a Roth IRA conversion. In both cases the IRA owner is paying taxes *sooner* to move money into an environment, either the Roth IRA or the insurance policy, where it will grow income tax-free. The advantage of the Roth IRA conversion is that it will benefit the IRA owner as well as his heirs. The benefit of the pension rescue is that unlike a Roth IRA, the proceeds of the policy, if set up correctly, will be outside the estate.

Income in Respect of a Decedent

There is an important concept that your heirs should know about if they do end up paying estate taxes on an IRA or other type of retirement plan. The concept is called *income in respect of a decedent* (IRD).

Though the double taxation is draconian, the alert IRA beneficiary (or advisor of the beneficiary) can take advantage of the IRD concept that many attorneys or tax preparers don't know about. IRD is a special deduction the IRA beneficiary is entitled to with every taxable distribution he receives from the inherited IRA. The deduction is taken as a miscellaneous itemized deduction and is not subject to the 2 percent of AGI limitation.

Let's look at this with a simple example. Bill dies in 2009 leaving an estate of $4 million—$3 million in after-tax money and $1 million in an IRA—to his son. His son must pay $225,000 in estate taxes.

Eventually his son will have to pay income taxes on the $1 million inherited IRA and its growth when he takes distributions. However, the IRD deduction allows for an income tax deduction calculated as follows. Since there wouldn't have been any federal estate tax if there hadn't been any IRA (just $3 million of after-tax money), the $225,000 of estate taxes paid can be attributed entirely to the inherited IRA. The $225,000 divided by the value of the IRA in the estate of $1 million is 22.5 percent. This means that for every dollar that the IRA beneficiary withdraws from the inherited IRA and must report as income, he can deduct 22.5 cents as an itemized deduction until his cumulative deductions claimed over the years equals $225,000. Though it is still exceedingly painful to pay the double taxes, the IRD takes out some of the bite.

Simultaneous Death

The odds of a simultaneous death, or even two deaths within 60 or 90 days of each other, are very small. But nonetheless the concern remains. In most cases, traditional couples share the same beneficiaries. If they both die, most of their money and assets would go to their offspring. So, if they have the same beneficiaries, their wills or trusts will direct the money where they want it to go. The point of the simultaneous death provision clause in your wills and trusts, even assuming the money and property will go to the children or grandchildren, is to address the critical issue of how to minimize the total estate taxes for both combined estates.

We believe the best way to handle the simultaneous death possibility is to carefully analyze the ownership of the couple's assets and then incorporate the desired survivorship presumptions into the wills, trusts, and the beneficiary designation of the IRA and retirement plan so that taxes are minimized. Lange's Cascading Beneficiary Plan or a similar arrangement that involves a series of disclaimers built into the documents will generally minimize the tax impact of a simultaneous death and, more importantly, provide the most flexibility for passing money to beneficiaries and minimizing taxes in more common situations.

The Exemption Equivalent Amount Trust (The B Trust, the Unified Credit Trust, or the Applicable Exclusion Amount)

One method of minimizing federal estate taxes has been to draft a trust whereupon the first spouse's death, one Applicable Exclusion Amount ($3.5 million in 2009) is moved into the trust and the estate is protected from estate taxes on that amount. This traditional estate plan uses two separate trusts: the A trust (Marital Trust) and the B trust (Unified Credit Trust). The surviving spouse has the right to use any and all income and principal from the A trust. Typically the spouse's access to the B trust is limited; he or she receives the income from the trust, but can only invade the principal for health, education, maintenance, and support. Sometimes there is a "5 and 5" clause, meaning the surviving spouse could also invade the principal of the trust for the greater of $5,000 or 5 percent of the corpus or principal of the trust. If, when the second spouse dies, his or her total assets, in combination with the A trust, equals more than the Applicable Exclusion Amount, the money will be subject to federal estate taxes. On the other hand, because the B trust was not owned by the surviving spouse, the B trust is not considered part of the second spouse's federal estate and is therefore not subject to estate tax at his or her death.

The B trust is typically funded with an amount up to, but not greater than, the Applicable Exclusion Amount. Typically, these trusts are drafted without specifying an amount. Instead there is a funding formula. Basically, the standard old-fashioned formula says that whatever the Applicable Exclusion Amount is in the year of death, that amount should go into the trust for the surviving spouse.

If you have one of these estate plans, you could inadvertently and unnecessarily be underproviding for your surviving spouse by transferring too much money to the B trust. In fact, the full use of this B trust may be downright stupid. In the above example, with a total estate of $4 million, if we had traditional documents using the B trust, only $500,000 would go to the surviving spouse since $3.5 million would be required to fund the B trust. Worse yet, what if the estate is smaller and all assets are in the name of the first to die? The surviving spouse might get nothing except an interest in the trust. Under the previous tax laws, an estate attorney may have drafted this type of trust to save estate taxes at the second death.

Now, however, with portfolios down and the Applicable Exclusion Amounts up, your surviving spouse's estate may not be subject to federal estate tax. Do you think he or she would want all the money in the estate going to a trust? These traditional plans pose harm to the comfort and/or convenience of the surviving spouse, and many people don't even realize what their estate planning documents invoke. That is a tragedy. It would be wise to take a look at your own plan after finishing this book.

> Wow! This can be a confusing chapter . . . but it is very important to complete your estate planning. Take your time and read this chapter twice if you need to. Although it is not pleasant to think about your passing on, it's important to anticipate the needs of your heirs. After all . . . none of us gets out alive. You want to be sure your family will continue to be taken care of after you are gone.

The Nastiest Trap of All

What follows is an analysis of how bad it can be if you have fairly standard wills and trusts. The quick analysis: It is nasty. The quick conclusion for clients with traditional documents and less than $3.5 million: It is time to review the will and trust.

If your will and/or trust uses a formula indicating the maximum marital deduction that has confusing language such as "the spouse shall receive an amount equal to the maximum marital deduction amount available after taking into account the applicable credit amount," chances are that, under current law, the document requires the dreaded mandatory funding of the B (exemption equivalent) trust, whether or not funding it is a good idea. Many wills and trusts contain this language, but with lower portfolios and higher exemption amounts you must take action and change your wills, trusts, beneficiary designations, or IRAs, etc. Don't let your inertia compromise your spouse's comfort.

The Details of the Nasty Provisions

Let's assume the will or revocable trust or beneficiary designation of the IRA or retirement plan creates a trust (B trust, Unified Credit Amount

Nastiest trap of all

Trust) as described above. Upon the death of the first spouse, the Applicable Exclusion Amount is automatically paid into this trust. Though this isn't mechanically accurate for the purpose of the IRAs or retirement plans, it is conceptually accurate. The trust will pay income to the surviving spouse for his or her life and provide the right to additional money for the health, maintenance, and support of the spouse. The trust may even allow the spouse to invade the principal for $5,000 or 5 percent of the trust, whichever is greater, and may have additional provisions allowing invasion of principal for children or grandchildren, if needed. At the death of the surviving spouse, the trust is usually distributed to the children equally.

Under the old law, this type of trust helped save on estate taxes, but unfortunately, under the new law, it creates a trap. Most of these trusts are structured so that:

1. The Applicable Exclusion Amount (it was $1 million in 2003, and now is $3.5 million in 2009) is distributed to the trust.

2. The balance of the estate (if any) is distributed to the surviving spouse.

The complication is that, as the Applicable Exclusion Amount increases, fewer and fewer second estates will be large enough to be subject to federal estate taxes. Thus, if the first spouse leaves everything to the second spouse, at the death of the second spouse the combined estates may still be under the threshold of the amount subject to federal estate tax. The raised exemption amounts mean fewer estates will be subject to estate tax, which means fewer estates will benefit from this trust. The spouse or family may not benefit from this trust, but the trust may be activated anyway.

> **... as the Applicable Exclusion Amount increases, fewer and fewer second estates will be large enough to be subject to federal estate taxes.**

Presuming an individual has the type of documents that will force an amount equivalent to (or less than) the Applicable Exclusion Amount into the B trust, this may mean that existing documents will put most—if not all—of the first spouse's assets into the trust at the expense of the surviving spouse. Even though funding the trust was critical when saving estate taxes was the issue, depending on the size of the estate and year of death, that logic may no longer apply, given today's higher federal Applicable Exclusion Amounts. An individual's current documents may ensure that a huge amount of money goes into the B trust and that only a small amount, or maybe no amount, will be left directly to the surviving spouse.

Unintentionally Disinheriting the Surviving Spouse

Consider an estate consisting of Husband's $1.3 million IRA with the exemption-equivalent-type trust as the primary beneficiary. If he dies in 2009 all the money would go into the trust (because the Applicable Exclusion Amount is $3.5 million in 2009). If that is the couple's main asset, we have just created a financial catastrophe.

Many surviving spouses will be unhappy to find that as a result of the increased exemption amounts, more money is going to a trust for their benefit and less money is going directly to them. There is a strong chance the surviving spouse would prefer to have the money directly rather than in trust, particularly where there is no tax-savings benefit of the trust. In this instance a simple "I love you" will or beneficiary designation of the IRA or retirement plan would have been sufficient to avoid estate taxes at the second death.

"I love you" wills are quite common and serve an important purpose. The will says, "I leave everything to my spouse, and my spouse leaves everything to me." At the second death the money is divided equally among the children.

In this example, having a simple "I love you" will would have been sufficient to avoid estate tax. At the first death, the surviving spouse would have received the $1.3 million and used the unlimited marital deduction to avoid estate taxes. At the second death, the surviving spouse's total estate would have been less than the exemption equivalent amount. Thus, there would be no estate tax and no messing around with an unnecessary trust. Not only was the entire complicated estate plan misguided and unnecessary, it also poses serious problems for the surviving spouse and the rest of the family.

Though it is not overly costly to draft these trusts, living with them after the death of the first spouse until the second death is far more costly in terms of fees (at a minimum you have to prepare a special annual trust tax return), aggravation, and restrictions on the surviving spouse. Most surviving spouses want control of all the assets of the marriage and don't want to deal with a trustee to get access to their assets. Although loss of control is less of an issue when the surviving spouse or family member is the trustee of the B trust, the trust can still be an unnecessary expense depending on the surviving spouse's circumstances at the time of the first spouse's death. With the rapidly changing estate tax exemption amounts, the vagaries of the stock market, and the big unknowns such as "When will you die?" and "How much money will be in your estate?," you could incur burdensome and unnecessary expenses *and* lose control of your money. Worse yet, there is no benefit at all from the estate plan for that couple. Individuals who have plans similar to the one referenced above are advised to consider the benefits of revising their estate plans.

While there are advantages and disadvantages to the B trust, a good solution to the problem is provided in Chapter 15.

What If Retirement Assets Will Fund the Trust? Yuck!

What if the assets that fund the trust are retirement assets (IRAs, 401[k]s, 403[b]s, etc.)? Then, after the IRA owner dies, the minimum required distribution from the trust is based on the life expectancy of the surviving spouse. At the death of the surviving spouse, the children are required to maintain distributions at the rate established when the surviving spouse was alive. The result is an enormous acceleration of distributions from the retirement plan. This produces taxable income for the family and an increase in taxes, and the family is deprived of the enormous potential they could have had from a stretch IRA, which I cover in Chapter 13.

A Key Lesson from This Chapter

Don't get caught with an estate plan that automatically transfers the Applicable Exclusion Amount into a B trust. Sometimes that type of plan is just bad, other times disastrous, although admittedly in some circumstances it may be okay.

12

The Most Certain and for Many the Best Way to Provide Financial Security for Your Children: Survivorship Life Insurance

*Money frees you from doing things you dislike. Since I dislike
doing nearly everything, money is handy.*
—Groucho Marx

*Money is one of the most important subjects of your entire life. Some of life's
greatest enjoyments and most of life's greatest disappointments stem from your
decisions about money. Whether you experience great peace of mind or constant
anxiety will depend on getting your finances under control.*
—Robert G. Allen

Main Topics

- What is survivorship life insurance?
- Who should consider the purchase of survivorship life insurance?
- Advantages of purchasing a survivorship life insurance policy

- Disadvantages of survivorship insurance
- Breakeven analysis using second-to-die insurance
- Which funds should be used to pay the insurance premiums?

KEY IDEA

Survivorship life insurance can be an excellent
strategy for transferring wealth to your heirs as well
as paying for taxes and expenses.

In Mini Case Study 11.3, we discussed in general terms how survivorship life insurance (also known as second-to-die life insurance) can benefit the family when the estate is IRA heavy. The insurance proceeds (the death benefit) are paid after the death of both the husband and the wife, or in insurance parlance, "when the policy matures." The death benefit, usually paid to a trust for the benefit of the children or to the children directly, can provide a liquidity that can be used to pay taxes and expenses without a fire sale, and to avoid the dreaded double taxation: transfer taxes on the estate and income taxes on the IRA withdrawals. The remaining proceeds, that is, what is left after paying taxes and expenses, will typically be used for the children's benefit. The classic advice for readers with an estate that is heavy with IRA and retirement plans is to purchase survivorship insurance. Estates with large IRAs and survivorship insurance are both good things, in and of themselves, but

> **The classic advice for readers with an estate that is heavy with IRA and retirement plans is to purchase survivorship insurance.**

a combination of the two often provides the best estate plan available. However, purchasing survivorship life insurance can also be a useful wealth-creating, wealth-preserving, and wealth-transferring technique even for estates that are not IRA heavy and that may never be subject to estate tax and high expenses.

Understanding the Basics of Gifting with Survivorship Life Insurance

Before we get into the nitty-gritty of analyzing survivorship life insurance, I thought I would report a recent conversation with Ed Slott, CPA, who wrote the Introduction for this book. Ed said that with all the financial uncertainty in our markets that life insurance was a certainty and a great investment and great way to pass wealth. Ed thinks that the reinsurance requirements, the regulations regarding the requirement for the life insurance company to maintain enough capital and surplus to satisfy their obligation along with other controls will protect beneficiaries. Even the life insurance side of AIG, a large life insurance company that was part of the bailout, the life insurance beneficiaries were never in jeopardy and there were provisions to pay claims. This is consistent with everything I have read since the AIG bailout. To date, there has never been a default for any beneficiary on any American life insurance policy.

1. Typically, second-to-die life insurance is a type of gift or transfer. You and your spouse pay for the premiums for the policy which is viewed as a gift under IRS rules. (Technically, to keep the proceeds out of your and your spouse's estate, you make a gift to a trust or your children and the trust or your children pay the premium.) Assuming it is done right, your children will get the death benefits income and estate tax-free. The purchase of second-to-die life insurance should be looked at as a technique to transfer wealth for the long-term benefit of your children in the most tax-efficient method possible.

2. It is only one type of gift and should not be the only type of gift for your family. In most cases, I usually like a three-pronged gifting strategy.

    *   Gifts of cash or securities for whatever purposes your children want (gifts for short-term use)

    *   Section 529 plans or the gift of education for your grandchildren

    *   Survivorship life insurance

3. The policies that we prefer are typically structured so that you pay a low fixed-rate guaranteed premium, usually paid annually, that includes a high death benefit when the policy matures, that is, after the death of both the husband and the wife. These policies have lower premiums because the insurance companies are calculating the mortality risks with two lives instead of one life. These types of policies generally don't have great cash surrender values because the costs of premiums are so low that typically there isn't a lot of equity in the policy—it is not designed to accumulate cash value. It is designed to have a low premium and a high death

benefit. Personally, I like the combination of a small premium and a large guaranteed death benefit for most, but not all, situations.

> **Survivorship life insurance is essentially a leveraged and tax-advantaged gift or transfer technique. If your overriding goal is to preserve all of your financial resources for your and your spouse's benefit and providing for your children after your death is not an important goal, then survivorship insurance is not appropriate.**

4. Survivorship life insurance is essentially a leveraged and tax-advantaged gift or transfer technique. If your overriding goal is to preserve all of your financial resources for your and your spouse's benefit and providing for your children after your death is not an important goal, then survivorship insurance is not appropriate.

Problems Facing Retirees That Can Be Solved Using a Survivorship Insurance Policy

What follows is a list of problems that suggest survivorship insurance as the solution:

1. You have more money than you are likely to need during your lifetime for you and your spouse, and you want to be able to transfer the money in the most tax-efficient manner.

2. You want to spend your money freely, but at the same time, you want to be sure you leave an inheritance for your children. Without life insurance, many of our clients feel like they may be spending their children's inheritance. Survivorship policies guaranteeing a death benefit for your children can give you the peace of mind to spend all the money you have freely, while knowing that your children will be provided for with the insurance.

3. Your assets are either not liquid by nature (real estate or closely held stock) or invested in equities that could decline in value, and you don't want your family to lose money in a fire sale to pay the taxes and expenses of your estate, which are generally due nine months after death.

4. On a related note, survivorship life insurance can also facilitate equalizing distributions among family members when one beneficiary is going to inherit the family business and cash is needed to make the other beneficiaries' shares equal.

5. Similarly, you may have a family-owned business or family real estate such as a vacation home that you would like to keep in the

family. After you are gone, there may be a continued need for cash investments to keep them from being liquidated. Survivorship policies can provide the needed liquidity to maintain the property in the family for many years. We had a client who had a beautiful second home on a lake that he wanted to keep in the family but didn't know where the money would come from to maintain the property. The solution was a second-to-die life insurance policy.

6.   Most of your assets are in retirement accounts. At death, cash will be needed to pay federal and state death taxes and the estate administration costs. Using retirement funds for that purpose will accelerate income and kill the stretch IRA. Survivorship insurance can help preserve the stretch IRA for the surviving family members.

7.   Life insurance is a useful asset to have as part of the estate plan if you have a disabled beneficiary. With life insurance, only the interest and dividends earned on the life insurance proceeds are taxable income to the beneficiary or the trust for the benefit of the beneficiary where distributions from retirement benefits (other than Roth IRAs) are 100 percent taxable. Because of high income tax rates for trusts, retaining taxable retirement benefits in a trust is generally undesirable for beneficiaries who generally pay taxes at a lower rate than the trust. However, a greater consideration for a disabled beneficiary is that a distribution from the trust may cause him or her to lose public assistance benefits. That means that the trustee of the trust for the disabled beneficiary is stuck with paying income taxes at very high rates on the retirement distribution to the disabled beneficiary's trust. By having life insurance as part of the plan the family can minimize taxes for the disabled beneficiary while providing the best income tax deferral possibilities from the retirement benefits to the other beneficiaries.

The Advantages of Survivorship Life Insurance

There are some tremendous advantages to survivorship life insurance, and it can provide a great deal of financial security for the family. Structured properly, it has a number of benefits that make it an excellent wealth transfer strategy.

There are some tremendous advantages to survivorship life insurance, and it can provide a great deal of financial security for the family. Structured properly, it has a number of benefits that make it an excellent wealth transfer strategy.

- The proceeds from the insurance are free from income taxes and, assuming it is properly set up outside of the estate, which is easy to do, it is free of state and federal estate, inheritance, or transfer taxes. Because of these tremendous tax-free features, some would say loopholes, survivorship life insurance is one of the best tax shelters around.

- The premiums for the types of policies we prefer are low relative to the face amount or death benefit (the annual premium *must* be paid every year until the death of the second spouse). The end result with this type of policy is that a portion of the total estate is guaranteed as a benefit for the survivors, creating a tax-free return for the family from the premiums invested in the policy.

- These policies are typically less costly in terms of annual premiums than single-life policies.

- The proceeds from the insurance can be used to pay estate taxes and other expenses when necessary. It provides a great source of liquidity for beneficiaries so they can keep the inherited IRA growing tax-deferred and the Roth IRA growing tax-free.

- When you analyze second-to-die insurance from a mathematical breakeven model, that is, how long you or your spouse must live before survivorship insurance death benefits equal the premiums invested plus growth, it is usually much longer than a normal life expectancy.

Those facts might cause a cynic to ask, "If the premiums are so low and it seems so advantageous for the family, how does the insurance company make any money?"

First there are tremendous tax benefits with the premium funds in the hands of the insurance company. The company does not pay income tax on the investment income on large reserves of premiums collected. If, instead of paying insurance premiums, you just invested the money yourself or if you made gifts to your children and your children invested the money, there would be income tax on dividends, interest, and capital gains.

Furthermore, there is something else that is going on in the pricing of second-to-die life insurance that heavily favors the consumer. As with all types of insurance, many policies lapse or lose their guarantee when people stop paying premiums. When the owner of a policy stops paying the premium, the insurance company is no longer obligated to honor the guarantee they have in the contract and the value of the contract to the owner could go down considerably. The insurance companies know that a large percentage of their sold policies will lapse or lose their guarantee, so they take that into consideration when determining the price of the premium. This allows the rates others pay for insurance to be lower.

But why would so many people let a second-to-die insurance policy lapse? Here's my theory. The math on the second-to-die policy usually seems extremely favorable and attractive to the more quantitative money person of the husband and wife team. Though that is changing, at least for now that is frequently the husband. The wife often would prefer her children get the money as gifts now instead of using it to pay premiums. (Our preference is that parents diversify their types of gifts to their children so the children will get some money now, even if they do opt for the insurance.) The wife grudgingly goes along with the decision to purchase the second-to-die insurance. As statistics would have it, the husband usually dies first and the surviving spouse, who never liked the idea of the insurance, then stops paying premiums. The insurance company becomes the big winner.

If you decide to go with the second-to-die insurance, please be prepared to pay premiums for the rest of both of your lives. If not, don't buy this type of insurance policy. The tendency for many buyers not to pay premiums to the end allows the insurance companies to offer policies at a great price for those of us who, once we start, will never let the policy lapse.

Alternatives to Letting a Survivorship Policy Lapse

Generally I don't recommend a survivorship policy unless I am confident the premiums will continue to be paid until the death of the second spouse. But occasionally, for whatever reason, someone doesn't want to continue paying the premium. However, if you purchase the kind of survivorship policy I recommend, there is little cash surrender value, so cashing them in to the issuing insurance company is not a great idea.

However, before letting the policy lapse, consider your original motivation for purchasing the policy, which was to benefit your children or heirs, and ask them if they want to continue paying the premiums themselves. If neither the parents nor the children have the money for the premiums, you should consider borrowing the money to pay the premium.

If these kinds of solutions are not workable, the reality is there is a relatively new trend in the insurance industry. You can potentially sell the policy to another underwriting company for much more than its minimal guaranteed cash surrender value. In most instances where this option is considered, many years will have passed before the sale of the policy would be necessary. Consider that as you have aged, it is likely that you will have developed health problems and perhaps you are a widow or widower. What would an insurance policy cost you now? Probably a lot more. But you have a policy with guaranteed low payments, no matter how poor your health is and how old you are. The underwriters know these facts and are willing to pay you a hefty sum, perhaps a large percentage of the death benefit, when you are older and more frail. The insurance company or investor buying the policy will collect the death benefit, but you get the cash now. The resale of these policies and other types of life insurance policies can offer you a way out of having to make the payments. However, this new market of reselling life insurance policies is likely to reduce the rate of lapsed policies which may lead to higher premiums for second-to-die life insurance in the future.

Disadvantages of Second-to-Die Insurance

When deciding whether it is appropriate to purchase a second-to-die policy, you have to consider the disadvantages of the second-to-die policy.

- First, let's go back to the basics. The second-to-die insurance is still a variation of a gift and if you don't want to or can't afford to make the gift, then second-to-die insurance is not for you or your family.

- Another problem with second-to-die insurance is that the heirs, usually your children, are likely to have better uses for money while they are young and you are still alive. Therefore, if you can afford a gift, the strategy of just making simple gifts to your children so they can spend and enjoy it while they are young has a natural appeal.

- Furthermore, if later in your lives, you can't afford to continue these gifts, you could potentially regret buying the insurance. This problem is partly tempered by the fact that if that happens, your children will probably want to continue the premium payments themselves, but then that is not a gift.

- Another disadvantage of this type of insurance is that both spouses must be committed to paying premiums all their lives.

- Another disadvantage is that the payment of the premium is still considered a gift. If you are purchasing a large policy, the premium for the policy might exceed the allowable gifting limit. This potentially could cause you to eat into your once-in-a-lifetime gifting exclusion. That's not a big problem, when you think about it. Or you could get a split dollar policy, which though it adds a layer of complexity, is a great idea for many wealthy taxpayers who need to preserve their gift tax exclusion.

Lower Risks of Investments with Survivorship Life Insurance

The return from a second-to-die policy is guaranteed. If you want to add safety to your estate, the second-to-die insurance will almost always have a better return than the vast majority of fixed-income instruments.

> The return from a second-to-die policy is guaranteed. If you want to add safety to your estate, the second-to-die insurance will almost always have a better return than the vast majority of fixed-income instruments.

Advantages of Survivorship Insurance if Estate or Inheritance Taxes Are Due

Whereas federal estate and state inheritance taxes are often avoided at the death of the first spouse, there could be a need to pay federal estate or state inheritance taxes at the death of the second spouse. A survivorship policy can provide the needed funds. This can be especially providential if the bulk of the remaining estate is in an IRA or other pretax investments. If federal estate or state inheritance taxes are due on the second estate, there are the multiple prongs of federal and state income tax and federal estate and state inheritance taxes, which could cause the marginal tax rate on the retirement funds in the estate to rise above 50 percent:

Potential income taxes on retirement funds	35.0%
Federal estate taxes	45.0%
State inheritance taxes (Pennsylvania, for example)	4.5%
Potential marginal tax rate	84.5%

Admittedly, there are tax-savings strategies to reduce this potentially high marginal rate. One such strategy is using the income in respect of a decedent deduction as more fully discussed in Chapter 11. Many taxpayers don't know that it is an income tax deduction specifically designed to reduce the double tax hit of federal estate and income tax on the same money. However, this deduction doesn't even come close to making up for the double estate and income tax hit that the heirs of the IRA owner will face.

(It should be noted that income taxes could be more in states that tax retirement fund withdrawals. State inheritance taxes could be more or less, depending on the residency of the IRA owner at death and whether the state has decoupled from the federal estate tax. Based on the current housing crisis that has reduced state property tax receipts and declining state tax collections from the repeal of the federal estate tax credit, it is conceivable that state inheritance or estate taxes will increase in the future.)

The solution that goes the farthest to avoid the double tax hit of federal estate tax and income tax is a second-to-die or survivorship life insurance policy. This is the classic solution for estates that will be subject to estate taxes and are IRA heavy. As a consequence, it is a common strategy for advisors to recommend taking withdrawals from the IRA, paying income tax now on the withdrawals, and using the net proceeds to purchase second-to-die life insurance. Conceptually, this is quite similar to making a Roth IRA conversion where you pay the income tax up front to get income tax-free growth in the future. In a way, the second-to-die insurance is better because if set up correctly, it is outside the IRA owner's estate, unlike a Roth IRA which is included in the Roth IRA owner's estate. In our practice, the Roth IRA conversion and second-to-die life insurance are not competing strategies, but complementary strategies.

In our practice, the Roth IRA conversion and second-to-die life insurance are not competing strategies, but complementary strategies.

The strategy of taking IRA dollars, paying taxes now, and using the proceeds to purchase second-to-die life insurance (with some variations) is commonly known as *pension rescue*. This strategy was previously described in the Chapter 11 discussion of the Dreaded Double Tax on IRA Assets at Death. While I agree there are many circumstances where pension rescue is appropriate, let's take a look at the best funds for paying the premiums on a second-to-die policy if we have a choice.

The Best Funds for Paying the Insurance Premiums

This is another area where we don't go with the flow of most advisors. Generally speaking, we recommend that you pay all your expenses, including premiums on second-to-die life insurance policies, from your after-tax money before using your IRA or retirement plan money. This strategy supports one of the basic principles we encourage everyone to adhere to: Pay taxes later. Does that sound familiar?

Some clients are able to generate the after-tax funds to pay the insurance premium by converting a CD or variable and fixed annuity into a joint immediate annuity that will make annual distributions over your and your spouse's lifetimes to cover the premiums to pay the returns. People do not feel like they are paying for the premium (even though they are) because they just use the annuity check to pay the premium. In addition, they know that the rate of return is better than what they were earning on their CD. Please see Chapter 8 regarding immediate annuities.

For those clients who do have a lot of after-tax funds, the pension rescue ignores the principle of pay taxes later. Yes, the numbers work using classic pension rescue. They work because the numbers on the second-to-die policy work. In most cases, however, I prefer using after-tax dollars to pay the insurance premiums before IRA or retirement plan dollars because the numbers work even better. However, as I have remarked before, it is quite common these days, especially among my clients, to see retirees with nearly all their wealth in their retirement plans and IRAs, plus their equity in their homes, but with very little extra after-tax money available. For people in this category, taking money from their IRA, paying taxes, and using the proceeds to pay for the second-to-die insurance probably makes the most sense. But if you have the after-tax funds available, use those first.

Some taxpayers who are younger than 70 might think, "When I am required to take minimum required distributions, there will be sufficient after-tax dollars to pay for second-to-die insurance, So I will wait." But waiting until age 70½ to buy the life insurance is frequently not a good idea. Simply by waiting, the annual cost of the policy goes up substantially. More importantly, if you are in good health and insurable now, it is risky to assume you and your spouse will enjoy equally good health later. Many health issues can arise between now and age 70½, which might mean that an individual's insurance rating goes from preferred to a more qualified rating with much higher premiums or, even worse, the individual can become uninsurable and lose the ability to get life insurance benefits altogether.

The best alternative for many IRA owners who have few after-tax funds and want to buy second-to-die insurance is to start distributions from the IRA now and use the funds to pay for life insurance. Although this goes against the general theme of "Pay taxes later," because we are accelerating income instead of waiting until age 70½ to take IRS minimum required distributions, in many situations the loss of tax deferral on the premium amounts is not significant in comparison to the great benefits and the financial security the life insurance provides.

For the fortunate people with sufficient after-tax accumulations to pay the premium, we recommend using those monies to pay the premiums because it preserves money in the tax-deferred environment.

Now we get into the nitty-gritty and we run the numbers to analyze a survivorship policy. We start with a case study where purchasing survivorship insurance is clearly recommended, almost a no-brainer, and proceed to situations where it is not as obvious, but still quite advantageous.

MINI CASE STUDY 12.1
Quantifying the Advantages of Purchasing a Survivorship Life Insurance Policy

Consider the case of Robert and Mary Jones. Robert has just retired at age 65. Mary is 64. Robert rolled his 401(k) plan accumulations into an IRA to provide him with more investment flexibility. Robert and Mary have spent their working lives making a comfortable living for their family and funding Robert's 401(k) with the maximum allowable contributions. Robert and Mary have saved additional money outside his retirement plans. Their lifetime of diligent savings has resulted in total accumulations of $2,500,000 in Robert's IRA upon retirement and $500,000 in after-tax money and investments. They receive Social Security income of $26,000 and $20,000, respectively, and Mary has a teacher's pension income of $50,000 per year. They spend $150,000 per year after income taxes, which includes a system of planned gifting for their children and grandchildren.

After going over their retirement and estate plan, Robert and Mary investigated the potential advantages of getting a life insurance policy for the benefit of their children and grandchildren. Robert and his wife are in good health now and can qualify for preferred rates on a survivorship life insurance policy. After a health examination revealed them to be healthy nonsmokers, their premium is $22,400 per year for a $2,000,000 second-to-die policy.

We have run the numbers using a sophisticated number-running program to project how much money the family will have left if both Robert and Mary survived until age 87 (their projected life expectancy). We have included state inheritance tax and federal estate tax in our analysis. Because this kind of life insurance policy has guaranteed maximum premiums and guaranteed death benefits, we have assumed a safe rate of return of 7 percent on investments.

We chose 7 percent to be more than fair to the cynics who start with the idea that the insurance isn't a good idea. Please keep in mind that 7 percent is a much better return than is currently available on most safe, long-term, fixed-income investments. If we picked a lower interest rate, it would make the purchase of second-to-die insurance even more favorable—but we want to prove its worth conclusively.

The following chart details how the children and grandchildren could be more than $1.5 million better off than they would be without the insurance.

Insurance	Total for Heirs *without* Life Insurance as of Age 87	Total for Heirs *with* Life as of Age 87
IRA balance	$ 4,656,243	$ 4,656,243
After-tax investments	2,193,659	1,305,171
Total assets	6,849,902	5,961,414
State inheritance tax 4.5%	(308,246)	(268,264)
Federal taxable estate	6,541,656	5,693,150
Federal estate tax	(1,368,745)	(986,918)
Life insurance proceeds	0	2,000,000
Total funds to heirs	5,172,911	6,706,232
30% Tax allowance on IRA	(1,396,873)	(1,396,873)
Total for heirs	$ 3,776,038	$ 5,309,359
	Advantage of life insurance	$ 1,533,321

This advantage is calculated assuming the second death occurs at age 87. If neither spouse survives that long, the advantage would be greater because fewer annual premiums would have been paid. If they survive longer, the advantage would be smaller. The graph of this advantage based on age is shown in Figure 12.1. The *Y* axis is how much better off the family is. The *X* axis is at what age both spouses are gone.

Please note that there is no breakeven point. The life insurance scenario is always better than the alternative of not getting

Figure 12.1

Advantage of $2 Million Survivorship Policy

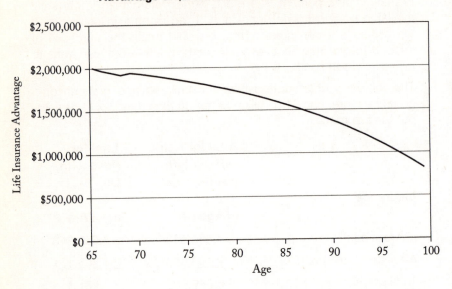

insurance, even if one spouse lives to age 100. One component of this analysis is the federal estate tax savings. For purposes of the above graph, we have assumed that the federal exemption equivalent amount available for use is $3,500,000 in 2009 and in future years. We have not assumed that the exemption equivalent amount will return to $1,000,000 in 2011 as is currently written into law.

Significant Advantages Even with No Federal Estate Tax

In considering the above case of Robert and Mary Jones, there are several additional assumptions that could be made that would result in zero federal estate tax at the second death. One such assumption is that both spouses are able to fully use their federal exemption exclusion amount of $3,500,000 for 2009. Another assumption would be a permanent estate tax repeal or a significant increase in the exemption equivalent amount. Another possible scenario might include a smaller estate but one large enough to afford the premiums. If we assume that federal estate tax is limited to zero at the time of the second death, the advantage of the life insurance policy based on age at the second death becomes lower as shown in Figure 12.2.

Figure 12.2

Advantage of $2 Million Survivorship Policy Assuming No Federal Estate Tax

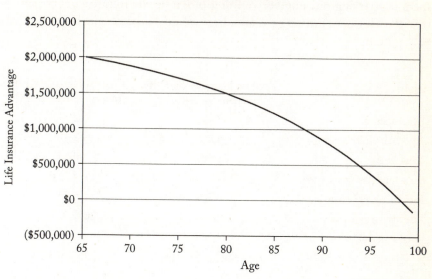

The advantage for the family, assuming the parents' life expectancy age of 87, now becomes $1,151,494. Figure 12.2 shows continued advantages for the family even if one of the parents lives to age 98 (even with the savings of no federal estate tax). Figure 12.2 shows a breakeven point near age 99, and since this is such an advanced age, it is an indication that the life insurance is a great idea. Since age 99 is well beyond the average life expectancy, using the insurance will leverage the estate to a much higher benefit for the family's heirs. However, we do not feel it is safe to plan on the full repeal of federal estate tax, so the advantages of life insurance may be even greater than shown in Figure 12.1.

Small or Large Estates without Federal Estate Tax Produce Similar Advantages

What if you do not have the financial resources that Robert and Mary Jones had in the above example? Let's assume their retirement assets were $1,000,000 instead of $2,500,000; that they had $200,000 in after-tax savings instead of $500,000; and that consequently their spending was

$100,000 per year plus income taxes instead of $150,000. They decide to take out a $2 million policy with annual premiums of approximately $22,000 per year (they can afford to do this without changing their annual spending). Using our number-running program, the following chart shows that the children and/or grandchildren would be better off by more than $1.1 million.

	Total for Heirs *without* Life Insurance as of age 87	Total for Heirs *with* Life Insurance as of Age 87
IRA balance	$ 1,862,498	$ 1,862,498
After-tax investments	1,566,391	677,910
Total assets	3,428,889	2,540,408
State inheritance tax 4.5%	(154,300)	(114,318)
Federal taxable estate	3,274,589	2,426,090
Life insurance proceeds	0	2,000,000
Total funds to heirs	3,274,589	4,426,090
30% Tax allowance on IRA	(558,749)	(558,749)
Total for heirs	$ 2,715,840	$ 3,867,341
	Advantage of Life Insurance	$ 1,151,501

If we ignore the additional advantages created when federal estate tax exists, the life insurance will provide essentially the same advantage as that created by the larger estate, as mentioned above. There are only rounding calculation differences of $7 between our advantage numbers for the large ($1,151,494) and small ($1,151,501) estates.

Different Amounts of Death Benefits

There is no rule that the death benefit must be $2,000,000. In our practice, purchasing $1 million policies is more common and most of the buyers are older than Robert and Mary. We also find that for many clients we determine the death benefit by working backwards. For example, we might have a situation where the family feels they can afford $15,000 per year in premiums and with that as a starting point, we see how much insurance they can get for that annual premium.

Advantages Are Greater in a Time of Lower Investment Returns

Part of the financial security provided for the family by this insurance is that the return on the premiums is guaranteed. If your family's investment returns are lower, the insurance will confer a greater advantage because the death benefit is not contingent on a particular rate of return. Assuming that investments only returned 5 percent annually instead of 7 percent and no federal estate taxes were levied, the life insurance advantage at age 87 is $1,241,896 instead of $1,151,501.

Furthermore, there is no breakeven point reached by age 100 as there is still an advantage of $426,450 if one spouse survives that long. Life insurance can go a long way toward ensuring a safe long-term return for the family.

Case Study with Health Risk Factors

In the above examples, both Robert and Mary Jones received preferred rates for their insurance policy. But what if you have health risk factors? Is insurance still a good idea if the premiums are higher? As we age, it is more common to have health problems than not. Our findings are that if it made sense to purchase a policy at preferred rates, it is probably still a good idea at standard rates.

The insurance companies will review your medical records and give you a physical when assigning you a rating. Generally speaking, minor problems are common and insurance can still be a good idea.

For example, let us reconsider Robert and Mary Jones, but assume Robert takes medicine for high cholesterol and Mary is overweight. Assume that these health conditions and other factors would result in a standard nonsmoker rate for both Robert and Mary for the survivorship policy. We have recently found, from a highly rated insurance company, a competitive quote of $26,908 per year for a $2,000,000 death benefit for this situation.

So, let's look at the numbers for our new—and not improved—Robert and Mary. They have a smaller estate: $1,000,000 in retirement funds, $200,000 of after-tax funds, and they spend $100,000 per year (over and above the policy premium). No federal estate taxes are considered. We used these higher annual premiums and have assumed returns on investments of

7 and 5 percent annually. Obviously, the advantages are somewhat smaller for the higher annual premiums but the result follows:

Advantage of life insurance at age 87:	Standard and Preferred Annual Premiums of	Standard Annual Premiums of	Smoker Annual Premiums of
	$ 22,400	$ 26,908	$ 32,355
Assuming 7% investment returns	$1,151,501	$ 980,742	$ 768,123
Assuming 5% investment returns	$1,288,243	$1,144,935	$ 961,834

This indicates that a survivorship policy can still offer a great financial advantage to the family even when the insured has health risks. I would not conclude that life insurance is less valuable based on the numbers above, because generally a shorter life expectancy is appropriate for individuals with health risks. After all, there is a reason why insurance companies charge more in these cases. An earlier death of both spouses would, of course, make the relative advantages even greater.

Three Ways to Make the Second-to-Die Life Insurance Even More Beneficial

Before wrapping up this chapter, I would like to let you in on some things we do in our own estate planning practice related to second-to-die insurance.

1. One strategy that I really like is to combine the second-to-die insurance with multigenerational planning. As we will discuss in Chapter 13, an inherited IRA is worth more to a young beneficiary than to an older beneficiary. In other words, an inherited IRA is worth more to your grandchildren than to your children. One of the benefits of the second-to-die insurance is that the insurance proceeds can be used to fund or partially fund the needs of your children and your inherited IRA, or at least a portion of your inherited IRA can go to well-drafted trusts for the benefit of your grandchildren. Better yet, you could let your children decide how much of your IRA should go to them and how much should go to your grandchildren after your death. Please see the disclaimer section in Chapter 15 with Lange's Cascading Beneficiary Plan. If we factored in the advantages of

a multigenerational strategy in our example above, the benefits of second-to-die insurance would increase significantly.

2. We believe it is best to purchase second-to-die insurance (or any type of life insurance, for that matter) from an independent broker rather than a captive agent. In one of the examples above, we assume a preferred rating for both husband and wife. Perhaps this is overly optimistic. A standard rating for both husband and wife would incur a higher insurance premium, which will still yield favorable results, but not as favorable as preferred, assuming the same life expectancy. The reality for most people in their sixties and beyond is that a rating of preferred or super-preferred for both husband and wife is unusual. One may have a health problem that will preclude such a high rating. It might be difficult for one or both of an older couple to be rated as standard.

In the real world, the person who decides whether you are rated super-preferred, preferred, standard, uninsurable, or somewhere in between, is the underwriter who is typically an employee of the insurance company. I am continually astounded by the different conclusions two underwriters will come to, given the same medical data, about an insurance prospect. As the death benefit and the premium are both easily quantified, I suggest that you shop for the best deal from among the well-rated companies.

However, looking on the Internet and finding the best quote isn't that meaningful for most people 60 and older. The real play in the joints of the cost of your premium will be determined by how the individual underwriter of the insurance company rates you in terms of preferred, standard, etc. One of the advantages of using a broker is that it is the broker's job to solicit quotes from multiple companies and negotiate insurance ratings with them as needed to get you the most favorable rate.

Another very practical reason to purchase life insurance from a broker is that it is likely that you will only want to subject yourself to one health exam. The exam usually entails a nurse coming to your home or office. He or she asks a bunch of questions, checks your pulse, your blood pressure, takes blood, and so forth. It isn't terrible, but it is better to only have to do it once. If you apply for the insurance with a bunch of different captive agents (agents that represent only one insurance company), you and your spouse will have to take multiple exams.

We have consistently found the best rates for our clients come from working with an ethical independent broker who represents many reputable insurance companies. The independent agent will schedule you for one health exam, and armed with that information and your medical history, will shop a number of different insurance companies. There is a good chance you and/ or your husband will have a health condition that will be looked upon differently by different underwriters. If the independent broker applies with eight different companies and seven give you a standard rating (or worse, rate you negatively) and one company gives you a preferred rating, then obviously, everything else being equal, it is best to go with the insurance company that is giving you the highest rating and the lowest premium. As I mentioned before, I am continually amazed at the different ratings conferred on people who have relatively common health problems, like being overweight or having high cholesterol. Using an independent agent who shops the policy to a number of insurance companies, I have seen people get standard and preferred ratings from some companies and negative ratings with other companies—all for the same health conditions. After the process is complete, the independent agent will recommend a company, and usually the company they recommend is offering the lowest premium.

In exploring options for our clients we have seen vast differences among quotes for practically identical insurance products for the same applicant. In one case, for a very large policy, one quote was for $180,000 payable for five years and the second best quote was for $230,000 for five years. (This was a slightly different product where the clients have a guaranteed death benefit if they pay for the entire policy with five years of premiums instead of paying a smaller premium annually until the death of the second spouse.) This type of policy often comes into play for charitable planning. Please see Chapter 18 for more information on charitable giving. In any case, the point is that by using an independent broker, the client saved $50,000 per year for five years.

There is one other factor that may sound sexist, but this is my clear observation and makes actuarial sense. The health of the woman, particularly if she is the younger person in the couple, is more important than the health of the man. Census data show that women on average live longer than men so it makes sense that the health of the woman is more important.

3. Finally, here is a tip many insurance professionals won't tell you. Obviously, you want the lowest possible premium. To be offered that, you (and your spouse) will need a favorable physical exam, and the exam has to be conducted by an examiner approved by the insurance company. Either the insurance company or the broker will pay for the exam, but you cannot substitute this exam with a physical from your personal physician—even if you just had your annual exam. You will also need to give the insurance company permission to ask your doctor (or doctors if you see specialists, too) for your medical records.

To get the best possible results from your physical, I have a couple of recommendations. The night before the exam, have your regular evening meal. Then, fast until after your exam—no snacks, no alcohol—water is fine. Personally, I like to get up and eat right away so I would schedule my exam very early, like 7:00 A.M. Whatever time you choose, it is important that there is no food in your stomach. No coffee either. You will get better results and a lower premium!

Summary of Indicators That Survivorship Life Insurance Should Be Considered

In conclusion, the following factors should be taken into consideration when deciding whether you and your spouse are good candidates for survivorship life insurance:

- *Estate or inheritance tax situations*: In situations where there is likely to be a federal estate tax, or a state inheritance tax, or other high expenses, the argument for using life insurance as a gifting method is really compelling. But even without an estate tax, the argument for second-to-die life insurance is still extremely favorable for the right IRA and retirement plan owners.

- *After-tax funds available*: Having the after-tax funds available to pay premiums on the life insurance is better than using IRA or retirement plan dollars. But the need for insurance may be compelling enough to fund the policy from your IRA if practically all your money is IRA and/or retirement plan dollars.

- *Good health status*: When your current health status is good, the insurance is available and at good rates. Locking in the premium amount protects against the risk of deteriorating health later in life that would make insurance unavailable or too costly.

- *Gifting strategy coordination*: A well-planned gifting strategy should consider the needs of the beneficiaries. Some may want gifts to be made for current use because the beneficiaries may need money now. Other gifts may satisfy needs for money in the future such as education funding for children or grandchildren. Survivorship life insurance should be considered as one component of an overall gifting strategy that will ultimately benefit your heirs after your death.

- *Sufficient assets in the estate*: Perhaps it seems somewhat obvious, but insurance is best used when there are more than enough assets in the estate to meet living costs. In other words, you should not starve to death, or spend your last dollar, or even compromise your lifestyle just to buy insurance. Running numbers may be useful to help decide the appropriate budget for insurance.

Disclosure

I am licensed to sell life insurance and that is part of my estate planning practice. When I am working with a client and I think my client would benefit from an insurance policy and the client agrees, I work closely with an ethical broker to help the client get the best deal. I do receive compensation from the broker.

In terms of the integrity of the information, you should also know that I have been a firm advocate of second-to-die or survivorship insurance for over 25 years. In 1986 I made a presentation touting the benefits of second-to-die insurance for clients with significant IRAs and retirement plans. This was 20 years before I made a nickel selling life insurance.

If you are interested in this type of insurance for your family, please visit www.retiresecure.com or go to the back of the book for more information.

A Key Lesson from This Chapter

For many married couples who are interested in protecting their children, survivorship life insurance is a classic, tax-favored, leveraged form of a gift that can be a great, if not the best, tool for creating and preserving wealth.

13

Laying the Foundation for Estate Planning

Using the Minimum Required Distribution Rules after Death

A man has made at least a start on discovering the meaning of human life when he plants shade trees under which he knows full well he will never sit.
— *Elton Trueblood (1900–1994)*

Generosity lies less in giving much than in giving at the right moment.
— Jean de la Bruyere

Main Topics

- What is an Inherited IRA and how does it work?
- How do beneficiaries calculate and stretch minimum required distributions?
- Why beneficiaries should continue to take the least possible amount out of their Inherited IRA.

KEY IDEA

Individuals profit from deferring income taxes during their
lifetime—so can their heirs.

Most people want to incorporate some planning for their heirs, beyond
that of their spouse. Providing for the surviving spouse is usually the
highest priority. Ultimately, after the second death, you might hope
to offer a cushion to children and/or grandchildren with the remaining
funds. So, how does maintaining money in the IRA environment accomplish those two objectives?

**Just as it was advantageous
for you to keep money in
your IRA, it is best for the
beneficiaries of IRAs to
retain the money in the
tax-deferred environment
for as long as possible.**

Don't pay taxes now—pay taxes later.
Just as it was advantageous for you to keep
money in your IRA, it is best for the beneficiaries of IRAs to retain the money in the
tax-deferred environment for as long as possible. Starting with that premise, let's examine planning for two types of beneficiaries.

What Is a Stretch IRA?

If you don't really know what a stretch IRA is, don't feel bad. Most financial
professionals don't know, either. Many readers and even many financial professionals could not give you a simple definition.

A *stretch IRA* is an IRA that has a beneficiary designation that provides for the possibility of maintaining the tax-deferred status of the IRA
after the death of the IRA owner. You might

**A stretch IRA is an IRA
that has a beneficiary
designation that provides
for the possibility of
maintaining the
tax-deferred status of
the IRA after the death of
the IRA owner.**

be thinking, "I wish I had a stretch IRA. I
only named my spouse as my primary beneficiary and my kids as my successor or contingent beneficiary." Well, guess what? You
have a stretch IRA. After your death, your
spouse and/or your children could continue
to defer income taxes for many years after
your death, as long as the right moves are

made by your heirs after your death. If someone does something really stupid, without extreme precautions, they may ruin the stretch IRA. Before we get into the mechanics of avoiding doing something stupid, let's look at likely beneficiaries.

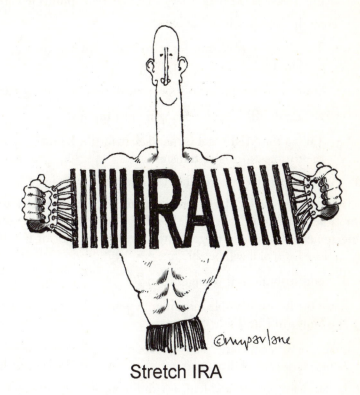

Stretch IRA

Who Can Inherit an IRA?

Just as at some point the IRA owner must take minimum distributions of his IRA, the beneficiaries of an IRA must also take minimum distributions after the death of the IRA owner. The minimum distribution rules for Inherited IRAs can be divided into two basic categories for individual beneficiaries:

- Spousal beneficiary
- Nonspouse beneficiary

Later sections of this chapter discuss the application of minimum distribution rules to estates and trusts.

Spousal Beneficiary

If the surviving spouse is the beneficiary, there are two options to consider:

1. Treat the IRA as his or her own

   - Trustee-to-trustee transfer to spouse's own new or existing IRA

   - Spousal IRA rollover to spouse's own new or existing IRA

   - Retitle the IRA (if not changing institutions)

   - Taking the MRD that is mandatory for the beneficiary prior to the trustee-to-trustee transfer

2. Act as beneficiary of an Inherited IRA from a spouse

It is generally best for the surviving spouse to treat the IRA as his or her own rather than as an Inherited IRA. By making it his or her own, the surviving spouse will be able to generate a greater amount of tax-deferred growth because he or she will be able to:

- Defer distributions if younger than 70½

- Take the lowest possible minimum required distribution based on the Uniform Life Table

- Name new beneficiaries on the account and give the newly named beneficiaries the ability to stretch the IRA after the spouse dies

If the surviving spouse is unhappy with the institution holding the IRA or with the investment choices, he or she can complete a trustee-to-trustee transfer. An IRA spousal rollover is also a possibility. I prefer the trustee-to-trustee transfer over the spousal IRA rollover for the same reasons that I like the trustee-to-trustee transfer while the IRA owner is alive (see Chapter 6). If he or she is happy with the institution and the current investments, the surviving spouse can inform the institution holding the IRA of the desire to retitle the account and treat the IRA as his or her own.

If a surviving spouse decides to treat the IRA as his or her own, ultimately the tax treatment is similar to the treatment of the deceased IRA owner. The difference is that the future minimum required distributions will be calculated from the Uniform Life Table based on the surviving spouse's age. The one exception occurs during the year the first spouse dies. If there is a minimum required distribution for that year, it will be based on the deceased spouse's previous distribution schedule and must be withdrawn by the surviving spouse prior to completing the trustee-to-trustee transfer. That specific minimum required distribution becomes the property of the beneficiary, not the estate (that goes for nonspouse beneficiaries also). By assuming ownership of the IRA, the surviving spouse can name his or her own beneficiaries (usually children and/or grandchildren who will become eligible to stretch the tax-deferral period over their individual life expectancies).

If the IRA is to be split among the surviving spouse and other beneficiaries, separate accounts should be established after the first death. Special care should be taken with the titling of the beneficiary accounts. Also, make sure to change Social Security numbers on the account.

Spousal Beneficiary Who Chooses the Spousal Inherited IRA Option

There are situations when the surviving spouse might choose not to be treated as a surviving spouse but instead assume ownership of his or her deceased spouse's IRA using the spousal inherited IRA option. This strategy is usually made by people who don't understand the implications or they would most likely opt to treat the IRA as their own. Usually the only time that choosing the spousal inherited IRA option makes sense is if the surviving spouse is at least 10 years younger than the deceased spouse and the surviving spouse needs the money. Perhaps the surviving spouse is younger than 59½, and he or she wants or needs the distributions but doesn't want to face the 10 percent penalty for premature withdrawals from an IRA for someone younger than 59½.

- If the surviving spouse takes over the IRA and is younger than 59½, he or she must comply with Section 72(t)—Premature Distribution Exceptions—to avoid the 10 percent penalty on early distributions.

- A spousal beneficiary who treats the IRA as a spousal inherited IRA, rather than as his or her own IRA, can take out as much as needed before age 59½ without penalty. The surviving spouse will not be required to take a distribution until the deceased spouse would have turned 70½.

There is a risk with this alternative: If the surviving spouse chooses to treat the IRA as a spousal inherited IRA, the long stretch for the ultimate beneficiaries, usually the children, will be gone unless the spouse rolls the

Inherited IRA into his or her own IRA at a later date. When the spouse acts as a beneficiary of an inherited IRA, the MRD will be calculated each year based on the single life expectancy of the surviving spouse. With the Inherited IRA, when that spouse dies, the beneficiaries who inherit the assets will be locked in to taking distributions based on the surviving spouse's remaining life expectancy, and the divisor will be reduced by one for each subsequent year. A full explanation of the rules and regulations for this option can be found below under the heading "Nonspouse Beneficiary."

Compromise Solution

In my practice, when we have a young spouse who needs the money, we have come up with a compromise. When a surviving spouse is younger than 59½ and he or she needs the proceeds from the IRA for normal living expenses, we make a projection of how much money he or she will need until turning 59½. I include in the calculation some growth of the assets. Then we treat that amount (the combination of his or her needs and the assumed interest and appreciation of those funds) as the inherited IRA, and for the rest we do a trustee-to-trustee transfer. The advantages are clear:

- He or she has access to the entire inherited IRA without penalty.

- There are allowances for immediate distributions.

- The portion that is rolled over into the IRA will continue to grow tax-deferred, stretching the IRA both before she is 70 and after she is 70½.

Sometimes it is a delicate calculation to figure out how much the surviving spouse will need and what interest rates are likely to do. I would probably prefer to err on the side of overproviding for the surviving spouse until 59½, even at the expense of some income tax acceleration.

If you are uncomfortable with that approach because you don't want to pay any extra taxes, you could underestimate and then plan to do a Section 72(t) periodic payment schedule before 59½ for a portion of the IRA that would be rolled over into the surviving spouse's IRA.

Spouses younger than 59½ who have a need for considerable money before they turn 59½ should seek professional help from someone who will run the numbers to help determine how to split up the IRA.

What if the Younger Spouse Dies First?

Another example when a spouse might choose to act as a beneficiary rather than assume ownership of the IRA occurs when the younger spouse predeceases the older spouse. The advantage here is that he or she may defer taking distributions until the IRA owner would have turned 70½. However, even though there might be some additional deferral period until the surviving spouse has to take the money out; I generally do not like this election. Unfortunately, when the time arrives to begin taking distributions, the surviving spouse must take out minimum distributions based on his or her sole life expectancy if he or she does not complete a rollover of the IRA.

Nonspouse Beneficiary

If the beneficiary is a nonspouse, and assuming no one botches it, the beneficiary has a new type of asset called an Inherited IRA. The nonspouse beneficiary may not roll the inherited IRA into his or her own IRA. Assuming proper drafting of the beneficiary designation and proper follow-through after the death of the IRA owner, the beneficiary of the Inherited IRA will also not have to pay income taxes on the Inherited IRA, at least not all at once. He or she will be able to stretch the Inherited IRA and take his own minimum required distributions based on Table I (Single Life Table) found in IRS Publication 590. Alternatively, that information can also be found at www.retiresecure.com, along with a calculator that will make the theory and the actual calculation quite easy.

The minimum required distribution for the beneficiary of the Inherited IRA is based on the beneficiary's life expectancy as of December 31st of the year following the year the IRA owner died. Please note, however, that the beneficiary must be determined no later than September 30 of the year following the year that the IRA owner died. The reason for the September 30 deadline is to give the IRA custodian sufficient time to make the minimum required distribution before the end of the year.

For example, assume that Judy (from the Tom and Judy example described in Mini Case Study 11.1) dies at age 88 and that her nonspouse beneficiary is then aged 63. The beneficiary would have a deemed life expectancy of 21.8 years (the life expectancy for a 64-year-old using the Single Life Table) for the first distribution, which would have to be withdrawn by December 31 of the following year. The minimum required distribution for the Inherited IRA is calculated by dividing the balance in the account as of December 31 of the previous year by the life expectancy of the beneficiary. For this example, assume an IRA balance of $1 million on December 31 of the year the IRA owner died. The minimum required distribution for the survivor would be $1 million divided by 21.8, or $45,871.56. As the beneficiary (survivor) ages, the factor is reduced by one year, that is, the next year's factor would be 20.8, then 19.8, and so on. Naming a younger beneficiary means a larger life expectancy factor and a lower minimum required distribution.

Thus, a younger beneficiary who inherits an IRA will have a greater potential for long-term tax deferral than would an older beneficiary.

> ...a younger beneficiary who inherits an IRA will have a greater potential for long-term tax deferral than would an older beneficiary.

Stated another way, the present value of the future cash flows to a younger beneficiary is greater than it is for an older beneficiary. Even when the surviving spouse uses a joint life expectancy (his or her life expectancy and a beneficiary 10 years younger) to calculate the minimum required distribution, the Inherited IRA has a greater tax-deferral potential for the surviving spouse's child than for the surviving spouse. The inherited IRA would have its greatest tax deferral potential in the hands of a grandchild (preferably via a well-drafted trust). A younger beneficiary means a longer life expectancy. A long life expectancy equates to lower annual minimum required distributions; the greater the portion of assets that remains in the tax-deferred environment, the greater the accumulation.

> A long life expectancy equates to lower annual minimum required distributions; the greater the portion of assets that remains in the tax-deferred environment, the greater the accumulation.

Later chapters tie the minimum required distribution rules for Inherited IRAs into the estate planning process.

Estate as Beneficiary

Naming an estate as the beneficiary of your IRA is almost always a mistake because the beneficiaries of an estate do not qualify as designated beneficiaries for purposes of the minimum required distribution rules. Thousands of misguided souls will cause their beneficiaries massive income tax acceleration unless someone or something intervenes.

- If the current beneficiary of your retirement plan or IRA is your estate, you should revise the beneficiary designation immediately.

- If you have not named a beneficiary and the default beneficiary of your IRA is the estate, then you must name a beneficiary.

In order to achieve the stretch for the beneficiary, you must have a designated beneficiary for your IRA. That used to be easier said than done. Now, it is hard to avoid, assuming you fill out the beneficiary form as recommended in Chapter 16. If the estate is named beneficiary of an IRA, a limited stretch for the remainder of the owner's unused life expectancy is available if the owner dies after the required beginning date without naming a designated beneficiary.

Trust as Beneficiary

There are many situations when a trust will be a good choice for a beneficiary of an IRA. The most common reason is if the beneficiary is still a minor. Another reason to name a trust, although usually not one I favor, as beneficiary of an IRA is to reduce or eliminate estate taxes. Finally, you may want to use a trust if your beneficiary is not responsible with money and you want to make sure your beneficiary doesn't do anything stupid with the money. If you want to ensure that the beneficiaries stretch the IRA, naming a trust as the beneficiary of an IRA will achieve your goal.

There are a growing number of estate attorneys who routinely draft IRA beneficiary trusts for the benefit of the IRA owner's adult children. They argue the trust forces the beneficiary to get the stretch effect and the trust protects against creditors. Though I think there is good reason to support their practice, I personally prefer simplicity and assuming the adult children are financially responsible and aren't experiencing financial strife, I would prefer the default be the children outright rather than a trust for the children. Part of the reason for my preference is avoiding the trustee fee and the accounting and tax return preparation fees associated with the trust.

Generally, we assume that a beneficiary will want to continue to defer income taxes after the IRA owner's death. We also know that a drafting error in the trust or a procedural error could prevent this from happening and lead to a massive acceleration of income taxes.

It is important that any trust that will serve as the beneficiary of an IRA or retirement plan be drafted with extreme care to ensure that:

- The retirement plan or IRA beneficiary designations are properly in place.

- The trust qualifies as a designated beneficiary.

If those two qualifications are met, the life expectancies of individual beneficiaries of a trust can be used for purposes of the MRDs.

Technical Requirements for a Trust to Get the Stretch IRA Treatment

For the trust to qualify as a designated beneficiary (and get the stretch treatment), it must meet the following five requirements:

1. The trust must be valid under state law, or would be but for the fact that it is not yet funded.

2. The trust is irrevocable or will become irrevocable at the creator's death.

3. The trust beneficiaries must be identifiable—that is, by the last day of the year following the creator's death, it must be possible to identify all the persons who could possibly be beneficiaries of the trust.

4. All the trust beneficiaries must be individuals.

5. Documentation about the trust must be provided to the plan administrator by October 31 of the year following the person's death. This consists of a copy of the trust instrument or a final list of all the beneficiaries.

Depending on the ages of the beneficiaries, the amounts, and the individual's situation, it may be worthwhile to establish a trust as the beneficiary of an IRA. If so, please be sure to comply with all the requirements so the beneficiary can enjoy tax benefits as well as the protection provided by a trust.

This is an area where an attorney's input is advisable. Unfortunately, many attorneys, even estate attorneys, just don't know this stuff. Since it is so easy to botch one of the requirements above, choose your attorney with care, and be sure to ask specifically about their experience with drafting a trust as a beneficiary of an IRA.

A Key Lesson from This Chapter

While you are alive, don't pay taxes now—pay taxes later. The same advice holds true for your beneficiaries. I encourage you to discuss this concept with your beneficiaries so that they are aware of the material advantages of stretching an IRA. Now, on to the ultimate solution for estate planning with IRAs and retirement plans.

14

Using Disclaimers in Estate Planning

If you cannot accurately predict the future, then you must flexibly be prepared to deal with various possible futures.

—Edward de Bono

Main Topics

- How disclaimers work
- Mistakes to avoid
- Advantages of disclaimers
- Comparing the disclaimer approach to the traditional approach

KEY IDEA

An individual who disclaims an inheritance simply steps aside and the next person in line (the contingent beneficiary or beneficiaries) inherits. Planning with this option in mind allows a family to assess and respond to the actual financial needs of the family after the death of the first spouse.

How Disclaimers Work

You can't force someone to accept an inherited IRA. In traditional families, the standard procedure is for the IRA owner to name his or her spouse as the primary beneficiary and their children equally as contingent beneficiaries (the same ingredients of the "I Love You" will). Here's the key: The surviving spouse always has the option to choose not to accept the inherited IRA and disclaim her entire interest or a portion of her interest in the inherited IRA.

> **The surviving spouse always has the option to choose not to accept the inherited IRA and disclaim her entire interest or a portion of her interest in the inherited IRA.**

Let's assume the surviving spouse's disclaimer meets the federal requirements for a qualified disclaimer and the applicable state law requirements for a valid disclaimer (as described later in this chapter). The IRA can be divided into as many inherited IRAs as there are children, and the surviving spouse will not be treated as making a gift for federal gift or estate tax purposes. Subsequently, each child can take minimum distributions from their inherited IRA based on their own individual life expectancy. Under the current rules, the beneficiary, whose age will determine the minimum required distribution, does not have to be determined until September 30 of the year following the year of the IRA owner's death.

Please do not misunderstand this concept. You cannot change beneficiaries after the IRA owner dies. If the three children were named equally as the contingent beneficiaries, the surviving spouse could only disclaim to all three children in equal shares. The surviving spouse could not pick and choose among the children nor alter amounts or percentages. If she disclaims, the children must receive equal shares. Disclaiming simply means that one beneficiary steps aside in favor of the next beneficiary. Should the first beneficiary disclaim, the contingent beneficiary is able to use his or her own life expectancy to calculate the minimum required distribution of the inherited IRA, allowing the IRA to be stretched.

> **You cannot change beneficiaries after the IRA owner dies. . . . Disclaiming simply means that one beneficiary steps aside in favor of the next beneficiary.**

Under most state disclaimer laws, the surviving spouse has nine months to decide whether or not to accept, disclaim, or partially accept and partially disclaim his or her interest. The requirements for a qualified disclaimer under federal law (which are generally the same requirements as under state law, although you must always review applicable state law to confirm that the proposed disclaimer meets the requirements) include the following:

1. The disclaimer must be irrevocable, unqualified (unconditional), and in writing.

2. The written disclaimer must be delivered to the owner of the interest or the owner's legal representative (i.e., executor or retirement plan administrator).

3. The disclaimer must be received by the owner of the interest no later than nine months after the date of death or nine months after the disclaimant attains age 21, whichever is later. (Even though the beneficiary is not finally determined until September 30 of the year following the year of the IRA owner's death, to be effective the disclaimer must be filed within nine months.)

4. The disclaimant has not accepted the interest (the interest can be either a partial interest or the entire interest) or any of its benefits. Also note that a disclaimer to a B trust for the benefit of a surviving spouse is a common exception to this rule because the surviving spouse's interest in the B trust is not considered to be an acceptance of any of the benefits of the IRA.

5. The property must pass to the alternate beneficiary without any direction on the part of the disclaimant.

6. The property must pass to either the spouse of the decedent or to a person other than the person making a disclaimer.

The death of a spouse is an emotional time. It's easy to make big mistakes when you're in an emotional state. Discuss, plan, and prepare ahead of time, and please make sure you have a flexible plan that will survive changes in both the tax code and how your investments do over time. Then your surviving spouse will have all the options at his or her disposal and will have an entire nine months to make decisions on what to do.

Avoid This Mistake

After a death, if the named beneficiary is even considering a disclaimer, the most important thing to do is *nothing*!

The surviving spouse should not take control of the assets. Do not transfer or roll the assets into the spouse's name until a final decision is made *not* to disclaim any portion of the account. Although the IRS has permitted disclaimers in certain situations after the spouse has partially accepted the assets, it is more prudent and considerably less expensive not to accept any assets until after consulting with a qualified advisor. I recently had a situation where the surviving spouse, in an attempt to save money, tried doing some of the estate administration on her own. She figured she could take care of making the trustee-to-trustee transfer of her husband's IRA over to her own name before she came in to see us. She filled out paperwork to complete the trustee-to-trustee transfer; later that month, she informed us of her husband's death and came to see us regarding the rest of the estate administration. I immediately saw the potential for the benefits of a disclaimer, something she forgot about. Unfortunately, I was too late. Before our office became involved, she took control of the IRA and transferred it into her own name. We could not do a disclaimer on any portion of her husband's IRA, something that would have provided great benefits to the family.

Advantages of Disclaimers

Trying to predict the future is like trying to drive down a country road at night with no lights while looking out the back window.

—Peter F. Drucker

A disclaimer offers several potential advantages. When reading the following examples, please assume that the surviving spouse is named as the primary beneficiary and the children equally as contingent beneficiaries of the first spouse's IRA. There are, of course, circumstances when disclaiming is not appropriate, and the surviving spouse would be wise to choose to retain the entire IRA. If, however, the surviving spouse has significantly more money than he or she needs, choosing to disclaim the IRA could be a powerful course of action. If the surviving spouse disclaims the IRA to his or her children, it accomplishes three objectives.

1. The IRA is not included in her estate, which could reduce estate and state inheritance taxes for the children at his or her death.

2. The second, and perhaps more important, advantage is that the minimum required distribution of the inherited IRA would be based on the life expectancy of the children rather than the shorter statutory joint life expectancy of the surviving spouse (longer life expectancy equals longer tax deferral).

3. The kids don't have to wait until both parents are gone to derive a financial benefit.

There is a good chance that the best solution will be for the surviving spouse to keep a portion of the IRA and disclaim the remaining portion.

The beauty of this disclaimer arrangement is that the decision of whether or how much to disclaim can be made after the death of the first spouse when a clearer picture of the surviving spouse's financial situation is available.

> There is a good chance that the best solution will be for the surviving spouse to keep a portion of the IRA and disclaim the remaining portion.

Comparing the Disclaimer Approach to a Traditional Approach

If you have the traditional retirement plan that includes a B trust, the following information is enormously important and similar to the analysis presented in Chapter 11 under the heading "The Nastiest Trap of All."

The problem with the fixed-in-stone traditional approach is that no one can predict:

*   The future value of the investments

*   Which spouse will die first

*   The needs of the surviving spouse

*   What estate tax laws will be in force at the death of the first spouse and/or the death of the second spouse

The traditional approach only allows you to guess at what might be an optimal plan for the surviving spouse and family.

The appeal of the traditional approach is that the bequeathing individual exercises control; he or she decides how to leave money at death and sees that the appropriate documents are drafted. This approach does not allow the surviving spouse to make nearly as many discretionary decisions as the more flexible plan.

One problem with this approach is that any traditional plan that is put in place today will likely be far from optimal within one or two years, let alone 10 to 20 years. As the laws change and the balances in the estate and other factors change, the traditional will or beneficiary designation must be redrafted. Please keep in mind that under the current law, the exemption amounts vary significantly from year to year.

Applicable Exclusion Amounts

2009	$3.5 million
2010	Estate tax is repealed*
2011	$1 million*

* Unless Congress takes action.

Please note that the shifting target of the Applicable Exclusion Amount (the amount of money you can die with before you incur federal estate tax) creates chaos for the estate planner. Traditional estate planners who do not use disclaimer-type planning will be forced to revise the will, trust, and beneficiary designation of the IRA every year to achieve the optimal result. (Of course, perhaps the traditional planner should not complain. All this revising brings in lots of revenue. The shifting Applicable Exclusion Amount could have been called "The Estate Planners' Full Employment Act" because it creates a steady need for redrafting and tinkering with the estate plan.

The use of disclaimers is controversial. There is a rapidly growing group of attorneys, including me, who love using at least some form of disclaimers in the plans of most of their clients. I have been using them in my practice for 15 years and they usually work out great and I believe in them for the reasons stated here. To be fair, however, the majority of estate attorneys don't plan to use disclaimers in their practice. I could be glib and say that is because many estate attorneys haven't considered the advantages of using disclaimers, which, at least for some attorneys, is unfortunately true. There are, however, a significant number of estate attorneys who fear the surviving spouse will fail to make a disclaimer. They believe it is better not to give the surviving spouse any choices. I obviously disagree. I think for many conventional families, giving the surviving spouse options is a sound course of action.

To be fair, however, I must report one situation where the disclaimer didn't work out. The estate attorneys who don't typically use disclaimers can gloat after reading this story because it validates their fears.

We did a cascading beneficiary plan known as Lange's Cascading Beneficiary Plan™ (LCBP) as more fully discussed in Chapter 15, for a client with $3 million in the husband's IRA. Other than a modest house, that was the only significant asset in the estate. When I heard about my client's death, it saddened me as I generally like my clients. The good thing was the surviving spouse was set up just the way I wanted with a LCBP.

This event happened when the exemption was $1 million. For some odd reason, I often remember the general holdings and configurations of my clients' estate plans. This family, as are many of my clients, was better at saving than spending. They lived a relatively frugal lifestyle and spent less than $60,000 a year. They also received Social Security.

As soon as I learned of his death, I remembered his holdings and knew what the best course of action would be. My plan was to recommend that his spouse disclaim $1 million to the children and grandchildren and keep the rest. I wasn't going to use the B trust at all.

It would have worked out beautifully, but despite my best efforts the surviving spouse insisted on keeping the entire amount. She did not change her spending and her estate is now $5 million and growing. The result of her failure to disclaim when she could have may potentially cost her children hundreds of thousands, perhaps more than $1 million because of estate taxes when she dies.

The moral of the story is that there is a genuine risk of the surviving spouse refusing to disclaim when he or she should. This is a legitimate downside of LCBP. Personally, I feel the advantages far outweigh the disadvantages. Ultimately, I think the best practice is to educate your clients and have the clients decide. The majority of my clients, perhaps due in part to my bias, choose LCBP over the traditional plan. I believe that if you have a long-term traditional marriage, the LCBP should be the starting point. Adjustments can be made if needed based on individual circumstances.

This situation notwithstanding, for most traditional families with spouses who trust each other, I am still a fan of using disclaimers in estate planning.

I suggest that the decision of whether the surviving spouse should keep all the funds or whether the children should receive some portion of them (not to mention other choices) can be most effectively made if the spouse is in possession of current facts and figures. Properly drafted documents and beneficiary designations using possibilities of disclaimers can provide the surviving spouse with options—not carte blanche—after the death of the first spouse.

> **The shifting Applicable Exclusion Amount could have been called "The Estate Planners' Full Employment Act" because it creates a steady need for redrafting and tinkering with the estate plan.**

Many planners use the Applicable Exclusion Amount trust to avoid estate taxes without considering disclaimers; that type of traditional planning can be harmful, even devastating, as shown in Mini Case Study 14.1. As if the limitations on the surviving spouse aren't bad enough with a B trust as beneficiary of an IRA, it can get worse.

MINI CASE STUDY 14.1
The Income Tax Hit of IRAs in the B Trust

Suppose Tom dies at the age of 70 with $1 million in an IRA. His wife, Judy, is 68 and has $1 million in after-tax assets. They have one child who is 43 years old, and one grandchild who is 13 years old.

Let's assume Tom went to a traditional estate planner. The planner named a revocable trust with the traditional A/B trust as a beneficiary of Tom's IRA, forcing the $1 million IRA to fund the B trust prior to the funding of the A trust. The minimum distributions from Tom's IRA will be distributed to the trust (technically the inherited IRA will not be transferred to the trust; the distributions from the inherited IRA go to the trust). Since Judy has her own $1 million and she doesn't want to accelerate income taxes, she elects to take only the minimum required distribution of the inherited IRA.

Since Tom's IRA is funding a spousal trust rather than going directly to Judy, the minimum required distributions will be higher than necessary. They will be based on Judy's single life expectancy, rather than on a combination of her life expectancy and the life expectancy of someone who is 10 years younger, as would be the case if he had solely named Judy. In determining the minimum required distributions to the trust, Judy's single life expectancy will be reduced by one year for every year throughout her lifetime and after her death. If Judy lives beyond her life expectancy, there will be nothing left in the trust. The consequences are accelerated income taxes for the family and probably no estate tax savings.

Assuming a 7 percent growth rate and that Judy will survive until age 88, it will take 19 years for the balance in the plan to be distributed to the trust, and distributions will stop before Judy's death. The total distributions received by the trust would equal $2,122,088, with a value of $1,488,070 in today's dollars as adjusted for 3 percent inflation (shown in the following table). Judy doesn't want to pay the trust's higher income tax rate and doesn't want the income from the inherited IRA to remain in the trust, so she makes annual withdrawals from the trust to transfer the income tax burden to her. Judy receives the distributions and pays her taxes. Whatever she doesn't spend over the course of her life is included in her estate.

Year	Distributions, $	Inflation-Adjusted Value of Distributions, $	Ending Trust Balance
1	$ 53,763	$ 52,151	$ 1,016,237
2	57,741	54,328	1,029,632
3	62,026	56,609	1,039,681
4	66,646	59,001	1,045,812
5	71,631	61,512	1,047,388
6	77,014	64,150	1,043,691
7	82,833	66,927	1,033,917
8	89,131	69,856	1,017,160
9	95,959	72,951	992,403
10	103,375	76,231	958,496
11	111,452	79,724	914,138
12	120,281	83,456	857,846
13	129,977	87,478	787,919
14	140,700	91,854	702,373
15	152,690	96,691	598,849
16	166,347	102,179	474,422
17	182,470	108,720	325,161
18	203,226	117,455	144,697
19	154,826	86,797	0
Total	$ 2,122,089	$ 1,488,069	

Using the same assumptions, however, if Tom names Judy outright, instead of the B trust, and Judy rolls the $1 million IRA into her own IRA and names her child as the beneficiary, total distributions to the family will be deferred over 43 years and increased by more than $3 million to $5,202,805 or, in inflation-adjusted dollars, $2,279,550—an increase of $791,480.

Using the same assumptions as above, except that Judy names her 13-year-old grandchild as beneficiary of her rollover IRA, the total amount of distributions from the IRA will be stretched over a period of 71 years (the life expectancy of the grandchild) and total $15,608,663 or $3,490,597 in inflation-adjusted dollars. Figure 14.1 shows the value of the distributions in inflation-adjusted dollars using these three beneficiary choices:

Figure 14.1

Value of Distributions

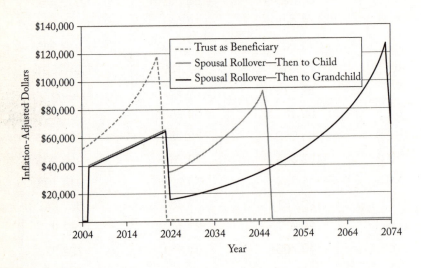

The reasons for the significant additional deferrals of distributions when Judy rolls the IRA over into her own name are:

1. There will be no MRD for Judy until she is 70½, so the IRA continues to grow fully tax-deferred.

2. When Judy is 70½, the MRD divisor factor will be based on a combination of her life expectancy and the life expectancy of someone who is deemed 10 years younger. That specific number is taken from the IRS Uniform Life Table. As a result, Judy's MRD will be much lower than the MRD for the trust that was based solely on her life expectancy.

3. Furthermore, if the IRA is rolled into Judy's IRA, the minimum required distributions after Judy's death are

determined based on her child's single life expectancy, which allows for even lower distributions. If the IRA is transferred to the trust at the death of the IRA owner, and if in our case Judy were to die prematurely, the minimum required distributions will continue to be disbursed based on the original projection of Judy's life expectancy, even after she has died!

"Hark! Hark!" One of our proper number-crunching reviewers is yelling. "I object." He screams that we are not presenting a fair picture. We must consider the value of the distributions from the IRAs and the potential growth even after income taxes have been paid. I agree. To do this, we look at the numbers using the following assumptions:

1. Distributions from the IRA funds are all taxed at a 25 percent rate.

2. Only minimum required distributions are taken from each IRA fund.

3. IRA distributions, net of this tax, are invested in after-tax funds to also yield 7 percent growth.

4. The after-tax fund is subject to net taxes of only 15 percent due to capital gains rules and rates.

5. Spending is made from each scenario's after-tax funds in the same amount beginning in 2011 when MRDs are required in Judy's (rolled-over) IRA. The spending amount is $30,000, increased 3 percent annually for inflation.

6. The remaining retirement assets are measured with a 25 percent income tax allowance.

7. The values of total remaining funds, both IRA and after-tax, are measured using 3 percent inflation-adjusted dollars.

Figure 14.2 shows the value of total funds using the trust, spouse and then child, and spouse and then grandchild, as beneficiaries.

The supporting calculations show that the trust alternative begins to become less favorable than the rollover IRA after the first year. After Judy's death, using the grandchild as beneficiary begins to become more favorable than using the child. Over time, due to the additional tax deferral in the IRA, Figure 14.2 shows that it is better to use assets other than IRAs to fund a B trust if possible. Please note, however, that this approach does not

Figure 14.2

Value of Inheritance from an IRA Using Different Beneficiaries and Taking Only MRDs

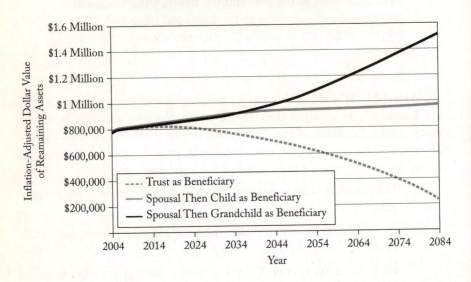

consider the potential estate tax savings. In some cases, there would be an estate tax savings if we used the B trust because we would avoid the double taxation of the estate tax and income tax in many situations. Because we do have a potential estate tax savings, we can't throw the idea of using the B trust as beneficiary of the IRA out the window.

Where does that leave us?

The Problem of Estate Planning in a Nutshell

- If we leave everything in the estate, including the IRA, to the surviving spouse, there might be an enormous estate tax at the second death. The damage will be compounded if there are no funds to pay the estate tax except by making distributions from the IRA that would trigger income tax—the payment of which would trigger more income tax, ad nauseam. We also may be accelerating income taxes by not naming children or grandchildren as beneficiaries.

- If we use a traditional plan and fund the B trust before we leave anything to the surviving spouse, we may have the problem of not sufficiently providing for the surviving spouse. In addition, if the underlying asset is an IRA or a retirement plan, we have the additional problem of the accelerated distributions during both the life of the surviving spouse and for the children at the death of the second spouse.

• If there are sufficient assets to provide for the surviving spouse, we also may want to have children or grandchildren as beneficiaries of IRAs in order to take advantage of their long life expectancies that would stretch the IRA.

The problem, of course, is that there are too many variables, and we cannot predict which ones will be relevant at the time of death. How much money will be there at the first death? Who will die first? What tax laws will be operative in the year of the first death? What will the needs of the surviving spouse be? Now that we understand the problem, what is the solution? The answer lies in the next chapter.

Special note to financial professionals: Understanding this concept is critical to your business. Please go to www.retiresecure.com for a special report designed to help you take better care of your clients and grow your business.

A Key Lesson from This Chapter

Any inflexible plan that we draft now will likely be in need of revision in a year or two. With constantly shifting circumstances, laws, and exemption equivalent amounts, it is extremely difficult to make a plan that will survive all foreseeable and unforeseeable events.

15

The Ideal Beneficiary Designation of Your Retirement Plan

Stretching and Disclaiming: Lange's Cascading Beneficiary Plan

The circumstances of the world are so variable that an irrevocable purpose or opinion is almost synonymous with a foolish one.

—W. H. Seward

Main Topics

- How Lange's Cascading Beneficiary Plan works
- Who should use the strategy
- Who shouldn't use this strategy

KEY IDEA

Lange's Cascading Beneficiary Plan's disclaimer strategy preserves the safety net for the natural heir of the IRA owner (i.e., the surviving spouse) by allowing complete discretion for the surviving spouse to keep funds for him- or herself, or to disclaim to the B trust or to children, or to trusts for grandchildren. The decision of whether and how much to disclaim can be made after the death of the IRA owner.

Critical Information: A Will or Living Trust Does Not Control the Distribution of an IRA or Retirement Plan

In my practice, clients often come with sophisticated and lengthy wills or revocable trusts covering every contingency, including a variety of trusts or subtrusts. When I ask clients where most of their money is, they often reply, "in my IRA or retirement plan." Then, when I ask about the beneficiaries of the IRA and retirement plan, I find that despite their long and complex wills, the beneficiary designation that controls the vast majority of their wealth is often two lines long:

1. Surviving spouse

2. Children equally

In this scenario, all the good planning that went into the will or revocable trust is of limited or no use to the client who has large retirement accounts, potentially the largest asset in the client's estate. This is because the will or revocable trust does not control the beneficiary designations of retirement plans.

This mistake is deadly and all too common. In my experience, effective planning for the retirement plan and/or IRA is the exception, not the rule. In the area of estate planning for IRAs and retirement plans, the difference between effective and ineffective planning can be hundreds of thousands, sometimes millions of dollars.

The will or revocable trust does not control the beneficiary designations of retirement plans.

Why do the *Wall Street Journal, Newsweek, Financial Planning Magazine, Kiplinger's, The Tax Adviser* (AICPA), and a host of other national periodicals sing the praises of Lange's Cascading Beneficiary Plan?

It's simple. It's a secure way for you to easily, safely, and with maximum flexibility, plan your estate and provide for your heirs before one of you dies. It's a plan that has stood the test of time! Read on and take notes: You'll want to implement this with the help of your attorney.

For discussion's sake, I am going to assume that you are married and that you are willing to answer the following question with an unequivocal yes. Are you ready for this? I love this. I ask this in my practice all the time. "Do you trust your spouse? Seriously, do you *trust* your spouse?"

Let's assume the answer is yes, that you trust your spouse. For discussion's sake, let's say that you have one of those traditional marriages: You and your spouse have only been married to each other and you have the same children and grandchildren. You have four natural choices for beneficiaries when it really comes down to it. Number one, you have your surviving spouse. We love our spouse. We want to provide for the comfort and security of our spouse after we die. I'm happy to report to you that in 30 years of practice nobody ever came in and said, "My goal for my estate is to have my grandchildren so stinking rich that they'll never have to work a day in their life." Nobody ever said that. I'll tell you what people say. "I want to take care of my spouse." That even comes before saving taxes. That comes before everything. I want to take care of my spouse. Let's leave that as the number one option. But one of the problems with that is you might end up with a big estate tax. Let's say you have $4 million in an IRA. You die. At the second death, your spouse's estate will have $4 million—a $3.5 million exemption and $500,000 that is taxable. There will be a $225,000 tax.

Maybe what you need is the classic A/B trust type of planning. The B trust essentially leaves income to the surviving spouse and provides the right to invade principal for health, maintenance, and support. At the second death the trust goes to the kids equally. The point of the B trust is to save estate taxes at the second death. It might be a reasonable strategy. It might save $225,000 in taxes. But it might be bad. It might be *really* bad. Your surviving spouse could face significant limitations that are totally unnecessary. Traditionally the amount of money that would go into the trust would be equal to the Applicable Exclusion Amount. If that were the case, for a death in 2009 the trust would get $3.5 million if there is that much in the estate. The Applicable Exclusion Amount has risen dramatically since a lot of these traditional plans were written. There are a lot of people who, if their spouses died right now, would be forced to have all their money transferred to the B trust and nothing would go directly to the surviving spouse. I call it "the nastiest trap of all." I promise you there are hundreds, probably thousands of people reading this book who have that as their estate plan, people who think that their spouse is the primary beneficiary. If you look closely at their will or trust, it is the B trust that is named as the primary beneficiary. So the trust might be good, or it might be a disaster.

The next beneficiary could be your children. They might be a good choice as beneficiaries, given that:

- You might have an estate tax if you leave everything to your spouse and she then dies with more than the applicable exclusion amount.

- The B trust may or may not be useful. If useful, it is more likely useful for after-tax dollars rather than IRA dollars.

- The children may need the money sooner than many years from now when both you and your spouse will be gone.

But the children may not need the money, in which case you'd want to give it to your grandchildren and let them stretch the inherited IRA. Or perhaps one child doesn't need the money and has children, yet another one of your children does need the money.

What are you going to do? How can you decide between these four choices?

1. Surviving spouse

2. B trust

3. Children

4. Grandchildren

Maybe do a little bit of each? Maybe try to figure it out? I know. Let's do a projection! Let's project how much money we are going to have when we die! Oh, come on! we don't know when we are going to die. I know, let's make a projection based on how much money we are going to have and what the tax laws are going to be! Oh . . . we don't know what the tax laws are going to be. Well, I'll tell you this, in 30 years I've done a lot of projections, and one thing is common to every single one of them. They are all wrong. Every time I've been wrong! People had *more* money than I thought. People had *less* money than I thought. The *tax laws* were different. The *wrong person* died first. So how can we handle this? How can we make this decision now if you don't want to come back and redo your will every year or two. I have an idea. Let's not decide. We just won't decide.

I refuse to decide.

Well, how do you refuse to decide? You draft the appropriate wills and trusts and IRA and retirement plan beneficiary designations to allow your surviving spouse to make these decisions within nine months after the date of your death. Then the surviving spouse will have answers to all of these questions. The surviving spouse will know what his or her needs are. He or she will know exactly how much money there is after the first death. The surviving spouse will know the current tax laws at the first death. If you were to look at my will or my IRA beneficiary designation, with the exception of money going to charity, if my wife wants it, she can have it all. End of story.

If she doesn't want it because she is worried about an estate tax, she could put it in a trust and get the income from it. At her death the remainder will go to our daughter. If my wife doesn't even want the income from the B trust, then the proceeds will go into a trust for our 14-year-old daughter. And if our daughter is grown up with kids of her own and she doesn't want it, it will go into a trust for her children. Perhaps best of all, my wife can choose to have the money directed in some combination of options.

I'm not going to decide now, because I trust my wife. She can do whatever she wants. I'm going to suggest that if you trust your spouse, don't decide now. Let your spouse decide. If you survive your spouse, then you decide.

I've been drafting these types of flexible documents for Pennsylvania residents since the early 1990s. Even though most of my clients are alive and kicking, we have had a sufficient number of clients who have died, and the plan works beautifully. It's always tragic when a client dies. But if they die with this plan in place, we almost always get a good financial result for the family. If you use a more traditional plan, decisions are fixed and set in advance. With the traditional plans that were drafted when the exemptions were $600,000, too much money is going into a trust and the surviving spouse is underprovided for. It happens all the time. And it is going to get worse as the exemptions go up.

By the way, I have a little story for you. When they changed the law in 2001, I knew instantly, within days of Congress changing the law, that this flexible estate plan was going to be the best estate plan there was. I was very excited. I had an e-mail newsletter, which at that time was going out to 50,000 readers. I wrote this little article called "The Ideal Beneficiary of Your IRA." I sent it out into e-mail land.

I was surprised by a call I received two days later when I heard, "Hi. This is Jane Bryant Quinn." I talked to her at length, and she put my plan in her column. Then *Financial Planning Magazine* asked me to write about this plan. I did, and they published my article. The American Institute of Certified Public Accountants (AICPA) published my peer-reviewed article and sent it to 60,000 CPA subscribers with this plan as part of the article. The *Wall Street Journal* also got ahold of this. They loved the idea. They've written four articles on it. *Kiplinger* also chimed in several times. I call it Lange's Cascading Beneficiary Plan, but it is also cited as a Cascading Beneficiary Plan in the professional literature. The concept of cascading beneficiaries appears widely in print and on the Internet. So this isn't just some crazy, fluky idea. This is something you should seriously think about putting in place for yourself.

How the Plan Works

First, a bit of background on terminology. To the best of my knowledge, I am the first person to have used the term Cascading Beneficiary Plan to describe the layering of beneficiaries through the use of disclaimers. Furthermore, Lange's Cascading Beneficiary Plan takes the technique to a new level of sophistication and flexibility. It is not uncommon currently to see references to cascading beneficiary plans in estate planning literature. Journals and magazines that originally published my articles on Lange's Cascading Beneficiary Plan continue to promote the concept, although some have dropped my name and simply refer to a cascading beneficiary plan. Using the cascade or disclaimer technique is a sound and excellent solution for many estate planning problems. I cannot attest, however, to how other financial professionals use the concepts and would not know if all the advantages to my particular plan are incorporated in the work of others. So, for the sake of clarity and because I have a vested interest in maintaining the integrity of my plan, I will refer to it as Lange's Cascading Beneficiary Plan, or LCBP for short.

LCBP recognizes the importance of providing for the surviving spouse and also the advantage of keeping options open after the death of the first spouse. LCBP accommodates the surviving spouse's need to take stock of his or her financial situation before deciding whether or not to disclaim. If he or she does decide to disclaim, the next question is how much and to whom? Relevant facts to consider include finances at the time of the first death, tax laws at the date of the first death, family needs, and perhaps most importantly, the needs of the surviving spouse. LCBP gives the spouse both the time to make decisions and the power to act on them. Many traditional families—that is, families without the complications of second marriages and stepchildren—would be wise to consider incorporating LCBP with disclaimer options into their estate plans.

Please note that LCBP, when appropriate, can and should be used for wills and living trusts as well as IRAs or retirement plans.

> **LCBP gives the spouse both the time to make decisions and the power to act on them.**

Typically, to take full advantage of LCBP, the IRA owner should name primary and contingent beneficiaries to their IRAs according to the following hierarchy:

1. The spouse
2. A unified credit shelter trust (or B trust)
3. A child (or the children equally)
4. A well-drafted qualifying trust for a grandchild (or grandchildren)

To preserve the surviving spouse's options, the participant should name the spouse as the primary beneficiary. The contingent beneficiary could be a unified credit shelter trust (or B trust) that is incorporated within LCBP. The unified credit shelter trust can be used to protect against a potential estate tax at the death of the surviving spouse. Money disclaimed to the unified credit shelter trust will not be subject to estate tax in the estate of the surviving spouse. As discussed in Chapter 14, a disclaimer to this type of trust will not violate the rule for a qualified disclaimer that says a taxpayer who disclaims can't directly benefit from the disclaimer. The surviving spouse could also avoid estate taxes at the second death if, at the first death, he or she disclaimed at least some of the inherited IRA to the children. That portion of the IRA would not be included in the surviving spouse's estate and would not be subject to estate taxes at the death of the surviving spouse.

LCBP contains provisions for the surviving spouse to disclaim some or all of his or her interest directly to the third contingent beneficiary, which would most likely be a child, or if there is more than one child, to the children equally. Then that child would be deemed a primary beneficiary, and the minimum required distribution of the inherited IRA would be based on the child's life expectancy.

I have written this chapter from the standpoint of the IRA or retirement plan owner who is planning his or her estate. What if you are the beneficiary of an inherited IRA or retirement plan? What should you do? At first, do nothing. I mean it. Don't do something quickly that you may later regret. If you inherit an IRA or retirement plan, it is absolutely critical to review your options with a qualified expert in IRAs and retirement plans. You might even need to take a couple of months to think over all your options and plan accordingly. Not only is this an area where thousands of people make mistakes, but the scope of the mistakes can often be measured in hundreds of thousands or even a million dollars or more.

When you are planning to leave your IRA and/or retirement plan to your heirs, you must impress upon them how important it is they get appropriate advice after your death.

Additionally, contained within the IRA beneficiary designation that I would recommend is language that allows an adult child to disclaim his or her interest in what had been disclaimed from his parent (the surviving spouse) to a trust for the benefit of his or her own child or children (the deceased IRA owner's grandchildren). Then, the trust for the grandchild would be deemed a primary beneficiary of the retirement account and could use the grandchild's own life expectancy for minimum required distribution purposes (the ultimate stretch).

The Ultimate Cascade of a Very Flexible Plan

In a perfect cascade, the surviving spouse:

- Could retain some of the participant's IRA, roll it over into his or her own name, and appoint his or her own beneficiaries

- Would have the option to disclaim a portion to the B trust (it may be more likely to disclaim after-tax funds into the B trust because of the income tax acceleration discussed earlier)

- Could disclaim a portion to an adult child or children, who would be the deemed primary beneficiary for that portion, which would allow the beneficiary to use his or her own life expectancy for MRD purposes

At which point, each adult child:

- Could retain some of the participant's IRA and take minimum required distributions based on his or her life expectancy

- Disclaim a portion to a trust for his or her own child, who would become the primary beneficiary for that portion and could then use his or her own life expectancy for minimum required distribution purposes

If the surviving spouse chooses to roll the entire IRA into his or her own IRA, then the path of distributions is fairly straightforward (see column one of Figure 15.1). The surviving spouse must begin taking minimum required distributions by April 1 of the year following the year that the surviving spouse turns 70½ based on his or her joint life expectancy and a beneficiary deemed to be 10 years younger. He or she would use Table III of the Uniform Lifetime Table, which is presented in the appendix. Using this table, the surviving spouse's life expectancy is recalculated each year, which means he or she can never outlive the IRA.

The surviving spouse will also be able to name his or her own primary and contingent beneficiaries. At the surviving spouse's death, the remaining IRA is included in the surviving spouse's estate for estate tax purposes. The minimum required distribution for the ultimate beneficiary of the inherited IRA—in traditional families, the children equally, assuming none of the children further disclaims—is calculated based on each of the different life expectancies of as many children as there are using the life expectancy of each beneficiary as of December 31 following the year of the death of the deceased spouse. The beneficiaries of the IRA would then use Table I of the Single Life Table, which is presented in the appendix. Unlike the surviving spouse, the beneficiary may exhaust his or her IRA even if only withdrawing minimum required distributions because his or her life expectancy is determined as of the surviving spouse's death and reduced by one for each subsequent year.

If the spouse disclaims into the B trust and retains the rights as income beneficiary, he or she will receive a steady income and the right to receive discretionary principal for health, maintenance, and support. Depending on how the trust was drafted, the surviving spouse could retain the power to withdraw the greater of $5,000 or 5 percent of the trust on an annual basis. Furthermore, those assets in the B trust will not be included in the estate of the second spouse to die, possibly saving estate taxes at the second death.

From a minimum required distribution or income tax perspective, the B trust is the worst alternative for an inherited IRA. During the life

Figure 15.1

Lange's Cascading Beneficiary Plan™

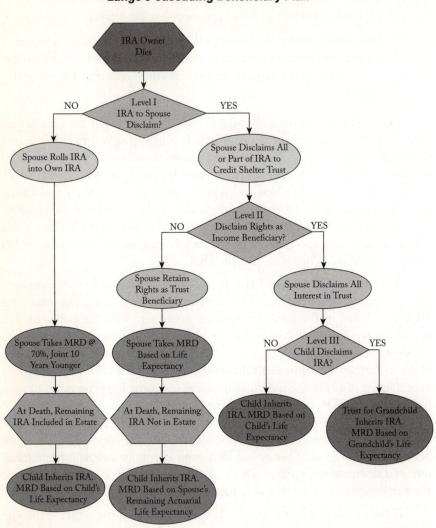

Copyright: James Lange

of the surviving spouse, the minimum required distribution is based on the surviving spouse's single life expectancy (see Table I in the Single Life Table), which forces a higher distribution than if the beneficiary would be the surviving spouse outright (see Table III, a joint life expectancy factor). Furthermore, it is quite possible that over the life of the surviving spouse, the entire IRA may have to be distributed and the resulting acceleration of income tax on the IRA would be extremely disadvantageous to the family. Remember that the surviving spouse cannot recalculate his or her life expectancy when the B trust is named as the beneficiary.

After the surviving spouse dies, the remainderman of the B trust (the person who receives the remainder of the trust, usually an adult child or adult children) must continue to take minimum required distributions on the same accelerated schedule as their parent if the IRA has not been exhausted during the surviving spouse's lifetime. These MRDs are based on the deceased parent's remaining single life expectancy, not the remainderman's much longer life expectancy. (See column two of Figure 15.1.) Thus, by using the B trust as a beneficiary of an IRA, the stretch is greatly reduced and the planner is condemning the survivors to accelerated income taxes.

As a practical matter, many people like the security of the B trust option because it provides for the living needs of the surviving spouse while ensuring that the trust assets will not be included in the estate of the surviving spouse, thus saving estate taxes at the second death. Though many attorneys often draft B trusts as the contingent beneficiary of an IRA, in practice upon the death of the first spouse, it is often wiser to attempt to find better alternatives than the B trust for the disposition of the IRA.

If the spouse is financially secure and chooses to disclaim either all or a portion of his or her interest as primary beneficiary to the contingent beneficiary, the B trust, and then simultaneously disclaims some or all of his or her income interest in the trust to the remainderman (the child), this continues the cascade. The long-term advantage of the lower minimum required distributions then moves to the foreground. The child, or the grandchild (assuming the child disclaims to the grandchild), can then take minimum distributions over the course of his or her own life expectancy (see columns three and four of Figure 15.1). A longer life expectancy means a lower minimum required distribution, which in turn means that a greater percentage of the assets in the inherited IRA can continue to compound and grow tax-deferred (or in the case of an inherited Roth IRA, tax-free).

LCBP protects or overprotects the surviving spouse. It allows the greatest flexibility to stretch the IRA and allows decisions to be made after the death of the IRA owner. However, this flexibility is a two-edged sword. By giving the surviving spouse that much power, the planner takes the risk that the surviving spouse will make inappropriately conservative decisions, such as failing to disclaim when he or she probably should. The family could end up with less-than-optimal results.

You can see why this plan might not work well in families with the complications of second marriages and stepchildren. The potential exists that your spouse will have no motivation to pass the money on to your children from your first marriage. Rather than disclaim any of the money to your children, your surviving spouse might be more inclined to keep all of the money and eventually leave it to his or her own children and grandchildren.

Perhaps the best short explanation of LCBP comes from Jane Bryant Quinn in *Newsweek*:

> For moneyed families, where the heirs won't need the IRA right away: When you die, your spouse could refuse to accept ("disclaim") all or part of the IRA. That money could go to a trust that pays your spouse a lifetime income and then passes to the children. Alternatively, your spouse could disclaim the IRA proceeds directly to your children, who could either take the money or disclaim to your grandchildren. They'd still have to take their minimum distributions, but the bulk of the IRA could be tax-deferred for generations.

Kiplinger's Retirement Report writes:

> If you're looking to stretch out your IRA's life but want to make sure your spouse is provided for when you die, you can use what Pittsburgh attorney and CPA James Lange calls a "cascading beneficiary" strategy.
>
> Lange paints this scene: You are married with children and grandchildren. You name your wife as the primary beneficiary and a bypass trust as first contingent beneficiary. The second contingent beneficiary is the children equally. The third is a trust for the grandchildren. At your death, your spouse could roll over all or part of the IRA into her IRA and could also disclaim a portion into the bypass trust.
>
> The advantage of disclaiming to the bypass trust is that upon your wife's death, the proceeds of the trust are

not included in her estate. She could also disclaim all or part to the children, who could then take withdrawals based on their longer life expectancy. Finally, if neither your spouse nor your children need all the money, they could disclaim all or a portion to a trust for the grandchildren.

Another interesting feature of LCBP is that it is also suitable and recommended for wills and revocable trusts. If you want the entire spectrum of options open for your surviving spouse, then drafting LCBP for the will (and/or revocable trust) and the IRAs and retirement plans is an excellent, probably the best, estate plan.

Are People Happy with Lange's Cascading Beneficiary Plan?

I developed and employed an early version of the cascade in the early 1990s. It has been tested and proven worthy. After determining that the fundamentals of the cascade were sound, I added the full Cascading Beneficiary Plan in January 2001, immediately after the overhaul of the IRA and retirement plan distribution rules, which increased the options for a stretch IRA. Most of my clients are still kicking. We have, however, been writing these plans long enough to have had quite a few deaths. The surviving spouses have appreciated the flexibility of our plan, and most of them who made decisions based on their personal circumstances at the time of their spouse's death were able to make better decisions—that is, more advantageous to them and their families—than the decisions that would have been forced upon them with the traditional A/B trust estate planning. People always say hindsight is 20/20. This plan offers a unique opportunity to actually use hindsight in deciding the best way to divide up the estate.

If you are interested in having Lange's Cascading Beneficiary Plan for your family, please see the information at the back of the book.

What if the Federal Estate Tax Laws Are Repealed?

As this book goes to press, there is proposed legislation to repeal or radically change the federal estate tax laws to make the exemption $3.5 million. Interestingly enough, no matter what the outcome or changes finally put into effect, LCBP is still sound. My advice regarding what type of will, revocable trust, or even beneficiary designation you should have for your IRA and retirement plan would be the same. That is, even in the event there is a full repeal of the federal estate tax or a major change in the exemption amount, I would still advocate LCBP for most readers.

Remember, the B trust is one of the options in the LCBP. Why would I still include the option of the B trust when apparently there would be no federal estate tax? Isn't the main point of the B trust to avoid federal estate tax at the second death? If there is no federal estate tax, why bother with the B trust? Yes, that's true. However, please keep in mind that whatever tax law changes are made, there will be more changes after this set of changes.

Three times our country eliminated the federal estate tax and three times it has been reinstated. So, even if it is repealed, who is to say that in five years it will not be brought back again?

So, if you have the LCBP in place and Congress subsequently repeals the estate tax, I would do nothing. There are no reasons to make any changes if you have LCBP in place. Even if there is repeal and no need to have the B trust, it can't hurt to have the B trust as an option.

If you were drafting a new document, would I recommend you retain the B trust as an option in the will and/or living trust? Yes. Why?

In short, why not? Other than the minimal additional cost of including the B trust as part of the LCBP, why not give the surviving spouse all the options that might be relevant?

In addition, you may live in a state that has separated its state death taxes from the federal estate tax and calculates the tax based on older rates. In those states, the LCBP is especially relevant because of the flexibility it provides for the beneficiary to disclaim the ideal amount calculated based on that state's law rather than having a more traditional estate plan forcing all assets into a B trust.

The last two administrations had relatively little respect for precedent in estate taxation. Why would we think any changes that will take place will be permanent? My best guess is that whatever Congress does, they will change it again, probably a number of times, in your lifetime.

If you have the LCBP and they change the law, you can shrug and say, "I don't have to redo my documents." If they change the tax laws again after the first set of changes, you can shrug again and say, "I still don't have to redo my documents."

If you don't have the LCBP but rather have a traditional estate plan and want to keep traditional "fixed in stone" estate planning documents (the A/B trust format), you should make changes if they repeal the law and you should make changes again when they change it again. You should make changes again if there is a change in your own personal financial circumstances.

In the event that the estate tax is not repealed but the exemption amount is raised, the B trust could be drafted as a precautionary measure and presumably would not be an important option. It would likely end up being an unnecessary option that will never be exercised.

On the other hand, in the event the federal estate tax is repealed and then brought back, the fact that you have a document that allows for those changes in the law would mean that you would not have to redo your wills, trusts, and other documents, again. Also note that, in the event of repeal, the impact of the nastiest trap of all (see Chapter 11) will certainly be more widespread than it is today.

The argument for a simplified LCBP without the B trust is also reasonable for smaller estates. If your estate is $1,000,000 or less, the LCBP without the B trust would seem to be a reasonable choice.

In conclusion, in the event of repeal, I would still recommend Lange's Cascading Beneficiary Plan for wills and trusts. For larger estates, I would still include the B trust possibility, even for IRAs and retirement plans, knowing that it will probably never be used. For estates of $1,000,000 or less, you could do the LCBP without the B trust. That way if the client and the drafting attorney prefer to keep things as absolutely simple as they can, you could leave the B trust out of the LCBP and have all of the options except the B trust. The overriding thought, however, is that the LCBP is the best and most flexible estate plan, and you should not have to continually change your documents every time there is a federal estate tax law change or if there is a change in your circumstances.

A Key Lesson from This Chapter

Having a flexible estate plan offers several advantages including providing the surviving spouse with multiple options for distributing the inheritance based on the family's circumstances at the time of the first death. By incorporating the cascade into an estate plan, you give yourself the best chance to stretch an IRA and pay taxes later.

16

|||||||||||||||||||||||||

Changing Beneficiaries for Retirement Plans and IRAs

When at last we are sure,
You've been properly pilled,
Then a few paper forms,
Must be properly filled.

—Dr. Seuss

Main Topics

- Filling out the beneficiary form
- Complex designations incorporating the cascade
- Trusts as beneficiaries
- Hazards of naming different beneficiaries to different accounts

KEY IDEA

Even the simplest beneficiary designation requires more than just a cursory review.

A Caution

Even though I have a disclaimer at the beginning of the book, I want to reemphasize that you should not rely on this information for filling out the beneficiary designation of your IRA or retirement plan.

I shudder at books and computer programs that help readers draft wills and fill out beneficiary change forms. There is often considerable judgment involved in filling out IRA beneficiary change forms and/or a will, and a generic book or software program cannot supply that judgment. Some of these consumer resources may be a good thing for people who can't afford an attorney and who want a simple will. Even then, I fear some type of mistake will be made. I recommend for most anyone reading this book that if there is real money at stake, professional guidance is recommended and a careful vetting of the professional is also recommended.

Plenty of people fill out the form incorrectly. Let's say you have a really simple beneficiary designation: I leave the money to my two sons, Jack and Tom. My secondary beneficiaries are my grandsons, Bob and John, who are Jack's boys. Unfortunately, something happens to Jack. Where is the money that Jack would have received if he was still alive? Is it going to go to your grandsons, Bob and John? No, under the default language of most forms, it's going to go to your son Tom. You don't want to disinherit your grandsons. Poor Bob and John don't have a parent. Now they don't have any money, either. Many people simply don't fill out the forms correctly. It happens all the time and creates catastrophic results. By the way, it's not just consumers filling out their own beneficiary forms who make mistakes. Financial professionals, attorneys, and CPAs who are not knowledgeable in this area also make costly mistakes. I don't let clients fill out these forms. As part of an estate planning engagement, we not only draft wills, trusts, etc., we also manually fill out the beneficiary designation for every IRA and retirement plan our clients own. I'm not going to do a wonderful plan for people and then let them ruin my masterpiece by filling out the beneficiary form incorrectly. The whole thing could just blow up.

Filling Out the Forms

Even the simplest beneficiary designation requires more than just a cursory review. An individual who wants to name adult individuals in his or her beneficiary designations needs to know the names, birth dates, and Social Security numbers of each beneficiary. But it goes beyond that. The individual must also decide where the money should go if a beneficiary predeceases the account owner.

Even the simplest beneficiary designation requires more than just a cursory review.

- If there is one primary and one contingent beneficiary and the primary beneficiary dies (or disclaims his or her interest), the contingent beneficiary inherits all.

- If the named primary and contingent beneficiaries die before the account holder and if no successor beneficiaries are named on the form, the proceeds could be paid to the estate of the account holder, or possibly to an intestate heir (the person who would have received the money had you died without a will). Resulting problems would include the wrong person getting the money and/or causing an acceleration of withdrawals and an income tax nightmare.

- If the children of the deceased first-named beneficiary are designated to inherit their parent's share, then the retirement account will be paid to those children—a much better plan. But again, you should probably have a trust for those children if they are young or can't handle money.

Clearly there are too many combinations for me to outline all possible scenarios. Furthermore, no two beneficiary forms and/ or change forms that are issued by different financial institutions are alike. It is critical to carefully read the form and instructions and develop, with the assistance of a qualified advisor, a strategy that is specific to your situation.

It is critical to carefully read the form and instructions and develop, with the assistance of a qualified advisor, a strategy that is specific to your situation.

MINI CASE STUDY 16.1
Filling Out the Forms—Simple Designation

Abe Account Owner is filling out his beneficiary forms. His first priority is to provide for his wife, Wanda, and, after her, his children Charlie and Charra. He also wants to ensure that, if either of his children should predecease him, their share will pass on to their children (his grandchildren). If the deceased child had no children, then the share would pass to his or her sibling.

1. He designates Wanda as the 100 percent primary beneficiary, inserting her Social Security number, date of birth, and where requested, her address. By designating her as 100 percent primary beneficiary, no other primary beneficiaries can be listed, and he will now move on to the contingent beneficiary section of the form.

2. He then designates his two children as the contingent beneficiaries, allocating 50 percent to each of them. He inserts their Social Security numbers, dates of birth, and, where indicated, their addresses.

3. He must now go one step further. Some forms (TIAA-CREF, for example) have a box that, when checked, directs that the money going to a child who predeceases the account holder should be paid to the children (the account holder's grandchildren) in equal shares. If the form does not have such a selection, then per stirpes should be written after the children's individual names. By using this term, the plan administrator will know to pay the share of that deceased child to the predeceased children's children in equal shares. This is true whether there is one beneficiary or two, and will ensure that the retirement account passes to the next generation rather than reverting to the estate of the account holder or even a sibling of the predeceased child who died with a child or children.

4. The account holder signs and dates the form where indicated and submits it to the plan administrator for processing. Usually within a couple of weeks the account holder will receive confirmation from the plan administrator that the changes have been effected.

An extra step must be taken if an account holder names someone other than his or her spouse as beneficiary to their qualified plan account. On ERISA type plans (401[k]s, for example, but not IRAs) the spouse must consent to a designation that doesn't leave all the proceeds to the surviving spouse. The spouse must sign a consent form, and this designation on the form must be notarized. This section of the form is usually below where the account holder signs. This step must be taken before the plan administrator will accept the form. Most qualified plans are subject to this spousal consent rule (with exceptions that are beyond the scope of this book) whereas IRAs and Roth IRAs are not subject to the rule.

The biggest problem with the simple designation is that:

- It does not contain the B trust option. You want the option if you want to give your surviving spouse more flexibility.

- If money passes to a minor or someone who needs a trust, the minor can use the funds to buy a fast car and have a party when he or she reaches 21 or even 18 in some states—there is no trust for the benefit of the grandchildren.

Complex Designations: Incorporating the Perfect Cascade

Now we address more complex designations. Some people might want more sophisticated beneficiary designations that name trusts as the beneficiaries of their retirement plans. For the purposes of this chapter, we assume that the account holder has designated his or her spouse as the primary beneficiary but wants to designate a trust as the contingent beneficiary. (See Chapter 17 for a discussion of the ramifications of designating a trust as the primary versus contingent beneficiary of a retirement plan.) This scenario is likely under four circumstances:

1. Where a credit shelter or B trust will be the contingent beneficiary for disclaimer and estate tax-savings purposes.

2. Where we want to provide for a spendthrift child and want to ensure the child enjoys the stretch IRA to the fullest.

3. Where an individual wants to allow for grandchildren or other young beneficiaries to receive retirement monies, but not outright. This can be accomplished with a standalone trust or a revocable trust or a trust within a will called a testamentary trust.

4. There is another purpose for a trust, such as when a beneficiary is disabled and you are trying to protect the proceeds from the government.

If the client wants to use a standalone trust (our office uses what is called a *Plan Benefits Trust*) to control the distribution of his or her retirement benefits, the beneficiary designation is relatively simple: The spouse is designated as the primary beneficiary and the Plan Benefits Trust is designated as the contingent beneficiary. The Plan Benefits Trust incorporates the perfect cascade to provide the option of the B trust: the option of children equally and the option of various trusts for grandchildren.

Alternatively, a client can preserve all of the distribution options of a Plan Benefits Trust through a standalone well-drafted beneficiary designation that includes all of the options. The beneficiary designation of the IRA or retirement plan would then refer to a will or revocable trust. Regardless of the mechanics, the key is that the money be directed where the IRA owner wants.

To introduce one more level of control, in some situations an account holder might want his or her spouse to be the primary beneficiary designation and the contingent beneficiaries to be their children, but the holder also wants their children to have the right to disclaim some part or all of their shares to their own children (the account owner's grandchildren). Rather than using the per stirpes designation, which would pay the money directly to the grandchild if the child disclaims (though subject to a custodian's control until the grandchild becomes 21), the account holder may want to designate separate trusts for the grandchildren as the beneficiaries. It is important to set up separate trusts for each grandchild.

One Consolidated Group Trust versus Individual Trusts for Grandchildren

If one group trust is used, then all beneficiaries are stuck taking distributions according to the life expectancy of the oldest beneficiary. Some clients, however, want to have one trust with several beneficiaries believing that there is no need for equalization and prefer having the flexibility to make unequal distributions.

For example, assume you are leaving money to three grandchildren, all children of your only child. You could leave the money in three separate trusts, or you could leave the money in one trust. If you choose three separate trusts, you would get the longest stretch for the youngest beneficiary. In addition, you would make sure or nearly sure that each grandchild would be treated equally. If one grandchild went to college, her trust could be used for college. If another grandchild didn't go to college, eventually he would get the money for other purposes.

On the other hand, if you weren't worried so much about equality and just wanted to emulate real life where you spend money on your children and grandchildren without keeping track of each dollar and equalizing at the end, the single trust may work well for your needs even though you are slightly accelerating distributions from the IRA. Many families prefer the flexibility of one trust if one of their primary estate planning goals is to educate their grandchildren. In a separate trust scenario for grandchildren, it is possible that one grandchild's education costs may not be fully covered due to insufficient funds while another grandchild takes his inheritance and drinks beer and buys a fast car. Since this result is not desired by most families, our clients are split regarding whether they prefer separate trusts for grandchildren to maximize IRA deferral or a single trust for grandchildren to permit unequal distributions.

Finally, you want to think about how you want your retirement plan to be distributed in the event that neither your spouse nor your descendants survive you. Under these circumstances you might want to do something for charity or give the assets to your siblings. All of these considerations must be spelled out in the beneficiary form, or else the assets might pass to someone you don't like.

Since no beneficiary change form allows for this kind of stepped planning, an attachment should be drafted that clearly spells out how the beneficiary designations should work. Most plan administrators are willing to accommodate such sophisticated planning when it is presented in a clear and concise manner.

The Hazards of Naming Different Beneficiaries for Different Accounts

It is quite common in my practice for clients to say they want one particular account to go to one beneficiary and a different account to another beneficiary. The accounts might reflect the relative proportionate value that the client wants each of the different beneficiaries to receive, but I think this can turn into a nightmare.

- You will have a terrible time trying to keep track of the different distribution schedules.

- As the different investments go up or down, the amount going to the different heirs would also go up and down, which is probably not the intent.

- A beneficiary designation may say, "I leave my Vanguard account to beneficiary B and my Schwab account to beneficiary A." If during your lifetime you switch or transfer money from Vanguard to Schwab, you have, in effect, changed who is going to get what, and that may not be your intention.

In general, I prefer one master beneficiary designation for all IRAs, retirement plans, 403(b)s, 401(k)s, and the like. In it I describe distributions as I would in a will or irrevocable or revocable trust. That way, we can avoid mistakes and simplify estate administration after the retirement plan owner dies.

I recognize that, for investment purposes, people use different accounts for different beneficiaries. For example, you might treat the investments of a grandchild beneficiary differently from those of a child or spouse. Under those circumstances I would be willing to bend and accept different beneficiaries for different accounts.

The one area where it might make sense to direct certain money to particular beneficiaries is FDIC insured deposits. At press time, the amount that the FDIC would insure rose from $100,000 to $250,000 through 2009. Assuming the money is outside the IRA (there are different protections for IRAs) one way to get more FDIC insurance is to have different beneficiaries with different paid on death designations. If you are a parent with four kids and you have four $250,000 CDs, you can do a pod account for each child and have the entire amount federally guaranteed. If the money was in an IRA, you are also insured up to $250,000 but you can't get additional coverage by naming additional beneficiaries.

Submitting the Forms

For any trust that is a beneficiary of an IRA the IRS requires that, by October 31 of the year following the year of the account holder's death, the plan administrator must be provided with either a copy of any trust designated as a beneficiary or a certified list of all the beneficiaries. As a matter of practice, we submit the trust to the plan administrator in a timely manner—and while the client is still alive—to give the plan administrator the opportunity to immediately lodge any objections to the trust, when the account holder can still make accommodations. Obviously, if the plan administrator does not get a copy of the trust until after the account holder's death and then makes a complaint, there could be problems. Therefore, after the account holder's death, we submit a final copy of the trust to comply with the IRS minimum required distribution rules.

A testamentary trust, where the contingent beneficiary is a trust contained in the account holder's will, is treated differently from a standalone trust. Then, a copy of the will should be provided to the plan administrator just as a standalone trust would be.

Where the trust is a tertiary beneficiary—that is, where the children are the contingent beneficiaries and the trusts for grandchildren receive money only at the death of the children or via the children disclaiming, then a copy of the will is generally not provided until it is determined that the trust will actually become a beneficiary.

On February 1, 2005, the IRS increased its fees to obtain a private letter ruling to $9,000. In the past, when taxpayers made a mistake they would ask the IRS to let them slide with a private letter ruling. Now, between the IRS fee and the professional fee to prepare the ruling, the cost could be $15,000 or more. Moral of the story: Pay close attention to the beneficiary form and submit it as early as you can.

A Key Lesson from This Chapter

Do not underestimate the attention to detail that is required to fill out a beneficiary designation. For many people, their IRA or retirement plans constitute the bulk of their wealth, and the beneficiary designation, not the will, controls the disbursement of those funds.

17

Trusts As Beneficiaries of Retirement Plans

Put not your trust in money, but put your money in trust.
—Oliver Wendell Holmes

Main Topics

- Whether to consider a trust as a beneficiary to your IRA
- Young beneficiaries
- Spendthrift trusts
- Unified Credit Shelter Trusts
- QTIPs (Qualified Terminal Interest Property)

KEY IDEA

Using a trust as the potential beneficiary of a retirement plan and/or IRA can be an excellent method of protecting the beneficiary. Creating trusts for minors, for spendthrifts, and for spouses can be appropriate under certain circumstances.

There are many types of trusts, and each one serves a particular purpose. As I mentioned earlier, many good estate attorneys routinely use trusts for adult children. Though I think this practice has merit, for responsible older adult children without marital problems, I believe the simplicity of leaving money outright outweighs some of the risks that the trust protects against. Please see Chapter 14.

Protecting Young Beneficiaries

The most prudent way to leave money to a young beneficiary is through a trust.

Typically I draft trusts for young beneficiaries with the following provisions:

- The trustee is given the discretion to make distributions for health, maintenance, support, education, postgraduate education, down payment for a house, seed money for a business, and if the parent or grandparent is a real sport, one summer in Europe.

- Then, at the age of 25 (not 21), the beneficiary is entitled to withdraw 33 percent of the principal of the trust.

- At age 30, the beneficiary is entitled to make a withdrawal of up to one-half of the remaining balance.

- At age 35, the beneficiary has unlimited access to the principal.

This example provides a reasonable starting point, but is not the only way to draft a trust for young beneficiaries.

Obviously, it is easy to vary the terms of the trust according to personal preferences. The type of trust I described works well when the beneficiaries are young, usually for grandchildren when it is unclear how they will turn out as young adults. Trusts are the most prudent way to leave money to young beneficiaries or spendthrifts. If the beneficiary is already in his or her late teens or early twenties, you can alter the terms as seems prudent. Some 25-year-olds are perfectly capable of handling money without the need for a trust. Some 35-year-olds are nowhere near ready for that type of responsibility. If

Trusts are the most prudent way to leave money to young beneficiaries or spendthrifts

your beneficiaries are old enough for you to make a reasonable judgment of their level of responsibility, then you don't have to rely on the general language recommended above.

Most of the trusts for minors that I draft are for the benefit of a grandchild (or grandchildren). The trust would take effect if the IRA owner dies and the child who was named before the grandchild either predeceased or disclaimed to his or her children.

MINI CASE STUDY 17.1
Protecting Junior

Tom, a retired IRA owner, has one son, Joe, and one grandson, Junior, age 3. He fills out his beneficiary form as follows:

1. My son, Joe

2. My grandson, Junior

Tom dies. Joe doesn't want or need the money. He disclaims. The money will then go to Junior. Since there was no trust, Junior will have complete access to the money when he reaches 21 (younger in some states). Tom's legacy might be a Corvette and a year of drunken partying for Junior.

Assume, instead, that Tom names his beneficiaries as follows:

1. My son, Joe

2. The Tom Family Trust for Grandchildren under Articles V & VI of the Last Will and Testament of Tom dated March 1, 2009

Obviously in Tom's will, he drafts the appropriate trust for Junior. With this structure, Joe can be much more comfortable. He disclaims to the trust that has reasonable restrictions for Junior rather than disclaiming the assets outright to Junior. Now Junior will not come into all the money at 21, but if he has legitimate needs—education, for example—they can be met. Joe could be named trustee. By going to the trouble of drafting the trust, Tom gave Joe a better choice with a better result for the family. He protected the money from premature taxation and frivolous spending. Another advantage is that the trust will protect the money from Junior's creditors. The trust money is protected from creditors of the beneficiary, which may range from an individual suing the beneficiary to the beneficiary's spouse if the beneficiary's marriage goes sour.

The Mechanics of Naming a Minor's Trust as Beneficiary

Please remember the basics. The beneficiary designation, not the will, controls the proceeds of the IRA at death. Therefore, the beneficiary designation of the retirement plan deserves attention.

An acceptable alternative is to direct the proceeds into a qualifying trust that complies with the five conditions listed in Chapter 13, and submit a correctly worded beneficiary designation form. If that is done correctly, we have the same result. If the beneficiary form is completed incorrectly or if the terms of the trust do not meet the five conditions described in Chapter 13, then we have enormous problems. Please refer back to Chapter 16 for details on actually filling out the beneficiary forms.

In our office we used to draft a special document to be used as the retirement plan or IRA beneficiary designation. Within that long document (see Lange's Cascading Beneficiary Plan) we draft a special trust or, more often, a series of trusts to be used as the beneficiary of the IRA. Currently, we typically refer to the will or a revocable trust that contains all the details. The trust within the will or revocable trust, however, always meets the five conditions required for the trust or beneficiary to stretch the IRA.

In my office, I do not allow clients to fill out beneficiary change forms for their IRA or retirement plan. Granted, it takes us additional time to do it. It requires even more work if there are many IRAs and retirement plans in different investment companies, all of which are likely to have their own beneficiary change form. I have seen enough instances where the client and/or his attorney were cavalier about the IRA beneficiary form and the form was filled out incorrectly. I have also seen situations where the attorney's directions to the client were not clear, or the client didn't follow the attorney's instructions. With large IRAs or retirement plans, there is too much at stake for errors.

My original intention was to include detailed sample language with this book, but after thinking it through, I fear I would invite mistakes and bad results. Get help from a competent attorney who understands about drafting IRA beneficiary designations. The attorney should understand your entire financial situation and have the core requisite technical knowledge of the law and the forms before being asked to properly fill out the forms. This is one instance when I think paying an attorney is money well spent. Some other financial professionals are competent to perform this task, but please make sure that filling out a beneficiary form is not incidental to a sale but rather is a job taken seriously by whoever is performing it.

> With large IRAs or retirement plans, there is too much at stake for errors. . . . Get help from a competent attorney who understands about drafting IRA beneficiary designations.

MINI CASE STUDY 17.2
The Perils of Inaccurate Beneficiary Designations

Tom fills out the beneficiary form with "My grandchild Junior, in trust." There is a will with a trust for Junior, but there is no specific reference to that will in this beneficiary designation. The result is that Junior may not be able to reach this money when he is 21 because, in effect, there is no trust as a beneficiary specific to the beneficiary designation. Although Junior's parents may successfully be able to argue that the trust mentioned in the beneficiary designation is the same as the trust under the will for Junior's benefit, considerable time and expense can be saved by initially completing the beneficiary designation properly.

Perils of a Trust That Doesn't Meet the Five Conditions

Tom fills out the beneficiary form with "The Tom Family Trust for Grandchildren, found in my will." Assuming the trust in the will meets all five requirements, the money will pass as intended in trust.

If, on the other hand, the trust in the will violates one of the five conditions, then we do not have a qualifying trust as a beneficiary. If that is the case, the income from the IRA is accelerated and Junior loses the ability to stretch the proceeds of the IRA over his lifetime.

Therefore, it is critical that the five conditions are met for all trusts with the potential to become beneficiaries of IRAs and/or retirement plans.

Spendthrift Trusts

This type of trust may also be referred to as a *forced prudence trust,* or, and this is my personal favorite, the "I don't want my no-good son-in-law getting one red cent of my money trust."

The basic spendthrift trust is usually drafted because not every child, even those beyond 35 years old, will have developed sufficient maturity or sense of fiscal responsibility to make wise choices after the death of their parent or parents. Parents may feel their children may never be financially responsible and will want to control from the grave for the remainder of their child's life. Since the greatest value of an inherited IRA is to stretch the benefits over the lifetime of the beneficiary, it would be a financial disaster to have an inappropriate and premature withdrawal of these funds.

A spendthrift trust will put a trusted relative, friend, or financial institution in control of the beneficiary's money and will ensure that the inherited IRA is used as a lifetime fund rather than an "I want a brand-new Porsche fund." In more severe cases, where drug addiction or alcohol abuse comes into play, additional special provisions are often recommended. Spendthrift trusts typically also include creditor protection language, and even though such language does not offer the beneficiary perfect protection, it does go a long way toward protecting the beneficiaries not only from themselves but also from their creditors or potential creditors. One set of common creditors for your children are your children's spouses in the event of a divorce. Other times, even without a divorce, a child's spouse may be pushing the child to act irresponsibly with the inherited funds. Sometimes a trust protects a child from his or her spouse's irresponsibility.

Our law firm is experiencing an ever-growing number of clients who love their kids, but who don't trust their kids' spouses.

True Story Ensuring the No-Good Son-in-Law Gets Nothing

One of life's greatest mysteries is how the boy who wasn't good enough to marry your daughter can be the father of the smartest grandchild in the world.
—Proverb

A couple came into my office, and the first thing the husband said was, "I don't want my no-good son-in-law to get one dime of my money." Only after discussing this issue could we proceed with providing for his wife, his other children, his grandchildren, and saving taxes. What we ended up with was, basically, leaving any money that his daughter might inherit to a trust for the benefit of the daughter. We named an independent trustee whose job is to make sure the money is protected from the son-in-law, even if the daughter wants to give her husband money. In terms of actual drafting, the language is similar to a traditional spendthrift trust.

Although I have no hesitation drafting a trust when the client thinks there is a significant need to protect the beneficiary, other practitioners go much farther in the direction of controlling from the grave. For some children, spendthrift trusts are certainly right, and it is far more prudent to leave money to a child in trust. Some practitioners see leaving money for adult children in trust as the norm rather than the exception. Personally,

I am a cheapskate and I like to keep things simple if I can. Therefore, my normal situation is not to draft a trust for an adult beneficiary.

One noted expert who recommends using a trust for an adult child as the rule instead of the exception advocates putting virtually all of an adult child's interest from an inherited IRA into a trust. As he correctly points out, this forces the child to stretch the benefits over his or her lifetime and protects the child from creditors. He claims that the adult children are happy with this arrangement. Many financial firms offer boilerplate trusts as beneficiaries of the IRA. I generally do not like this approach.

I prefer the simplicity of trusting the adult child's judgment unless there is a reason not to. The idea of forcing the adult child to stretch the IRA, and not permitting optional withdrawals, to maximize creditor protection is a reasonable idea under some circumstances. If you do choose to use this idea (or even in a spendthrift situation), the trust should go beyond just providing the minimum required distribution. It should also have a provision for health, maintenance, support, education, and so on.

A relevant issue when naming a trust as a beneficiary of an IRA is whether the drafter wishes to treat the required minimum distribution as income, or part income and part principal for the trust's accounting purposes. Pennsylvania and some other states in accordance with the Uniform Principal and Income Act of 1997 (UPAIA) have adopted tracing rules which require the trustee to allocate the portion of the minimum required distribution determined to be income as income and the remainder of the minimum required distribution as principal. If the income portion of the minimum required distribution cannot be traced, the UPAIA states that a minimum required distribution payable to a trust will be treated as the 90 percent principal and 10 percent income for trust accounting purposes. Accordingly, if the objective is for the income beneficiary of the trust to pay the income tax due on the minimum required distribution (my usual preference because the income tax rates for individuals are lower than the rates for trusts), drafters should opt out of the UPAIA by mandating that minimum required distributions payable to the trust be treated as income and paid out to the income beneficiary.

Unified Credit Shelter Trust, or B Trust, as Beneficiary

As mentioned at the beginning of the estate planning section of this book, a frequent contingent beneficiary of a retirement plan is the B trust, or the Unified Credit Shelter Trust. This type of trust gives the surviving spouse all of the trust income and the trustee the flexibility to distribute principal for the health, maintenance, and support of the surviving spouse. The surviving spouse is also often given a "5 and 5 power," meaning that each year the surviving spouse could withdraw the greater of an additional 5 percent of the corpus (assets excluding profit and interest) of the trust, or $5,000. At the death of the surviving spouse, the trust proceeds generally go to the children equally. The purpose of this type of trust is to ensure that, for federal estate tax purposes, the proceeds of the trust will not be included in the estate of the second spouse to die.

As we previously discussed, despite the potential estate tax savings, using this trust will cause the minimum required distributions to be based on the age of the surviving spouse, thus accelerating income taxable withdrawals, both during the surviving spouse's life and after the surviving spouse dies. As a result, we never recommend this type of trust as the primary beneficiary of an IRA or retirement plan and only use it as a contingent beneficiary available for disclaimer purposes. For more about disclaimers, please see Chapter 14.

Assume an IRA or a 403(b) or 401(a) participant owner dies. Also assume that either a well-drafted B trust, or Unified Credit Shelter Trust, is the primary beneficiary, or that it becomes the beneficiary because the surviving spouse, who had been named as the primary beneficiary, disclaims and the B trust is the secondary beneficiary.

We have discussed the minimum required distribution rules for the inherited IRA owned by the trust both during the life of the surviving spouse and after the surviving spouse dies. What perhaps is not clear is the mechanics of how the account should be handled after death in order to avoid a massive acceleration of income taxes.

Mechanics of the B Trust as Beneficiary of the IRA

After death, the IRA will be transferred into an account titled something like "Joe Schmoe, deceased, for the benefit of Bill Schmoe, Trustee of the Joe Schmoe Plan Benefits Trust." However, the money is not actually transferred to the trust at that point. The name of the account is retitled, but this is not an income taxable event.

The money sits in this newly named account held by the plan administrator. The MRD rules for that inherited IRA are based on the life expectancy of the surviving spouse. If, for example, the surviving spouse has a 20-year life expectancy, we would divide 20 into the balance as of December 31 of the year the IRA owner died in order to calculate the minimum required distribution. In the subsequent year, the life expectancy factor would be 19, then 18, and so on. Even after the death of the surviving spouse, the children would still have to take withdrawals based on the surviving spouse's remaining life expectancy according to the tables, if any money remains.

When any trust is the beneficiary of an inherited IRA, whether the end beneficiary is a trust for children or the spouse, income taxation occurs when the money is transferred from the inherited IRA to the trustee of the trust, usually only on a minimum required distribution basis. The trustee will receive the check from the plan administrator and deposit it into a checking account in the name of the trust. If the money is retained by the trust, the trust must pay income taxes on the distribution at trust income tax rates. More commonly, the trust will distribute the MRD it receives to the trust beneficiary, the surviving spouse. The reason for distributing the minimum required distribution amount (or other amounts withdrawn) in whole is to avoid income taxation to the trust, which is usually taxed higher than individual income tax rates.

Mechanically, you may choose to follow our example from a recent estate plan. We calculate the MRD early in the year. We have a monthly automatic transfer of one-twelfth of the minimum required distribution from the inherited IRA to a separate trust checking account. Then we have an automatic transfer from this trust account to the bank account of the surviving spouse.

At the end of the year, the plan administrator issues a 1099 (or multiple 1099s) to the trust. The trustee files a Form 1041 reporting the distribution as income and deducts the same amount as a distribution deduction via a K-1 issued to the surviving spouse, thus paying no tax. The surviving spouse includes the K-1 income on her own 1040 for the year and pays the income tax accordingly.

Therefore, what you may have heard in the past—that when the money goes to a trust it becomes taxable—is accurate. However, it is important to understand that after the death of the IRA owner, the money is transferred into an inherited IRA account and not a trust account until minimum distributions or other distributions are incurred. Simply renaming the account to the name of the trust is not a withdrawal of the entire IRA.

The QTIP (The A Trust of the A/B Trust)

I hate QTIP trusts (Qualified Terminal Interest Property) and/or B trusts as beneficiaries of retirement plans and IRAs. It is typical to see QTIP trusts in second marriages. Basically, the trust says to pay the surviving spouse an income for life, but at the second spouse's death have the principal revert to the children of the first marriage.

The terms of the QTIP trust have provisions for the surviving spouse that are similar to the provisions for the surviving spouse in the B trust. Like the B trust, it provides income to the surviving spouse and the assets revert to the children at the surviving spouse's death. The purpose of the QTIP trust, however, is not to avoid estate taxes at the second death. Rather the purposes are to provide an income to the surviving spouse, to preserve a marital deduction at the death of the first spouse, and to preserve the assets for the children from the decedent's first marriage. The marital deduction allows the first estate to escape federal estate taxation on the assets transferred to the QTIP trust. But unlike the B trust, the balance of the QTIP trust is included in the estate of the second spouse to die. As a result, there is no estate tax savings with the QTIP trust.

It is natural to want to protect your second spouse and then have the money revert to the children. For after-tax assets, QTIP trusts, though not a perfect solution, are often the best solution. In reality, for IRA owners using this type of plan, the biggest question in my mind is who will be most unhappy: the surviving spouse, the children of the first marriage, or the poor trustee.

This type of trust accelerates income taxes by forcing both the surviving spouse and the children of the first marriage (generally the ones who inherit the remainder of the trust at the second death) to take minimum required distributions based on the surviving spouse's age. Because QTIP trusts are usually the primary beneficiaries and the interests of both spouses are usually different because they each have their own set of children, there are few disclaimer opportunities providing alternative ways to reduce income taxes.

As a result, during the surviving spouse's life, minimum distributions are accelerated faster than if the surviving spouse had been named outright. When the surviving spouse dies (assuming the surviving spouse predeceases the children), the children of the first marriage will also have an accelerated minimum required distribution schedule based on the life expectancy of their stepparent, not their own life expectancy (the same situation as the MRD of a Unified Credit Shelter Trust). (See Mini Case Study 14.1.)

An Alternative Solution to the QTIP

Instead of setting up a QTIP trust, provide:

- X percent of your IRA to your surviving spouse
- $100 - X$ percent of your IRA to the children of your first marriage

For example, if the value of an income stream for a 65-year-old surviving spouse based on a 6 percent rate of return is worth roughly 58 percent of the principal of the IRA (based on the life expectancy of the surviving spouse and depending on what tables you use), then it is simpler and preferable in the vast majority of cases to leave the surviving spouse 58 percent of the IRA and the children 42 percent of the IRA.

Upon the death of the IRA owner, the surviving spouse takes her share and rolls it into an IRA. Until the surviving spouse reaches 70½, there is no MRD. When she reaches 70½, she will take minimum required distributions based on the Uniform Life Table (see the appendix). The children take their shares as an inherited IRA and stretch distributions based on their own life expectancies. Clean. Simple. Cheap. No trusts, no fuss, no muss.

This solution may not fit with the IRA owner's goal of making sure the surviving spouse always has an income. In some circumstances, particularly for an older and less sophisticated beneficiary spouse, it may be prudent to direct the executor to buy an annuity that will guarantee the second spouse an income for life (see Chapter 8).

Another solution is to buy life insurance. But please, no QTIPs for IRAs.

A Key Lesson from This Chapter

Establishing a trust as a beneficiary is most successful for protecting minors and spendthrifts. B trusts and QTIP trusts, though sometimes an interesting option, are usually not best for IRA and retirement plan beneficiary designations.

18

‖‖‖‖‖‖‖‖‖‖‖‖‖‖‖‖‖

How Donors Can Do Well by Doing Good

As I started getting rich, I started thinking, "What the hell am I going to do with all this money?"... You have to learn to give.

—Ted Turner

Main Topics

- Charitable lifetime planning with IRAs
- Charitable estate planning with IRA and retirement assets
- Charitable trusts in general
- Lifetime charitable remainder trusts
- Alternatives to charitable trusts
- Testamentary charitable trusts

KEY IDEA

By understanding a few concepts, you can do far more for charity than you may have expected, while still providing for your family.

Charitable Lifetime Planning with IRAs

On October 3, 2008, Congress passed and President Bush signed into law the Emergency Economic Stabilization Act of 2008, which extended the charitable IRA rollover provision for taxpayers who are age 70½ or older through 2009. The provision allows these taxpayers to directly donate up to $100,000 from their IRAs to charity. To be eligible to benefit from this provision, you must be 70½ or older, make your minimum required distribution from an IRA (not a qualified plan), and the distribution must be to a public charity (not to a private foundation or a donor advised fund).

The charitable IRA rollover provision is a welcome addition to charitable lifetime planning. Frequently, my clients take minimum required distributions from IRAs not because they need them but because they are required to take them. This provision gives these taxpayers a way to benefit charity while helping their families.

Many people have asked why is it better to donate your minimum required distribution directly to charity rather than withdraw your minimum required distribution and then donate it to charity. The primary reason is that donating your minimum required distribution directly to charity provides you with greater income tax benefits.

The first benefit to your family is that the charitable deduction for the direct IRA donations to charity will be 100 percent deductible. A charitable donation of the same amount of after-tax funds might not be fully deductible in the year of the gift due to adjusted gross income limitations. In addition, donating directly to charity may minimize the amount of a retired taxpayer's Social Security benefits that would have been subject to tax if the taxpayer had withdrawn his minimum required distribution and then donated that amount to charity. Furthermore, the charitable IRA rollover provision gives non-itemizers a way to deduct their charitable contributions.

An additional benefit for your family includes using the income tax savings from the charitable tax deduction to convert a greater amount of dollars from traditional IRAs to Roth IRAs assuming that you are eligible to do the Roth IRA conversion. For example, a $100,000 IRA donation may save $25,000 on federal income taxes which you could then use to make a $100,000 Roth IRA conversion. Please run the numbers with a qualified advisor before doing the conversion but I wanted to illustrate one idea of how you could use the savings from the charitable IRA donation to help your family. In conclusion, I believe that donating the minimum required distribution from your IRA (cannot exceed $100,000) to charity is a great way both to benefit charity and to help your family by using the income tax savings to do a Roth IRA conversion.

Charitable Estate Planning with IRA and Retirement Assets

Some people have charitable intentions, and regardless of any tax benefits, they plan on giving large amounts of money during their lives and at their deaths to worthy charities. Some people are not charitable at all and make neither lifetime gifts nor death transfers to charity. Then, there are the rest of us, including me, whom I will label, tongue-in-cheek, as greedy givers.

The greedy giver's primary concern is providing for our family and ourselves. We do, however, have some charity in our soul and want to make some provision for charities both while we are alive and at our death. If we can make a large impact with our charitable dollars, particularly if we get Uncle Sam to significantly subsidize our charitable intentions, we are that much happier. To this group we address this chapter.

Sometimes simple planning goes a long way toward providing great value to the charity, great value to your heirs, and eliminates or at least reduces funds going to the IRS.

A Simple Example of Which Dollars to Leave to Charity

Assume you have an estate consisting of $500,000 in an IRA and $500,000 in after-tax money. Assume further that you want half to go to charity and half to your heirs. Many planners, in an attempt to keep things simple, would prepare wills and beneficiary designations leaving one-half of the IRA and one-half of the after-tax funds to the charity and one-half to the heirs. Or worse, they would leave their entire IRA to their heirs and make a bequest of their after-tax money to the charity.

Charities don't care in what form (IRA, after-tax, highly appreciated dollars, Roth IRA, etc.) they get their money, because they do not pay income taxes. Individuals do care because of the different tax implications of the different types of inherited funds.

> Charities don't care in what form (IRA, after-tax, highly appreciated dollars, Roth IRA, etc.) they get their money, because they do not pay income taxes. Individuals do care because of the different tax implications of the different types of inherited funds.

In the above example, it makes sense to give the IRA to charity unless the beneficiaries are 40 or under and would actually use the stretch IRA for their entire lives. If the beneficiaries of the IRA are 40 or younger, the advantages of the stretch IRA usually outweigh the fact that income tax has to be paid on the money. In other words, for a 50-year-old, I would rather he get the after-tax funds and the charity get the IRA. For a 30-year-old who plans to do a stretch IRA, I would prefer she get the inherited IRA as opposed to the after-tax funds. In either case, the charity doesn't care because it is all the same to them. In the more common situation where you have a beneficiary who is older than 40 or there is some question as to whether the IRA beneficiary will take advantage of the stretch IRA, it is best to leave the IRA to charity. In that case, no one will ever have to pay income tax on the IRA or the growth on the IRA. Give the after-tax money to the heirs. That way, the heirs will pay less income tax than if they received the proceeds as an inherited IRA.

It is quite common for me to see bequests to a charity in a will, and I usually advise the client to switch gears and leave the charity money from the IRA or retirement plan.

Charitable Trusts in General

Next, we graduate to split-interest gifts. *Split-interest gifts* are gifts where the donor or his family maintains some interest in the property and a charity (or charities) also receives an interest. They are often found in some form of a charitable trust. These trusts can be established and funded either during your life or at your death. The living or inter vivos trust involves a transfer of assets to a charitable trust while you are alive. Testamentary charitable trusts take effect at death and are created in a will, a revocable trust, or even the beneficiary designation of an IRA and/or a retirement plan.

In a charitable trust the people or charity receiving distributions while the donor is alive receive what is commonly referred to as an income interest. The income interest is the recurring annuity payments that last either a number of years, or for the life of the donor or spouse or other noncharitable beneficiary, or the joint lives of the donor and spouse or other noncharitable beneficiary. The remainder interest is what is left in the trust at the end of the term or at the end of the life (lives) of the donor (donors). If the charity gets the remainder interest (which by far is the most common), it is a charitable remainder trust. If the charity gets the regular payments but the donor's family gets the remainder, it is a charitable lead trust.

The term *unitrust* is used when the annuity amount is calculated as a percentage of the value of the trust assets, so unitrust payments typically vary in amount as the investment values change (hopefully, they grow), and distributions to the income beneficiary increase. If the value of the trust goes down in a unitrust, the payments to the individuals will decrease. This unitrust is properly called a *charitable remainder unitrust,* or CRUT. If the payments to the income beneficiary are constant, then you have a *charitable remainder annuity trust,* or CRAT.

If the donor creates a trust where the charity gets the regular payments and at a certain time in the future, the principal is returned to the family, that is called a *charitable lead annuity trust,* or CLAT. If the payments to the charity vary based on the value of the investment, it is called a *charitable lead unitrust,* or CLUT.

A donor is entitled to a charitable income tax deduction based on the value of the income or remainder interest irrevocably pledged to the charity. In these trusts, the donor is taxed only on distributions from the trust as he receives payments from the trust. This can create income tax-deferral advantages as shown in the following mini case studies.

MINI CASE STUDY 18.1

When a Donor Should Consider a Charitable Remainder Annuity Trust

Paul and Mary, a married couple, both 62, want to receive a regular income during their upcoming retirement which they anticipate will occur when they are 65. They have $500,000 worth of GE stock that has a basis of $100,000. (This is not IRA or retirement plan money, and they have other assets besides this stock.) They have been worrying about the lack of diversification and heavy concentration of their portfolio for years, but did not want to sell the stock and incur a large capital gains tax.

They are charitably inclined. They have been approached by their local charity and told if they make a gift of the $500,000 of stock using a charitable remainder annuity trust, they will receive an income tax deduction of $86,650 on the value of the remainder interest and a fixed income of $30,410 per year for the rest of their lives. This is the maximum annuity amount permitted in this case (over 6 percent of the initial value of $500,000). At their death their heirs would not receive any of that money; it would go to the charity.

Paul and Mary figure if they sold the stock without the charitable trust they would have $440,000 left. (Capital gains of $500,000 − $100,000 = $400,000 gain × 15% = $60,000 tax. $500,000 − $60,000 = $440,000) If the $440,000 is invested at 6 percent, the income would be only $26,400, and they have no guarantee the money will earn 6 percent.

With the charitable remainder annuity trust, however, they will receive:

- An upfront $86,650 income tax deduction of the remainder interest while avoiding the initial $60,000 capital gains tax.

- A fixed stream of income equal to 6 percent of the assets will continue even if the trust value declines. This annuity income will be taxed at capital gains rates if there is no ordinary income in the CRAT. While they are still working and in a high ordinary income tax bracket, they will invest the CRAT portfolio for capital appreciation and after they retire, when they plan to be in a lower tax bracket, they can invest the portfolio for income.

MINI CASE STUDY 18.2
When a Donor Should Consider a CRUT

Paul and Mary, from the preceding example, are more optimistic about potential investment returns, and want a higher annuity income. They are willing to risk lower future annuity receipts if the investments decline but want to get larger payments if the investments do well. They can choose a CRUT that will pay them 10.4 percent of the annual value of the trust each year, which yields $52,095 in the first year. This is the maximum percentage of the CRUT payment permitted in their case, based on their ages and a Section 7520 interest rate of 4.2 percent. This results in the minimum charitable deduction of $50,000 or 10 percent of the initial trust value. The future annuity payments will increase in amount if the CRUT earns over 10.4 percent or decrease in amount if earnings are less than that.

For people with charity in their heart, the CRAT and CRUT approaches are good deals. After the transfer of the stock to the charitable trust, the stock is sold and there is no capital gains tax, except for the annuity payments, and no federal income tax for the trust or the charity. (It should be noted that in states like Pennsylvania, which does not recognize charitable trusts as tax-exempt, there can be state income taxes on the trust earnings.) Then, with the proceeds of the stock, the trustee of the charitable trust purchases a well-diversified portfolio. The charitable remainder interest's value is a good current tax deduction, and the annuities provide a great retirement income benefit.

MINI CASE STUDY 18.3
Using a NIMCRUT—a Variation of a CRUT

A *Net Income with Makeup CRUT* (NIMCRUT) is a CRUT that stipulates that the annuity payments are only to be paid to the extent of the current year's realized income. If the income is less than the payout percentage, the deficiency is withdrawn in addition to the annual percentage amount in future years when there is sufficient income. From Mini Case Study 18.1, assume Paul and Mary funded the trust with cash. If the trust was a NIMCRUT, they could defer any annuity income while they are working and in a high marginal tax rate by investing only in appreciating securities. After they retire, and before they are again in higher tax rates due to MRDs on their retirement income, they can sell the appreciated securities in the NIMCRUT and get the annuity payments along with deficiencies of amounts not collected in prior years. Since they will be in a lower tax bracket between retirement and minimum required distribution years, this strategy, though more complicated than a regular CRUT, is an interesting variation that should be considered. If there are remaining deficiencies at their deaths (i.e., the actual returns were lower than the stated amount on the CRUT, and they would have been entitled to take more money from the trust in future years), the heirs of Paul and Mary are entitled to the deficiency amounts with the remainder of the trust value going to charity.

Here is a summary of possible scenarios for Paul and Mary and the charity (or charities) by using a CRAT, CRUT, or NIMCRUT.

- If the donor and his spouse live long enough, there may be little for charity, and it will have been a major plus for Paul and Mary.
- If Paul and Mary don't live long, the charity will do quite well.
- With normal life expectancies, both Paul and Mary and the charity will do well, but Paul and Mary will do better than the charity.

Given a normal life expectancy, will Paul and Mary do better than if they had invested the money and left the proceeds to their children with no charity involved? Probably not. I don't encourage charitable trusts for people who are not at all charitably inclined.

Charitable remainder trusts work out so well in terms of taxes and what the family gets that you don't have to be extremely charitable to make this work for everyone. Some CRUTs are designed to retain 90 percent of the benefits (the projected value of the annual payments) for the family, and the charity receives only 10 percent of the benefits (the projected value of the remainder interest). Not bad for donors who want to provide for themselves and their family, but also want to provide for charity. In addition, the donor:

- Receives a current charitable deduction for the percentage of the transfer to the CRUT allocated to the charity's remainder interest (10 percent, in this case)
- Avoids a large capital gains tax on the sale of the appreciated assets used to fund the trust
- Receives a regular income for life (some or all of which may be taxable at capital gains or ordinary rates). However, the income to the donor can be much higher than many people realize.

At the donor's death (or subsequent to more than one income beneficiary, at the death of the last income beneficiary), the remaining proceeds go to a charity. The NIMCRUT election can also be used for CRUTs to provide additional tax-deferral opportunities by careful investment planning.

Less commonly used are CLATs and CLUTs when remainder interests are transferred to heirs that result in lower estate taxes upon death by moving future appreciation out of the taxable estate. Since federal estate taxes are less common now, these are less frequently used. CLATs and CLUTs, however, also provide larger initial charitable deductions at formation, so they can become useful when current tax deferral is appropriate.

Charitable trusts are often packaged together with life insurance. One strategy is the insurance proceeds, often a second-to-die policy, which constitute the replacement trust, replacing what the children would have received had the donor not established the charitable trust. Life insurance and charitable giving go well together in a variety of circumstances.

Alternatives to Charitable Trusts

Charitable trusts come with inherent administrative burdens including setting up the trust, preparing annual income tax returns for the trust, annual calculations of the withdrawal amount, and investment management. Although CRTs have advantages for large transfers of money, simpler alternatives are available for those who would rather avoid these burdens. These include charitable gift annuities, pooled income funds, and life insurance owned by charities under certain circumstances.

Charitable Gift Annuities

Charitably motivated individuals may enter into a charitable gift annuity contract with charitable organizations that offer the option—a common practice for many universities. This is an agreement contract between the charity and the donor. It is similar to a CRT in that:

- The donor transfers a sum of money to the charity.
- The donor gets a regular (often annual) annuity income from the charity.
- The donor gets a partial income tax deduction for the gift.
- The charity gets the remainder interest.
- The agreement is irrevocable.

The charitable gift annuity differs from CRTs in that:

- Smaller amounts can be contributed. Minimums may be as little as $10,000 or $25,000, whereas CRTs are usually only done with hundreds of thousands of dollars or more.

- No annual tax returns have to be filed.

- No investment management by the donor is necessary.

The annuity income to the donor must be fixed in amount and does not vary from year to year. This is similar to the CRAT, but unlike the CRUT where the income could change with the change in value of the trust. The annuity payouts are often determined using guidelines set up by the American Council of Gift Annuities. For example, a 65-year-old individual transferring $25,000 would receive a $1,500 per year annuity (6 percent of the initial amount) and get an up-front charitable deduction of $8,882.

Charitable gift annuities are great for people who like the idea of CRTs but want to participate on a smaller scale. Charitable gift annuities are typically more generous to the charity than CRTs, which are often more generous to the family.

Pooled Income Funds

Pooled income fund giving is similar to charitable gift annuities, except the annual income paid to the donor is variable and consists of the interest and dividends earned in a pooled investment account. The payout does not include capital gains income, so the payout is typically smaller, but the up-front charitable deduction is larger. Therefore, more money eventually goes to the charity. For example, a 65-year-old individual transferring $25,000 may receive a smaller annuity, $875 per year (3.5 percent of the initial amount), and an up-front charitable deduction of $13,564.

Often people want to continue their pattern of charitable giving after their deaths but do not want to deprive their family of an inheritance or want to minimize the impact of their charitable gift on their family's inheritance.

Charitable Life Insurance

Often people want to continue their pattern of charitable giving after their deaths but do not want to deprive their family of an inheritance or want to minimize the impact of their charitable gift on their family's inheritance. The following two examples will illustrate two strategies that profitably employ life insurance in charitable planning.

Suppose that Joe and Mary feel they can afford to give $10,000 to a charity of their choice on an annual basis. Joe and Mary, however, would prefer to make a major impact with their gifts. In addition, Joe and Mary would like to continue supporting the charity after their deaths. Their trusted advisor suggests that they restructure their annual charitable gift by giving $5,000 directly to the charity of their choice and giving another $5,000 to the charity for the charity to purchase in its own name and to name itself as the beneficiary of a $500,000 survivorship life insurance policy on the lives of Joe and Mary. Joe and Mary would still get the same annual charitable income tax deduction as they were getting when they were just giving the $10,000 to charity each year. Therefore, Joe and Mary do not lose any tax benefits by considering this approach. Joe and Mary might have a specific charitable purpose for the $500,000 death benefit that will go to the charity. They may set up a fund within the charity that would be used for the purpose they specify and that fund could continue into perpetuity.

Charitable life insurance is also a wonderful way to fund a large endowment or scholarship for a charity of your choice. We recently worked with a couple whose family was very financially comfortable and they really wanted to make a significant charitable gift at their death to endow a university chair in their names. The only way it worked for the client and the university was through life insurance. The couple had the following benefits:

> **Charitable life insurance is also a wonderful way to fund a large endowment or scholarship for a charity of your choice.**

- There was a tax deduction for all the gifts to the university.

- The donors met their goal of providing sufficient money to the university to endow a chair.

- The couple received a flood of kudos from their peers and the university for making this gift during their lifetimes, which reinforced their positive feelings about the gift.

In conclusion, charitable life insurance can be a wonderful way to continue a pattern of charitable giving beyond your lifetime and/or to make a significant charitable gift with often fewer dollars than having to contribute the entire principal at the death of the donor or donors.

If you are interested in using life insurance for charitable purposes, please see the back of the book, or visit www.retiresecure.com

MINI CASE STUDY 18.4
Testamentary Charitable Trusts

May your charity increase as much as your wealth.

                                                              —Proverb

Now the fun really begins. Let's assume the parents of a 40-year-old child have a large estate including a substantial amount of money in their IRA.

Freddy and Frieda have given a lot of money to their child already. They think Frank is too carefree with his money, and they are worried that he may blow his inheritance. At the same time, they don't want Frank to end up living under a bridge when he is 70 years old.

Freddy and Frieda are charitably inclined. When Frank was young, they made sure he did volunteer work because they consider charitable involvement a blessing. They are not blind to estate planning nor do they scorn effective tax planning. They want all the tax benefits they can get. Though they ultimately want a significant amount of their money to go to charity, they also want Frank to have access to a regular income during his lifetime. In addition, they want to encourage Frank to have the option to direct some of their money to the charity or charities of his choice at his death.

After a lengthy conversation with their advisor, they establish a charitable trust as the secondary beneficiary of their IRA. (They are each other's primary beneficiary.) Their advisor is a good woman so she clearly outlines all the benefits of their decision.

- During their lives, it is their money and they can do whatever they want with it.

- If they ever reconsider their decision, they can change the beneficiary to Frank; they can choose to give all the money to the charity; or they can devise something completely different.

- At their deaths, assuming they don't change the beneficiary, the money would go to a trust. If they die this year when Frank is 40, Frank will get an income of 7.29 percent of the principal every year for the rest of his life.

- At Frank's death, whatever is left can go to a charity of Frank's choosing.

The numbers work out pretty favorably, and Freddy and Frieda's wishes are respected. The charity must wait to get their money, but they will get it. The loser is the IRS because of all the income and estate tax they couldn't collect.

This chapter provides only a small glimpse into the window of charitable giving. It is one of my goals to present objective information and encourage individuals who would not have otherwise considered charity or charitable trusts to do so after realizing all the tax and other benefits.

If you haven't any charity in your heart, you have
the worst kind of heart trouble.

—Bob Hope

A Key Lesson from This Chapter

I believe there are many donors who have charity in their hearts but whose interest in themselves and their families comes first.
If after reading this book, you have some incentive to explore some charitable options, even if the charity has to wait, then there will be charitable value as well as commercial and educational value to this book.

19

|||||||||||||||||||||||

A Point-by-Point Summary
of the Whole Process

Money isn't everything, but it sure keeps you in touch with your children.

—J. Paul Getty

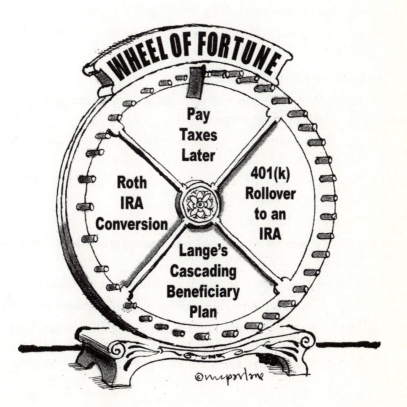

If you are still working, please:

1. Contribute the maximum amount to your retirement plan that your employer is willing to match or partially match.

2. Contribute the maximum allowed to Roth IRAs and/or Roth 401(k)s or Roth 403(b)s.

3. If you can afford it, contribute nonmatching funds to your retirement plan.

4. Deduct retirement plan contributions on your tax return, Form 1040. (Another way to look at it is that you don't have to pay income taxes on the wages earned that are contributed to the retirement plan.)

5. Allow these funds to grow income tax-deferred or in the case of the Roth, tax-free.

6. Continue to make new contributions.

7. Continue deferring taxes by deferring distributions.

8. If your income is too high for Roth IRAs, consider nondeductible IRAs.

At retirement when you need money:

9. Consider a trustee-to-trustee transfer from your company 401(k) to an IRA or a one-person 401(k).

10. Spend nonretirement assets (money you already paid income tax on).

11. Then, when your after-tax assets run down, spend your retirement plan money (IRAs, 401[k]s, etc.).

12. Spend your Roth IRA last.

13. Plan for needed or required minimum distributions during your lifetime.

14. Keep your minimum required distributions to a minimum.

15. Pay income taxes only when retirement funds are distributed to you.

16. Put in place a specially drafted Change of Beneficiary Form for your retirement plan and IRAs. The plan recommended in *Retire Secure!*, Lange's Cascading Beneficiary Plan, could allow continued

tax deferral up to two generations after your death while at the same time providing or overproviding for your surviving spouse or other heirs.

17. Determine if you are eligible for a Roth IRA conversion and, if so, determine whether and when it would be advantageous for a conversion to be made.

Thank You, Readers

A Letter to All Readers

Dear *Retire Secure!* Reader:

First, I want to thank you for purchasing the book and congratulate you for making it this far. It's no secret that plowing through this information can be challenging.

But . . . the most important decisions remain to be made. "What are you going to do with this treasure trove of newfound knowledge?"

You could respond in several ways after reading *Retire Secure!* You could decide:

1. I am going to take action. Tax reduction and long-term security are important for me and my family.

2. This information is important, but . . . (and then some excuse for not taking action).

3. I am really busy right now. I will get on this as soon as things calm down (a variation of No. 2).

You really can't afford to have the second and third responses. You need to take the next step: find an appropriate advisor with a lot of experience in distribution and estate planning for IRAs and retirement plans, and set up an appointment. If you can't find an appropriate advisor, refer to the back of the book to see if it makes sense for us to work together or if we can refer you to an advisor.

Perhaps you could plan your retirement and your estate on your own and maybe it would turn out fine, but . . . maybe you would make a huge mistake that could be enormously costly.

And wouldn't you agree that gambling with your retirement and estate planning is too risky? True, you do have more knowledge now than before you read this book, but this is an area where lack of expertise can lead to a financial disaster.

I can't tell you how many people have been to one of my seminars or read the first edition and decided to take matters into their own hands. Fortunately, some of them come to me after they made some huge mistakes and sometimes I can salvage the situation. Every time I see it happen, however, it makes me wince. Once mistakes have been made, it can be difficult to ever fully recover financially, especially if my client is already retired.

If you already have a qualified, experienced, and proactive IRA and retirement plan distribution expert who you trust, that is great; you're ahead of the game. Please make that call and carry through until your planning is complete.

If you do not have a qualified advisor, it is my most sincere recommendation that you seek one out. Please make sure he or she is qualified for your type of assets—IRAs and/or retirement plans. Many CPAs, attorneys, or financial planners are not IRA and retirement plan distribution experts, so please be careful.

But now that you bought this book and read it, you can approach the task of finding an advisor with some confidence. You now have the requisite information to be a better judge of your candidate's qualifications. Doing due diligence in choosing an advisor is absolutely crucial. The goal should be to enter into a long-term relationship where you can receive not only the best advice for your situation as it stands today but proactively receive the best advice on an ongoing basis as time passes and your situation and the tax laws change.

You see, with your new knowledge, you're uniquely able to *fully* participate in your retirement planning. No longer will you just have an uneasy feeling that you would like to understand why you are getting the advice you are getting.

Depending on your situation and the capabilities of your advisor, you may be better off with a CPA, an attorney, a financial planner, or some other type of financial professional. You may even want more than one advisor on your team. My point is . . . don't read this book, pat yourself on the back for making it through, and then put it up on the shelf and do nothing.

If, however, you don't have a trusted advisor and can't find anyone who you feel has the appropriate expertise in retirement plans and IRAs, there is another option for some readers. I am offering a number of free consultations and taking on a very limited number of private clients who will work with me directly. Please see the information at the back of the book.

If you would enjoy the benefits of *hearing* some of the material presented, please turn to the back of the book for the free MP3 offer. Don't forget to sign up for the free reports as well.

I wish you a long, happy, healthy, and secure retirement!

To your prosperity,

James Lange

CPA, Attorney at Law

A Special Note to Financial Professionals

Thank you for taking your valuable time to read *Retire Secure!* I urge you to apply this information to your practice in a proactive way.

In the beginning of this book, I urged you to have a printout of your clients with you as you read. I suggested that you think about how the different strategies could be used by individual clients to significantly improve their financial picture. If you did that, wonderful. Really, that is great. Now take the next step and plan how to communicate relevant ideas to your clients. Many advisors will make calls. Obviously, if you schedule appointments with clients, that will be significantly better.

If you didn't make notes for your clients while you were reading, I would urge you to get your client list out now, and make some notes while the ideas are fresh. By reviewing the individual chapters and looking at a list of your clients, it should trigger associations—different ideas that would work for different clients.

Finally, whether you made a list before or are doing so now, please don't read this book and go back to your old routine. Apply this information to your clients' situations and communicate with them.

We have developed tools for financial planners so you can educate your clients and prospects and attract new business. Go to www.retiresecure.com for more information on resources we have developed for you.

Every financial professional who has clients with significant IRAs and/ or retirement plans should have a copy of *Retire Secure!* If you have responsibility for other financial professionals, consider purchasing a copy of this book for all the financial professionals of your organization as well as using it as a premium for your favored clients.

Providing appropriate advice on IRAs and retirement plans is no longer a luxury. It is a necessity. Jerry Reiter, CEO and Chairman of Financial

Advisers Legal Association, said that *Retire Secure!* will help provide the education that financial advisors need to reduce their potential liabilities.

Thank you for your business. I hope you and your clients reap tremendous benefits from your having taken the time to read and implement the ideas in *Retire Secure!*

I wish you the best,

James Lange

CPA, Attorney at Law

Appendix: Life Expectancy Tables

TABLE I

Single Life Expectancy Table
(For Use by Beneficiaries)

Age	Life Expectancy	Age	Life Expectancy	Age	Life Expectancy	Age	Life Expectancy
0	82.4	28	55.3	56	28.7	84	8.1
1	81.6	29	54.3	57	27.9	85	7.6
2	80.6	30	53.3	58	27.0	86	7.1
3	79.7	31	52.4	59	26.1	87	6.7
4	78.7	32	51.4	60	25.2	88	6.3
5	77.7	33	50.4	61	24.4	89	5.9
6	76.7	34	49.4	62	23.5	90	5.5
7	75.8	35	48.5	63	22.7	91	5.2
8	74.8	36	47.5	64	21.8	92	4.9
9	73.8	37	46.5	65	21.0	93	4.6
10	72.8	38	45.6	66	20.2	94	4.3
11	71.8	39	44.6	67	19.4	95	4.1
12	70.8	40	43.6	68	18.6	96	3.8
13	69.9	41	42.7	69	17.8	97	3.6
14	68.9	42	41.7	70	17.0	98	3.4
15	67.9	43	40.7	71	16.3	99	3.1
16	66.9	44	39.8	72	15.5	100	2.9
17	66.0	45	38.8	73	14.8	101	2.7
18	65.0	46	37.9	74	14.1	102	2.5
19	64.0	47	37.0	75	13.4	103	2.3
20	63.0	48	36.0	76	12.7	104	2.1
21	62.1	49	35.1	77	12.1	105	1.9
22	61.1	50	34.2	78	11.4	106	1.7
23	60.1	51	33.3	79	10.8	107	1.5
24	59.1	52	32.3	80	10.2	108	1.4
25	58.2	53	31.4	81	9.7	109	1.2
26	57.2	54	30.5	82	9.1	110	1.1
27	56.2	55	29.6	83	8.6	111 and over	1.0

TABLE II

Joint Life and Last Survivor Expectancy Table
(See IRS Publication 590)

TABLE III

Uniform Lifetime Table
(For Use by Owners)

Age	Distribution Period	Age	Distribution Period
70	27.4	93	9.6
71	26.5	94	9.1
72	25.6	95	8.6
73	24.7	96	8.1
74	23.8	97	7.6
75	22.9	98	7.1
76	22.0	99	6.7
77	21.2	100	6.3
78	20.3	101	5.9
79	19.5	102	5.5
80	18.7	103	5.2
81	17.9	104	4.9
82	17.1	105	4.5
83	16.3	106	4.2
84	15.5	107	3.9
85	14.8	108	3.7
86	14.1	109	3.4
87	13.4	110	3.1
88	12.7	111	2.9
89	12.0	112	2.6
90	11.4	113	2.4
91	10.8	114	2.1
92	10.2	115	and over, . . . 1.9

About the Author

James Lange, CPA, Attorney, and registered investment advisor is a nationally recognized IRA, 401(k), and retirement plan distribution expert. With 30 years of experience, Jim offers unbeatable recommendations when he tackles the #1 fear facing most retirees: running out of money. Jim has also developed Lange's Cascading Beneficiary Plan™, which is widely regarded as the gold standard of estate planning for many IRA and retirement plan owners.

Jane Bryant Quinn introduced the country to Jim's mantra, "Pay taxes later," in *Newsweek*. Jim's recommendations have appeared 30 times in *The Wall Street Journal*, and his articles have appeared in *Journal of Retirement Planning, Financial Planning, The Tax Adviser (AICPA), The Bottom Line*, and other top financial, legal, and tax journals.

In 1998, Jim wrote the definitive article on Roth IRA conversions for *The Tax Adviser*, the peer-reviewed journal of the American Institute of Certified Public Accountants. Much of that analysis is updated and included in *Retire Secure!* One of Jim's web sites, www.rothira-advisor.com, is consistently ranked in Google's Top 10 for people who search using the words *Roth IRA*. Jim is the founder of The Roth IRA Institute.

Jim is the principal member of Lange Legal Group LLC, Lange Accounting Group LLC and the Lange Financial Group LLC. Jim's companies serve over 1,300 clients. Jim has presented 229 workshops for taxpayers and financial professionals throughout the country, and his workshops consistently get the highest ratings. Please see www.rothira-advisor. com for additional information about Jim's workshops.

Overall, Jim's web sites have registered 35 million hits (at press time) and they offer readers hundreds of pages of analysis, videos, and audios, and an e-mail newsletter that goes to more than 5,000 opt-in subscribers.

Jim lives in Pittsburgh, in the home he grew up in, with his wife, Cindy, and their 14-year-old daughter, Erica. When Jim is not devising new strategies for retirees to save taxes and accumulate wealth (which is most of the time), he enjoys bicycling, hiking, skiing, and traveling with his family. Jim also plays chess and bridge both online and with his friends.

Index

A

A/B trust, 283–284
Accelerated lump-sum distribution, contrast, 100f
Adjusted gross income (AGI)
  conversion amount, addition, 125–126
  limit, earning, 32
After-tax assets (generation), income source
    (usage), 79
After-tax dollars
  spending exception, 81
    usage, importance, 191–192
After-tax funds
  assumptions, 100
  availability, 223
After-tax investments, return rate, 154
After-tax money
  bequest, 290
  spending, case study, 75–77
    After-tax purchasing power, example, 12
After-tax savings, spending
    benefits, 75f
  tax cost basis, absence, 78f
Annual gifting, importance, 184–185
Annuities. *See* Longevity annuity
  basis, 150–151
  usage, case study, 157–158
  variation, 152
Annuitizing. *See* Partial annuitizing
  conservative strategy, 142–143
  defining, 140–141
  fixed monthly amounts, providing, 150–151
  investor advantage, 149–150
  risk, 150–152
Annuity
  definition, 140
  option, comparison, 145
  payments
    income tax treatment, differences, 140–141
    insurance companies/retirement plans
      calculations, 142
    schedules, 141–142
Applicable Exclusion Amount, 182–183, 197–198
  concern, 193–194
  estimates, 240
  increase, 252
  target, shift, 240
Assets
  annuitizing, 143–147
  list, case study, 172
  retirement accounts, 207
  spending
    classes, optimal order (case study), 79–81
    priority, 74
Attorney fees, avoidance, 184–185

B

Balance of funds. *See* Funds
Bankruptcy Abuse Prevention Act of 2005,
    107
Beneficiary form. *See* Retirement plans; Individual
    retirement accounts
  completion, 266–267
    case study, 267–268
  designation
    complexity, 269–270
    inaccuracy, problems, 279
    problem, 269
  language specificity
    case study, 118–119
    importance, 118
Beneficiary gifts, 185
Beneficiary naming hazards, 271–272
Beneficiary protection, 275–276
B trust, 197–198
  alternative. *See* Inherited IRA
  beneficiary
    mechanics. *See* Individual retirement
      accounts
    role, 281–283
  IRA, income tax (impact), 242–245
  LCBP option, 262
  usefulness, 252

C

Capital gains tax
  caution, case study, 77
  rates, example, 7
Cash balance plan, 21
Cash flow problems, 26–27
Certificates of deposit (CDs)
  conversion, 213
  FDIC insurance, 104
  investments, 144
    lifetime annuities, contrast, 146f
  management, 103–104
  option, comparison, 145
Charitable estate planning, IRA/retirement assets
    (usage), 289
Charitable gift annuities, 295–296
Charitable lead annuity trust (CLAT), 291
Charitable lead unitrust (CLUT), 291
Charitable life insurance, 296–297
Charitable lifetime planning, IRA (usage),
    288
Charitable remainder annuity trust (CRAT),
    291
  donor consideration, case study, 292

Retire Secure! Exclusive Offers:

FREE PODCAST

(Easily downloadable audio file)

"How to Keep More Money for Your Retirement"

As a reader of *Retire Secure!*, you are entitled to a free podcast by James Lange. Recorded during one of Jim's well received retirement planning workshops, this audio file highlights his wealth-building strategies and offers real-life examples not found in the book, including what he did with his own money.

Hear Jim explain best practices **for the three critical stages of retirement planning:**

- *The Accumulation Stage:* Steps you can take now, while you're still working, to save taxes and build wealth for you and future generations.

- *The Distribution Stage:* Proactive strategies you should be pursuing after you retire to ensure that your money lasts as long as you do.

- *The Estate Planning Stage:* Steps and measures you can implement with advance planning to safeguard your family after you are gone.

Also learn more details about Jim's favorite tax-saving strategies:

Roth IRA Conversions:

- Jim explains **the secret** to understanding the power of the Roth IRA conversion and how this tool can create wealth for you, your children and your grandchildren. Knowing the secret (not in the book) will give you a new way to look at Roth IRA conversions.

- *Lange's Cascading Beneficiary Plan™:* A traditional estate plan could leave your surviving spouse with little or **no control** over your hard-earned money. Lange's Cascading Beneficiary Plan™ gives the surviving spouse total flexibility and control to make prudent decisions going forward.

This is an EXCLUSIVE, free offer for Retire Secure! readers.
Download it Now!

Please go to **www.retiresecure.com** and click on the Podcast link!

Radio Show

Get Jim's latest advice by listening to his radio show starting March 25, 2009. It runs every other Wednesday evening from 7-8 pm EST, and repeats Sunday mornings at 9 am EST. The show streams live on *www. kqv.com* so anyone with an internet connection can listen. For more details and for excerpts of the show, please go to *www.retiresecure.com*.

Professional Speaking

Jim presents his well received strategies in person to financial professionals and consumers all over the country. Find out how you can book Jim for your next event at *www.retiresecure.com*.

What to Do After Reading Retire Secure!

**Throughout the book, I have recommended readers
seek help from financial professionals who have solid
backgrounds in IRAs, retirement plans, Roth IRA
conversions and estate planning for IRA and retirement
plan owners.**

True, reading *Retire Secure!* is a great start to building a solid financial future. However, until you implement the appropriate strategies, and address questions on how much money you can safely afford to spend and how to invest your money, you haven't finished the task.

We recommend you see your advisor or advisors. But be sure that they have the expertise to make good recommendations for your specific situation. If they do not, or if you don't have a trusted advisor, or if you are interested in a second opinion, James Lange's office may be able to help you.

Jim Lange and members of his dedicated team of CPAs and attorneys offer a variety of services that may be appropriate for you.

**To schedule your Complimentary Assessment to
determine if it makes sense to use the services of Jim's
office, please:**

Call 800-387-1129

Or click on the link at www.retiresecure.com